THE MOST OF

John Held Jr.

FOREWORD BY

Marc Connelly

INTRODUCTION BY

Carl J. Weinhardt

DIRECTOR, INDIANAPOLIS MUSEUM OF ART

THE STEPHEN GREENE PRESS

BRATTLEBORO, VERMONT

For
John Locke

Grateful acknowledgment is made to:

Thomas Y. Crowell Company, for permission to reprint illustrations that appeared in *Held's Angels* by John Held, Jr. and Frank B. Gilbreth, Jr. Copyright © 1952 by John Held, Jr. and Frank B. Gilbreth, Jr. Reprinted by permission of Thomas Y. Crowell Company, Inc., the publisher.

The Liberty Library Corporation, for permission to reprint drawings that appeared originally in *Liberty* magazine. Copyright © 1931 by Liberty Publishing Corp. Reprinted by permission of Liberty Library Corporation.

David McKay Company, Inc., for permission to reprint drawings that appeared in *The Dublin Letters*, published in 1931 by Ives Washburn, Inc.

The New Yorker, in which nineteen of the drawings in this collection originally appeared, and which were copyrighted © in 1927, 1928, 1930 and 1931, by The New Yorker Magazine, Inc.

The New York Times, for permission to reproduce "The Yell." © 1954 by the New York Times Company. Reprinted by permission.

The Penn Central Transportation Company, for permission to reproduce a travel poster originally drawn for the New Haven Railroad.

Mr. Henry T. Rockwell, for permission to reproduce illustrations that appeared in *Life* magazine, copyright Old *Life* Magazine, est. F. Berry Rockwell; and for permission to reproduce an illustration that appeared in *Judge* magazine, copyright Old *Life* Magazine, est. F. Berry Rockwell.

Vanguard Press, for permission to reprint drawings that appeared in *Grim Youth* (1930), whose collected stories had been published in *Scribner's*, 1929; *Harper's Bazaar*, 1930; and *College Humor*, 1929 and 1930; and for permission to reprint drawings published in *The Flesh is Weak* (1931) and *A Bowl of Cherries* (1932).

This book has been produced in the United States of America: designed by R. L. Dothard Associates; composed by Syracuse Photo Comp, Inc.; color separations and plates by Rainbows, Inc.; printed by Holyoke Lithograph Company, and bound by Robert Burlen and Son.

It is published by the Stephen Greene Press, Brattleboro, Vermont 05301.

Library of Congress Catalog Card Number: 72-81525

International Standard Book Number: 0-8289-0167-8

Throughout in boldface italic are quotations from the published writings of John Held Jr., used with permission from his wife, Margaret Janes Held, and memoirs of his boyhood in Salt Lake City, which have never before been published. Interspersed in lightface roman are specific valuations of John Held's technique by Bartlett Hayes, Director of the American Academy in Rome, adapted from his essay "Optical Allusions," written especially for the Smithsonian Institution's exhibition "The Art of John Held Jr.," which travelled throughout the United States and to Canada from January 4, 1969, to January 16, 1972.

WHERE THE BLUE BEGINS   Watercolor, 9-9/16 x 11-1/8″: *Judge*, April 7, 1923: Collection of Mrs. John Held Jr.

The Doings at Cockroach Glades

Remembered by MARC CONNELLY

The winter of 1916–17 was a bitterly cold one, especially for the five congenial young men who lived in a dingy New York rooming house on West 37th Street. The quintet occupied a front room on the second floor. Its two windows kept out neither the bone-chilling air nor the racket of Sixth Avenue El trains a few yards away.

Our sleeping equipment consisted of one large double bed and two single cots. Red Smith—he did *not* later become a sports writer—worked on the night shift of the Associated Press and somehow managed to sleep during the day on one of the cots. The repose of John Held Jr., Hal Burrows, Paul Perez, and myself was sporadic, even though the noisy daytime traffic was diminished, and drowsy heads were tolerant to the less frequent rumble and racket of the El. Our sleep was most frequently interrupted by the little bedmates in whose honor our dormitory was named, and whose activities we tried to discourage by moats of kerosene in the saucers under the legs of our bed and cots.

John had come to New York from Salt Lake City, his birthplace, where he wasn't making much money as a newspaper cartoonist. When I joined The Glades' inhabitants, John and Hal were using the room in the daytime as a studio. Bundled up with scarves and sweaters, the two young men sat by the drafty windows, their drawing boards propped against the kitchen table between them, both engaged in making colored portraits of onions, asparagus, tomatoes, and ears of corn for a seed company's catalog. John's vegetables brought him enough livelihood to allow him time to work on sculpture. As I remember, he won one or two modest prizes offered in contests for animals and human figures carved from cakes of Ivory soap. I thought John's were beautiful.

Mrs. Roselle Knott was our landlady. In her youth, she had played important parts with Richard Mansfield. Now she and her daughter, Viola, were finding it difficult to make ends meet. Their sympathy and

Mr. Connelly is a distinguished writer, a graduate of the Round Table at the Algonquin, and a Pulitzer Prize–winning playwright (The Green Pastures, 1930) *whose name has always meant the best of the musical and the legitimate theater.*

kindness would not permit the dispossession of several nonpaying guests, who included half a dozen out-of-work actors and actresses. One of them, the daughter of an old friend of Mrs. Knott, had come to New York to begin her own theatrical career. She was in her very early teens and her name was Miriam Hopkins. When she was stricken by appendicitis John easily carried her 75 pounds down four flights of stairs to await the arrival of an ambulance.

My own income was certainly meager. I had been a newspaper reporter in Pittsburgh. A musical comedy for which I had written the lyrics had been so successful in its amateur production in Pittsburgh that I had been commissioned to write an original libretto for professional production in New York. My backer, a Pittsburgh steel man, took on an experienced New York theater man as a partner, who convinced him that the libretto needed complete rewriting. My original script was no doubt pretty bad, but professional doctoring did it no good. When it closed immediately after its New York opening I didn't have the train fare back to Pittsburgh. I was now subsisting on returns from the light verse I occasionally sold to newspapers and magazines. Most of my time I spent making the rounds of the city rooms of newspapers, none of which ever needed a staff replacement. Luckily it didn't take much to keep going in those days. A novel kind of restaurant, called the Automat, had opened around the corner on Sixth Avenue. Now and then I had enough cash to buy food there. Excellent beefsteak pies cost ten cents; rice pudding, five. Topping it off with a good cup of coffee brought the expenditure to twenty cents. When the price of beefsteak pie went to fifteen cents I relinquished the coffee and still dined famously for less than a quarter.

Despite constant self-denial, I probably was more in arrears than any of Mrs. Knott's roomers. Compared with me, the others in The Glades were affluent. Even Paul Perez was frequently finding work over in Fort Lee, New Jersey, as a movie actor. Pride kept me from disclosing my financial condition to my roommates. One day Hal, Paul, and I accepted John's invitation to have a beer with him at our corner saloon. John looked at me oddly when, having had no breakfast, I wished him good health as I bit into a dill pickle. My weekly share of the rent was two dollars. One morning as I was about to make the rounds of the newspapers I encountered Mrs. Knott in the hallway. Her solemn greeting made me acutely aware that I was at least two months behind in my rent. I waited to be told that my tenancy had ended.

"Young man," said Mansfield's former leading lady, "You don't look as though you're getting enough to eat." Before I could make any rejoinder she had hurried away leaving two dollars in my hand.

The Glades' illumination came from two single gas jets that protruded from the wall between the two windows. After a community conference the Welsbach mantle over one of them was replaced by a metal heating device that threw off perceptible warmth for anyone within two or three feet of it. The room had a fireplace that had burned no fuel for many years. For psychological effect John filled a large piece of cardboard with a drawing of flaming logs which was put over the hearth.

One day in the early spring John encountered a friend who had come in from his farm in Connecticut with a basket filled with Airedale puppies. He intended to sell them to a pet shop.

"They won't bring you much right now, will they?"

"No, but my wife and I are moving to California."

"Then sell them to me," said John. "I know a lot about dogs and can get a good price for them when they're grown."

John's roommates were dubious when he assured us the puppies would cause no trouble while occupying a box in a corner of The Glades. His promise that we would all share in their eventual disposal quieted objections.

Besides a community concern with the puppies, a lot of our time went into keeping down the insect population of The Glades. The kerosene augmented by roach powder seemed only to make the little fellows thrive. At first the puppies' whining did not interrupt our sleep as frequently as the bugs, but as they grew older the whines threatened to turn into barks. They learned to crawl out of their container, and we knew it would be only a matter of time before they would join us as bedmates. As our anti-roach campaign was proving itself hopeless, a council-of-war vote of four to one ended our investment in Airedales. I forget how much John got for them, but they added little to the community wealth.

When I could afford it I joined John and several of his artist friends on their weekly visits to the Chinese Delmonico's restaurant in Mott Street. Four of them had already made names for themselves. Perhaps the best known was Mahonri Young, the sculptor, grandson of Brigham, the founder of the Mormon church. He had known John all his life and was his constant adviser. Paintings of Robert Henri, Louis Boucher, and Ernest Haskell can be seen in great galleries throughout the world. Haskell, up to then best known for his pen and ink drawings, was about to leave that medium to work in oil, and in the traditional manner he had begun his *pièce de congé,* a great oak tree composed entirely of stippling. It required many months to complete. To keep from going mad while applying its myriad of small dots, he listened while his wife read him the writings of several authors, including the complete works of Zola. I believe the tree can be seen today at the Metropolitan Museum in New York.

When we entered World War I in April, 1917, Haskell was commissioned to help develop the new science of camouflage. I remember the astonishment of John, Hal and myself one day that summer when Haskell, on leave, told us of the remarkable achievements of the Camouflage Corps.

"We can paint battleships in such a way that at sea they seem invisible a mile away, or even less. We're also devising camouflage for arttillery concealment and even uniforms. Come over to my flat and I'll show you a raincoat a Heinie can't recognize two hundred yards away."

Haskell left his living room a moment and reappeared wearing a doughboy helmet and raincoat, both painted with a dadaistic confusion of reds, greens, yellows, blues, and browns. He stood about 6′2″ and now gave the appearance of a nightmarish Pierrot. While the rest of us stared at his weird appearance, John stretched out his hands like a man groping in the dark.

"My God!" John cried. "Where's Ernie?"

JOHN HELD JR. IN THE TWENTIES   Photograph by Nicholas Muray

The Rise of the Mormon Kid

By CARL J. WEINHARDT

Some artists, writers and actors do one thing so well, so perfectly and essentially for its moment, that they are condemned to live in its particular shadow for the rest of their years. With time, their other achievements—both earlier and later—are quite unfairly passed over or are forgotten entirely. Such a false assessment of John Held Jr. and The Flapper misled a recent uninformed critic to write that Held did not deserve to be compared in his own field with that other observer of Flaming Youth, F. Scott Fizgerald, in his. But he does: Held was an important and uniquely American artist of the first half of our century.

Looking back twenty or thirty years is exactly like gazing into the wrong end of a telescope. The view is dim and the figures are very small. In those years when I started to caricature the time and foibles of the younger generation, I had no idea that it would ever be called 'The Flapper Period'; I was merely commenting on what I saw going on around me. I must confess that I was mainly bent on making a living. Then due to the vicissitudes of the day and the subjects that I drew, my drawings hit upon what was—I say this in all modesty—a popular note. I made so many drawings that I grew to loathe the little

Mr. Weinhardt for the past decade has been a devoted scholar of and friend to the art of John Held Jr. He is former associate curator of the Metropolitan Museum of Art; has been director of the Minneapolis Institute of Art and of the Gallery of Modern Art in New York; and is now director of the Indianapolis Museum of Art.

characters. But time has dimmed that loathing, so I look back now with amusement, and not a little amazement, to think, in this day and age, that a young girl smoking or drinking or necking—and 'parking' as it was called—or cutting her hair short, were subjects for editorial comment, and the nation cried, 'What is going to become of the younger generation?' Time has also answered that question.

Thus John Held Jr. wrote in 1952 about the Twenties, at the peak of the first revival of that endlessly fascinating decade, now inevitably resurfacing again in the guise of "nostalgia" (or, according to more moralizing critics, "escapism").

But looking back forty or fifty years is somewhat easier. The view is less dim, and certain figures now appear very large as the rest have shrunk. In this new light, Held is clearly among the important commentators on his time.

In the flush of our relatively recent coming-of-age in the visual arts, shedding, at last, the inferiority complex we had nurtured for too long about our home-grown artists, a great deal of foolishness has been written about what is "distinctively American about American Art." The obvious, and usually most accurate, statement is simply that it was created by an artist living in America. Most serious American artists from the eighteenth century until World War II were fully aware of what their European contemporaries were doing, and worked in more or less the same vein with more or less success; and more frequently than we knew or yet know, they surpassed their models. But

Held was one of the few exceptions. Not remotely impressed by his foreign peers, he expressed what he felt in his own unabashed, independent way. Yet he had no inverse snobbism: he was not at all opposed to experimenting with a European "style" if it appealed to him and suited his purposes at the moment—as witness the conscious (but not self-conscious) pointillism in a number of his finest watercolors. He was thoroughly familiar with the general vocabulary and heritage of the Western tradition in the arts, and drew on it as he chose. He frequently referred to Greek vase painting as the earliest form of caricature. (His favorite sculpture was the Metropolitan Museum's famed Greek bronze horse—which has subsequently turned out to be less than purebred). Had he seen and known the cave paintings at Lascaux, he might have moved that genesis earlier by several millennia. Essentially he was right, however, though "modern" caricature as we know it re-emerged after a long medieval hiatus in the peripheral work of major artists in Italy and the North during the Renaissance.

As is true in almost any of the arts, caricature in the hands of supreme masters—like, say, Goya and Daumier—can be raised to the highest level of profundity and social relevance. Goya and Daumier, of course, were activists who attempted, partly through the sheer savagery of their attacks, to reform the society of their time. In this attempt they failed; yet they influenced permanently the way posterity has since viewed their times. Ironically, though John Held Jr. was far from being an activist on the same level, he too was able, through the popular appeal of his benignly satiric view of American life in the early years of this century, to mold the way successive generations have seen his time—especially the "decade of glamour." And more than this, his everlasting image of that decade was unique—unique in being recognized as valid in its *own* time. This should be proof enough of his particularly creative genius, and of his contribution to American art.

The word *glamour* is suddenly terribly old hat, I learn from my teen-age sons. If anything, it means to them "superficial" and, naturally, totally "irrelevant"—the current curse of curses. They have forgotten that Webster's first synonym for glamour is *magic*, and magic is exactly what was felt by their grandparents in the Twenties and their parents in the Thirties. The optimism, the sudden freedom, the apparent progress, and the enlightenment about old-fashioned mores and morals—all were new. It was exciting, it was daring, it was beautiful all at once; in short, too good to be true—it was magic. How do you explain Gertrude Lawrence's indefinable attributes to a teen-ager in the Seventies? I don't know; but I find that if you just keep her records on the phonograph long enough, youngsters get hooked in their own way: but only because she is still magic. Let's hope that relevance can accommodate a little magic, if not glamour—it needs it!

Unfortunately, Held's posthumous critical reputation has been until now more or less equal to what Scott Fitzgerald's would have been, had Fitzgerald been judged solely on the basis of his best and brilliant and very superficial short stories. Admittedly, Held experienced little of the prolonged lower depths and personal tragedy that caused Fitzgerald to live much of his life "in the dark night of the soul where it is always three o'clock in the morning." By *his* prime Held had had no real crack-up, and was for the most part a remarkably happy man. The content of his work is therefore more generally surficial, though at its best it has no less integrity and skill than that of his literary counterpart.

I have had the enlightening and unmitigated pleasure in recent years of going over the innumerable scrapbooks compiled by John Held's widow. They are a happy and somewhat haphazard compendium of memories, thoughts, observations, clippings, and quotes from other friends and contemporaries of John's which she had compiled in the years since his death. The picture that emerges is rich and bubbling, diverse and lively. Held was at once simple and complex; the one absolutely consistent component being the deep and abiding affection that he inspired in everyone who knew him well. He seems to have maintained a perhaps subconscious control of exactly how well he let his friends know him, depending on the depth of his feelings about them. Those who knew him best, however, simply knew more and more of the same engaging personal qualities as did those who knew him less well. About him, the opinions of his friends were neither conflicting nor different, but were, rather, depending on how close was the friendship, merely stronger, reinforced by the numbers and depths of the insights he had given them. He was a rare "character" in the best British sense of the term. People said of him:

"No one ever thought of John as being old."

"He read *everything*."

"John loved everyone, and everyone loved him."

"The definitive illustrator of the Jazz Age."

"He was as American as firecrackers in July."

"Tall, dark, handsome and tatooed."

"He liked to tap dance in public."

"He turned his second wife into a lady blacksmith making weather vanes."

"He ran for Congress as a Democrat, but never left his farm to campaign, and lost— to his great and publicly articulated relief."

"When he went to Atlantic City to judge beauty contests, he spent most of his time fishing—for fish."

"He was the first man to wear gray flannel trousers and tweed jackets with leather elbow patches."

"To Held, people are obviously funnier than animals."

"Mr. Held is a pickling and canning expert . . . he is proudest of his pickled scallions."

"He always kept a dictionary handy, and at one point started memorizing it, page by page."

"He gave marvelous parties—particularly when he did his 'acts'."

"He read every book of William Faulkner, John Steinbeck, and Stephen Crane—to name a few."

In short, "rich and bubbling, diverse and lively." Not such schizoid fragments as they may appear to be when simply strung together like beads of wildly different colors, in Held these were facets of a remarkably coherent whole.

He came from talented and energetic Mormon stock. His father, John Held Sr., met his mother, Annie Evans, at a church social, and their union, duly blessed by the Church, produced six children, John Jr. being the eldest. John Jr. wrote later: " . . . I was somewhere in the nowhere at the time of the accident [before he was born, a sled overturned and his mother suffered a cut nose], But I think that was when I made my decision to be born, high on the hills of the Twentieth Ward on D Street in the Territory of Deseret." John's mother was a gentle, sweet soul who loved the theater, but was completely and eternally devoted to her family. She spent her last years happily reading books with John Jr. and his wife on their farm in New Jersey.

John Held Senior was born in Geneva, Switzerland, the son of Jacques Held, a Swiss watchmaker, and when only nine years old was a skilled penman in an era when penmanship was classed as a fine art. At that early age he was discovered by John R. Park, on one of the great Mormon educator's excursions to Europe in search of brilliant youngsters to grace the thriving new community on the shores of the Great Salt Lake. When he heard of the highly gifted boy, Dr. Park without further ado adopted him along with several other European prodigies and brought them back to Salt Lake City.

In the 1870's, in addition to the true faith, the Mormon Church offered its communicants sustenance and a broad education.

GIRL DANCING ON STAGE [Salt Lake City, 1890's] Watercolor, 6-5/8 x 4-1/4": Collection of Mrs. John Held Jr.

PERFORMER WITH HOOPS [Salt Lake City, 1890's] Watercolor, 7/8 x 6-3/8": Collection of Mrs. John Held Jr.

Under the progressive guidance of Dr. Park, the elder Held's instruction in art and music continued until he was nineteen. At that point, John Sr. opted *not* to be an educator, and struck out on a diverse career, which included making copperplate engravings, manufacturing fountain pens, and operating a stationery shop. He acquired a cornet, and, helped by his boyhood experience on the Flügelhorn, went into a five-year period of solitary practice. After mastering the instrument he organized Held's Band, a company of some fifty musicians who played at virtually every important occasion in Utah during the next half-century.

If he grew up with the sound of a cornet in his ear, John Jr. also always had a drawing pencil in his hand. When asked later how he happened to originate "this new woodblock style," he answered, "That's not new. That is an old idea. Dad taught me engraving and woodcutting. The first I ever did was for the Politz Candy Kitchen on Main Street away back in the early Salt Lake days."

Held's rewards, like his father's, came early. John, too, was "discovered" at the age of nine—when he sold his first drawing to a local newspaper for the perhaps apocryphally coincidental sum of $9.00. He became a professional illustrator at fifteen with the sale of his first cartoon to the old *Life* magazine. The following year (1905) he became the sports illustrator and cartoonist for the *Salt Lake City Tribune*, and soon joining the staff was a boyhood friend named Harold Wallace Ross, three years his junior. There the young cartoonist and the precocious cub reporter shared, with wide eyes, the by-play of city room and the drama of police blotter, honing their wit and talents against the day when they would set their benchmark on America's art and letters—the one as limner of The Jazz Age, the other as founder of *The New Yorker*. To Ross's delight, Held began making blockprints parodying, in Gay Nineties style, the denizens of what he later called "a wild, free existence in an inter-Rocky Mountain settlement with my friends the whores, the pimps, the gamblers, the hop-

heads and the lenient police who used to know [me] The Mormon Kid."

While he was on the *Tribune* he studied with Mahonri Young, the well-known sculptor and a grandson of Brigham Young. This period constitutes John's first, last, and only formal art instruction. While it undoubtedly refined his techniques and heightened his three-dimensional sensitivity, it left him unencumbered by rigid formulae and concepts.

When he reached his majority in 1910, The Mormon Kid married Myrtle Jennings, society editor of the *Tribune*, and left the West for the big city, where he soon became a man about town. But New York was not prodigal during the years before the First War (as witness Marc Connelly's recollections of Cockroach Glades), and to make ends meet he undertook commissions for streetcar posters and ads for Wanamaker's department store, and experimented with designs for theater sets and costumes. He continued with the blockprint caricatures of his earlier memories, and executed his justly famous "Frankie and Johnny" series in his old Salt Lake City style. (The linocuts—which took "many hours and a strong right arm"—were finally published in a very limited edition in 1930, and at last in appropriate numbers in 1971.) In 1915 his illustrations began to appear in many popular magazines, usually under the name of "Myrtle Held." This harmless subterfuge has never been completely explained, but it has been suggested that Held thought a pretty girl like his wife could peddle the drawings more successfully than he. I am inclined to think it was just typical Heldism—he did it because it struck him funny.

When the United States entered World War I, Held was hired by U.S. Naval Intelligence as an artist and cartographer. He joined two Mayan experts, archaeologist Sylvanus Morley and anthropologist Herbert Spinden, on an expedition to Central America. The expedition, co-sponsored by the American Museum of Natural History and the Carnegie Foundation, was to study

Mayan inscriptions and art forms with one eye and keep the other peeled for German submarine activity off shore. John's mission was to make coastal maps and to sketch installations and possible sites for additional military operations, as well as to record the Mayan hieroglyphics and to sketch the expedition's finds. Morley wrote in his diary for 1917: "John is working hard on new ideas for comic pages of war stuff. He is getting away with it in a rather whimsical way of his own. He's undoubtedly awfully clever at this sort of thing and infuses into his 'stuff' a sort of sophisticated humor, which must appeal to the worldly, smart New York palate." Held's special gift, discovered early, never failed him, even in a jungle during a world war.

After the Armistice, Held returned to New York armed with a portfolio bulging with sketches and drafts, an indefatigable sense of comedy, and a desire for some of the better things in life.

And he found them. Reminiscing in the middle 1950's, he said, "It doesn't make any sense. I used to work all day, days and nights. Nobody believes me now, when I tell this, but people used to send me blank checks to make drawings for them. I could write in my own price . . . . What could I do? I came to New York from Salt Lake with just four dollars in my pocket. I was looking for success and I found it . . . . I guess I knew then it didn't make sense. But I couldn't let go. I had a tiger by the tail."

His tiger was The Flapper, alias Betty Co-ed, escorted by Joe College in a coonskin coat to Midwestern U's big game, there to drink moon through straws from a hip flask, and thereafter to wrestle on the Zeke house porch while couples just like them danced to "Fascinatin' Rhythm" inside. Despite the fact that he was doing other work that was well received, it was his picture of Flaming Youth in the nation's most popular magazines that America couldn't get enough of. Then, in 1925, Harold Ross started *The New Yorker*.

According to James Thurber's brilliant pseudo biography (really a hilariously incisive psychoanalysis), Ross was a "genius and a plodder, obstinate and reasonable, cosmopolitan and provincial, wide-eyed and world-weary." In large part much the same could be said of Held, and it thus not surprising that the relationship between these two boyhood friends from the West, who reached the top of the ladder of Eastern sophistication in the New York of the Twenties, should have been less than easy and somewhat hard to assess. Still, it is known that Ross urged Held to return to the early blockprints of their youth for his work in the infant *New Yorker*. Held was already more bored with The Flapper than Ross was, and turned to this "new" genre with alacrity and brilliance. In a long series of these cuts he created the popular visual image of the so-called Gay Nineties that still persists, and which will always color our ideas about that decade. Just as he invented The Flapper, he translated the Gibson Girl into a simple, memorable graphic image that could, and still can, travel.

Meanwhile, in his more timely work for *Vanity Fair* and *Harper's Bazaar*, although he remained fundamentally a draftsman, he was extraordinarily sensitive to color, and his outrageous combinations of violent hues did much to heighten the hilarity of his best cartoons. It is hard to think of any other artist who understood, as well as Held did, the comic potentialities of color alone.

In the Thirties he returned to his landscapes and cityscapes, and turned to children's books and animal fantasies (which, although they must have influenced Disney, make Disney's look mindless by comparison). His always-present interest in sculpture emerged more strongly in his later years, and the relatively few bronzes that were cast are highly accomplished works, demonstrating clearly that he could have made his mark as a sculptor, had he chosen that route. He once told a reporter, "Serious art is my vice."

Held had a love of life and a love life as varied and peripetic as his art. In his fourth and final love, however, he found in Margaret Janes the perfect wife, and their intensely happy marriage ended only with his death in 1958.

The art movement that probably had the greatest impact on Held when he arrived in New York in 1910 was the so-called Ashcan School, the realistic treatment of the American scene by The Eight, a group of iconoclasts led by Robert Henri and containing several former newspaper illustrators. He did not remain under their sway for long, however. His own vision was happier and unencumbered by the often overly self-conscious insistence on social comment that was at the heart of such movements. He was a "realist," yes, because he shared a newspaperman's amiable acceptance of the foibles of life around him, and his eye, too, was like a lens that recorded what he saw—but Held's was a frantically warped lens that recorded what he saw in its own hilarious manner. His peculiar astigmatism heightened rather than diminished the reality, and he distorted nature only to make it funnier. And if the distortion failed in its result, it was only because the people he caricatured were too bemused by his light-heartedness to feel any wound. Gentle as he was, Held no doubt counted on this anaesthesia.

Inevitably, Held's work has had to be placed in the new hierarchy of what a number of scholars and recent exhibitions have somewhat mistakenly tried to establish as "Art Deco," which they see as the successor to, or a delayed outgrowth of, Art Nouveau. They have been able to create a niche for Held there, but not for the right reasons. He had been fascinated and influenced by Classical Greco-Roman geometric ornament from childhood, and was a brilliant draftsman at age nine. He was later further fascinated by the then relatively unknown Mayan geometric ornament, which he discovered on his own during his "military career" in Central America. Both of these sharp angular styles had great appeal for the more self-conscious "modernists" of the Twenties and Thirties (who were trying to escape the "fin de siècle" taffy tentacles

of the Art Nouveau), but they never became the basis of a style for Held. They just added more elements to his repertory. Over the years, this repertory became a storehouse crammed with a diverse variety of forms and styles and ornament that came from any period of art history and that attracted or interested him for its own peculiar beauties. Whenever it suited his purposes, Held would pull one out and use it, like a magician pulling a scarf from his sleeve. He still used, for example, more or less pure pointillism à la Seurat as late as 1931.

Only when the general mood of his country was at a low ebb during the depths of the Depression did a sense of true sadness appear in his work—and then not in terms of people, but in a series of empty, lonely, and lovely watercolors of the Manhattan skyline created during a period of about three years beginning in the early Thirties. He was acutely aware of the often strange but intense beauty of his adopted never-never land, and Mrs. Held remembers the irrepressible excitement he expressed as late as the Fifties when driving back to Manhattan in the late light of summer Sunday afternoons. He would shout, "Look at the towers—they're all silver!" or "pink!" or "gold!"

The unity present in all Held's work is one of effect rather than style, for style to Held was only a tool that evolved and oscillated with the passing fashions. He was, in a sense, a twentieth-century Rowlandson in recording with biting accuracy the spectrum of social and other foibles of his time, but he depicted them with much, much more heart. There was no cruelty, no very real venom, and no desire to reform or destroy his subjects whom, for the most part, if anything, he loved. And, when the chips are down, Held may emerge as the greater artist, with more dimensions on the level of caricature alone than Rowlandson could have dreamed of.

In his visual sensibilities, Held was like litmus paper, responding to and recording what he saw; but along with a heightened visual awareness, he had an extraordinarily imaginative and inventive mind, and the

18

results, which you will see in this book, range from more or less accurately observed topography to gentle or outrageous—and often inspired—flights of fantasy.

Three of the works in this book are dated prior to 1910; of the rest, perhaps 10 percent were executed between 1910 and 1920; about 25 percent during the Twenties proper; roughly 50 percent, surprisingly, between 1930 and 1940; and the remainder during his last productive period—from 1940 until he died eighteen years later. In writing to an old friend shortly before his death, he said: ". . . It's getting so I can't write any more. My hand jumps the wrong way." This book should be magnificent testimony to the fact that for more than fifty productive years his hand had jumped exactly the right way.

I suppose his portrayal of the Twenties will always mean "Held" for most readers, but the half-century of this irrepressibly creative artist's career, and particularly his intense creativity during the Thirties, should dispel once and for all the false notion that his work began and ended with the period of bathtub gin. Once this point is established, it is possible to savor his work of the Twenties for what it is—the peak of a long and fruitful career. *The* decade provided a uniquely fertile ground for his special talents. Corey Ford said it well in *The Time of Laughter* (Little, Brown and Company, Boston, 1967): ". . . But at least we could laugh at ourselves, we could make fun. Whatever else may be said of the era—and certainly it was materialistic and self-centered—it was a time for and of laughter."

Held loved nature and animals deeply, and usually treated them with considerable respect. Although he loved people too, he always found them irresistably funny, and their antics in that manic decade gave him the perfect material for his ever-so-gently acid pen. He captured the Twenties with a line as no one else ever could or did. Mr. Ford in his perceptive but light-hearted chronicle of the era couldn't get past page four without mentioning Held:

Fitzgerald christened it [the Twenties] the Jazz Age, but John Held Jr. set its styles and manners. His angular and scantily clad flapper was accepted by scandalized elders as the prototype of modern youth, the symbol of our moral revolution. . . .

Week after week in *Life* and *Judge* and *College Humor,* they danced the Charleston with ropes of beads swinging and bracelets clanking and legs kicking at right angles. . . . So sedulously did we ape his caricatures that they lost their satiric point and came to be a documentary record of our time.

Although he drew them as he knew them or vice versa, his real opinion of what he recorded inevitably emerged from time to time, as we can deduce from his caption of a drawing focusing on a witless male collegian: "One mother, one father, one tonsil expert, four general practitioners, three trained nurses, five governesses, fifty-six ordinary teachers, thirty-two professors, and three athletic trainers combined their efforts to produce *this.*"

The Twenties certainly brought Held fame and fortune, and though these were not really his driving goals, he instinctively managed to enjoy them thoroughly, within his self-imposed limits. Along with Maurice Ravel, Lawrence of Arabia, Ellen Terry, Grace Coolidge, Al Smith, and his old friend Harold Ross, Held was nominated for the 1927 Vanity Fair Hall of Fame. The citation read: "Because, as a caricaturist, he invented the modern flapper; because last year he was almost elected a member of Congress from Connecticut; because he is a syndicated artist who has not lost his flair for drawing and satire; and because he is a born comedian."

The last phrase was most true and provided the unique quality of most of Held's art, for it was this rare element that produced his peculiar and very special genius. How may other artists in history were also "born comedians"?

19

BALLOON ARTIST AND CROWD [Salt Lake City, 1900]   Watercolor, 7 x 11-5/8″: Collection of Mrs. John Held Jr.

BUY ME FOR A DOLLAR   Pen and ink, 8-3/8 x 6-13/16": [*Vanity Fair*, 1915]: Collection of Mrs. John Held Jr.

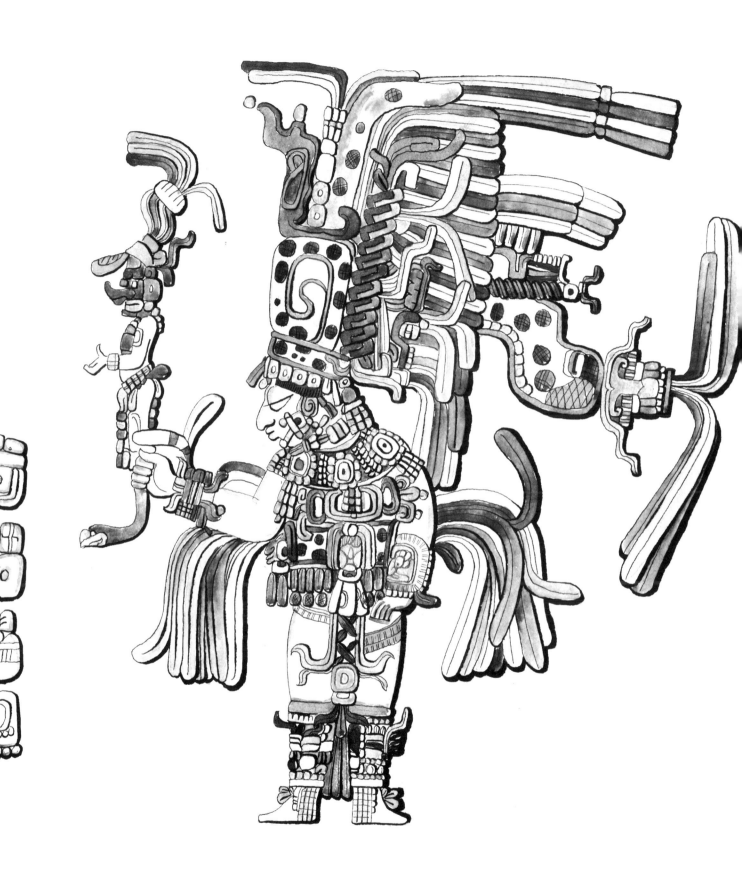

PAGAN IDOL [*ca.* 1918]   Watercolor, 11-1/4 x 11": Collection of Mrs. John Held Jr.

PALENQUE. May 13, 1918   Watercolor, 8-15/16 x 12-5/8″: Collection of Mrs. John Held Jr.

GIRL WITH TWO SOLDIERS   Pen and ink, 6-15/16 x 8-1/8″: [*Vanity Fair*, 1918]: Collection of Mrs. John Held Jr.

ON THE TOWN   Pen and ink, 7-1/4 x 8-7/8″: [*Vanity Fair*, 1918]: Collection of Mrs. John Held Jr.

LEONIA, NEW JERSEY [Spring 1918]   Watercolor, 9-5/8 x 12″: Collection of Mrs. John Held Jr.

Out of Uniform   Pen and ink, 5-9/16 x 9-3/16": Collection of Mrs. John Held Jr.

Scratchboard, 14 x 10-7/8″: *The New Yorker*, September 24, 1927: Collection of Mrs. John Held Jr.

Blockprint, 11-7/8 x 10-3/16″: *The New Yorker*, March 31, 1928: Collection of Mrs. John Held Jr.

Blockprint, 14 x 11-11/16″: *The New Yorker*, May 12, 1928: Collection of Mrs. John Held Jr.

A MENACE TO LIFE AND LIMB ON THE HIGHWAYS
The SCORCHERS
Eng By JOHN HELD JR. – Who is the toast of the town

Scratchboard, 10-3/4 x 9-1/2": *The New Yorker*, August 16, 1930: Collection of Mrs. John Held Jr.

In the archives of my memories the bicycle fills many pigeonholes, and my archives go back to the old high-wheel job that Father rode before the introduction of the "safety" model. It was the days before the streets of Salt Lake City knew the smoothness of paving. The sidewalks were more level, and the bicycle was used on the sidewalks, unless forbidden.

The next bicycle highlight came with the "safety" type of wheel. Pleasure-riding was the mode, and it was the era of the "century," or one-hundred-mile ride. Father equipped himself with a White, and for Mother he imported the last word in a Victor. I need not emphasize the sensational attention that Mother attracted. She made her bicycle debut in—bloomers. They were long and baggy, but exceptional enough to bring out long editorials in the press. Thus Mother became Salt Lake's first Bloomer Girl.

Salt Lake City was a focal point for professional bicycle riders. Down at Ninth South Street and State was the Salt Pal-ace, a medium-sized amusement park. The Palace was a large frame structure, stuccoed with coarse rock salt, and very glittering at night with arc lights playing on it. In the grounds of the Salt Palace was a quarter-mile saucer bicycle track, used on Tuesday and Friday evenings for bicycle races.

Father's band was the musical attraction. Between the heats of the races he conducted selections popular with concert bands.

I was always able to crash the gate at the bicycle races by lugging in the music to be used in the concert, in a large leather portmanteau. The parts for full band for an evening's concert in most cases weighed more than I did at the time, but my custodianship of the sheet music always admitted me to the races.

The "Echo Quartet" was a feature of these concerts. Dad was also very fond of a composition called "My Creole Sue," and he would beat the living bejesus out of it on his cornet:

THE VOYAGE   Watercolor, 9-3/16 x 10-1/4″: [*Vanity Fair*, 1920's]: Collection of Dr. and Mrs. Frederick W. Schweizer, Ithaca, New York

I had been attending Sunday school in the vestry of the Twentieth Ward Meeting House of the Church of Latter Day Saints for quite some time before I realized that the Jordan River that flowed north on the western city limits was named for the river in the Bible. Matter of fact, we always pronounced it Jurdan.

Somewhere in my early childhood, places and localities were always associated with people who were important in the Mormon Church. Brigham Street was named for Brigham Young. Cannon Ward was named for a dignitary named Cannon. Parley's Canyon was named for Parley Pratt, and Calder's Park belonged to a man named Calder. So the Jordan River must be named for someone named Jordan.

The Jordan rose as an outlet for Utah Lake, a fresh-water lake forty-odd miles to the south. It was slow moving and muddy as it drained Salt Lake Valley and emptied into Great Salt Lake.

To me it was a place to fish for carp and suckers. It was treacherous, as every summer it claimed the lives of young adventurous swimmers.

When I discovered in Sunday school that our river was named for the one of the same name in the Bible, I also discovered that both were in The Promised Land, and both emptied into a Dead Sea—Great Salt Lake being the Dead Sea in this land.

I don't know if religion urged me into an interest in geography or vice versa; I think it was the first. To me as a boy, religion was not important other than it was part of life as we lived it.

Religion touched me first when I was a few weeks old. I was born in January, and in the early part of March, as soon as the crossing muds had dried, Mother carried me down the hill to the Meeting House, and there I was blessed in the Name of the Holy Ghost. I don't remember any of the ceremony. I only know of it, as I have the Certificate of Blessing.

When I was nine I was baptized by complete submersion in the baptismal tanks in the basement of the Mormon Tabernacle. I remember enjoying this, as the water was warm and pleasant and it was the most water that I had ever been in at one time.

The Mormon religion was no different from any other to me, until early youth, when I came in contact with outside influences and it became different.

To all of us, anyone that was not a Mormon was a Gentile. In our teaching even the Jew was a Gentile. I don't think I heard the word polygamy mentioned until I was ten or twelve years old, even though many of the children in our neighborhood whom I played with were the fruits of such unions.

In my childhood there were no religious prejudices, nor were there any racial prejudices. I remember in my Kaleidoscope of childhood, among my playmates were Mormons, Catholics, Jews, Protestants, a couple of Ute Indian children, a Negro, a Chinese, and several Hawaiians. The only religious prejudice that any of us youngsters were conscious of was the feeling on the part of inquisitive strangers who were curious of the religion of Mormonism. To us there were only Mormons and Gentiles.

WHEN THE THEATRE WAS FRAUGHT with ROMANCE
THE STARTLING INNOVATION OF THE MAGIC-LANTERN SLIDE
IN CONJUNCTION WITH THE SERPENTINE DANCE
ENGRAVED BY JOHN HELD JR WHO IS GAME TO THE CORE

Scratchboard, 10-3/4 x 9-5/8″: *The New Yorker*, November 8, 1930: Collection of Mrs. John Held Jr.

TAXI! Pen and ink, 8 x 10″: [*Vanity Fair*, 1920's]: Collection of Mrs. John Held Jr.

MAY I SAVE YOU?   Pen and ink, 9-11/16 x 9-3/4″: From *Held's Angels*, 1952: Collection of Mrs. John Held Jr.

Apart from their present day meaning, as well as historical interest, these erstwhile illustrations may serve as useful studies of the art of drawing. There are several salient, yet subtle devices, which characterize them. One is the accuracy with which the anatomical structure is both incisively described and emphatically exaggerated. Yet withal, despite the caricature, the anatomy of the human figure is superbly expressed; only when it is accurately understood may intelligent liberties be effectively taken.

HORSE SENSE   Watercolor, 10 x 13-5/16″: *Life* cover, *ca.* 1920: Courtesy Addison Gallery of American Art, Phillips Academy, Andover, Massachusetts

CHINESE WITH BABY [ca. 1922]   Pen and ink, 7-9/16 x 9-11/16": Collection of Mrs. John Held Jr.

MAP OF GREAT NECK   Pen and ink, 17-5/8 x 24-3/4": *The New Yorker*, July 16, 1927: Collection of Mrs. John Held Jr.

LARGEMOUTH BASS Watercolor, 10-5/16 x 13-5/8″: *Life* cover [mid 1920's]: Courtesy Mr. and Mrs. Thomas Link, Englewood, New Jersey.

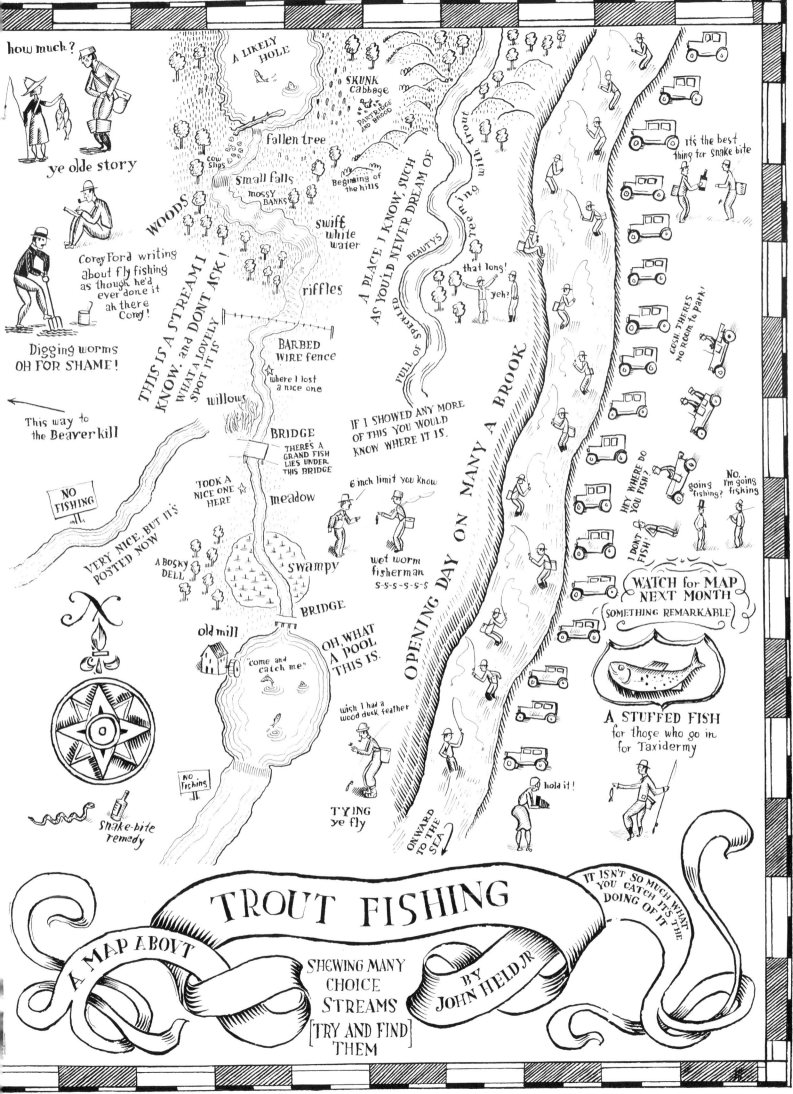

A MAP ABOUT TROUT FISHING—SHOWING MANY CHOICE STREAMS, TRY AND FIND THEM Pen and Ink, 12-15/16 x 16-3/4″: [*Country Life in America*, 1920's]: Collection of Mrs. John Held Jr.

NAVAL OFFICER   Pen and ink, 3-3/8 x 9-1/2″: [*Vanity Fair, ca.* 1919]: Collection of Mrs. John Held Jr.

BACK SCRATCHING AT THE ALGONQUIN FROM AN OLD ENGRAVING BY JOHN HELD JR MADE IN 1926

Blockprint, 20 x 16″: Collection of Mrs. John Held Jr.

Oh, this isn't a portrait. This is to be what the editor calls a caricature. It isn't really a caricature in the true sense. It's one of those quick-impression things. You know, a quick impression that only takes days to do and that you sweat blood over. [Crosstown].

I guess I've folded more magazines than any man in the country. Whenever a magazine got into trouble, the editor would come to me. He'd say, "I need Held. Held'll pull it out for me." I couldn't pull it out for them. Nobody could. But they came. [From an interview in the New York Post, *September 9, 1957.*]

41

Golf Series—THE NEST OF HORNETS [*ca.* 1922]   Watercolor, 11-3/8 x 15-1/4″: Collection of Mrs. John Held Jr.

Golf Series—THE EAGLE [*ca*. 1922]   Watercolor, 10-5/8 x 14-5/8″: Collection of Mrs. John Held Jr.

NEW YORK HARBOR   Colored blockprint, 11-7/16 x 13-3/4": Collection of Mrs. John Held Jr.

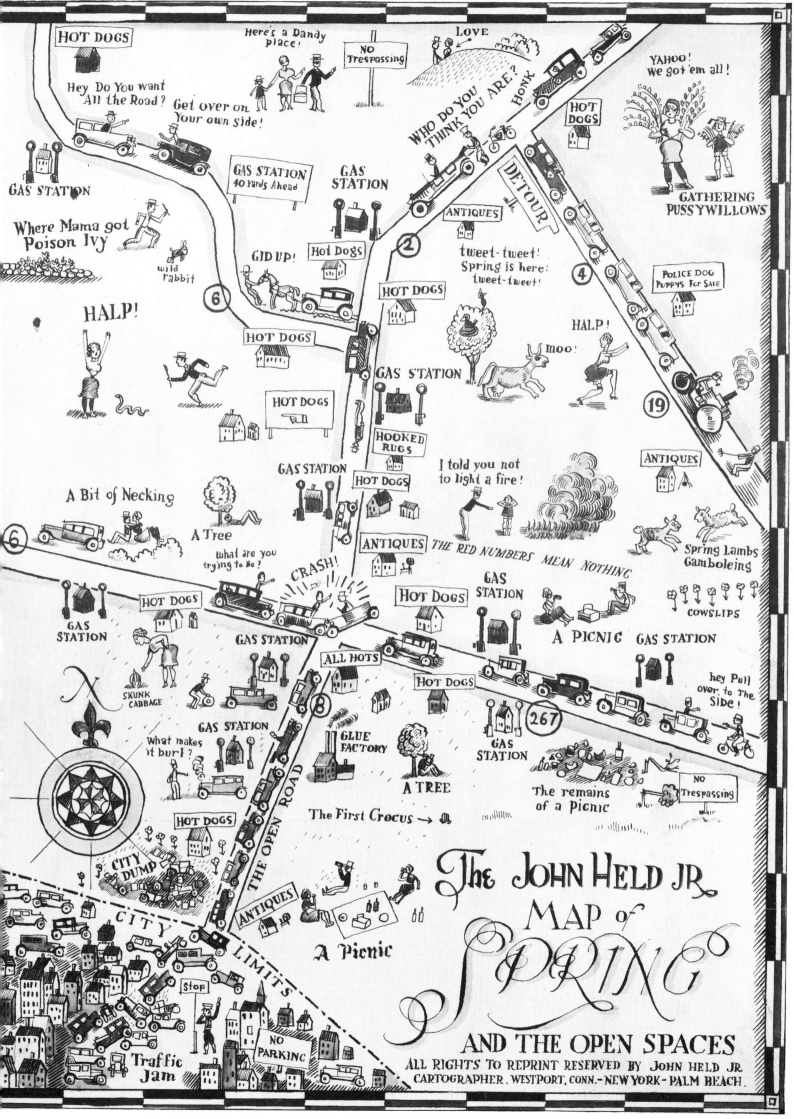

A Map of Spring and the Wide Open Spaces [Early 1920's]   Pen and ink, 11-1/4 x 15-1/16": Collection of Mrs. John Held Jr.

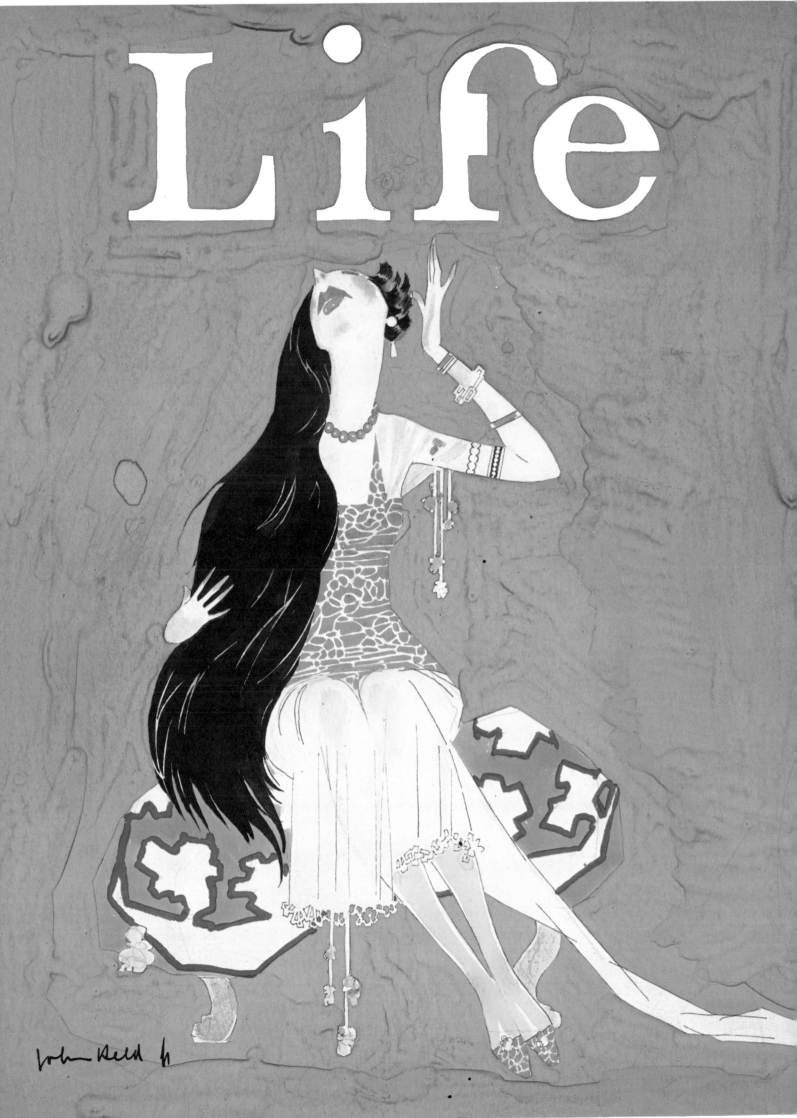

THE LONG AND THE SHORT OF IT Watercolor, 10 x 12-13/16″: *Life* cover, December 18, 1924: Collection of Mrs. John Held Jr.

A Sheik in Wolf's Clothing [*ca.* 1925]   Pen and Ink, 11-1/8 x 8": Collection of Mrs. John Held Jr.

WITH BEST WISHES FOR A MERRY CHRISTMAS

Blockprint, 5-1/8″ x 3-5/16″: Christmas card, mid 1920's: Collection of Mrs. John Held Jr.

Mother conceded that my drawing was a distant relative of the Arts, but in it she saw a living for me, perhaps in a garret. Yet even at that time I was making small money with my cartoons and I was engraving initials on the popular fad of the day, Friendship Hearts. These were small silver or gold bangles that the younger female set collected. The donor always had his initials engraved on the gift. I got to be pretty expert at engraving these at two and one-half cents a letter, after school in Dad's shop.

To clear up this last sentence: Father was a copper-plate engraver as well as a band leader and cornetist. He ran an engraving and embossing shop in the city.

THE FATE OF THE CIGARETTE FIEND
ENGRAVED BY JOHN HELD, JR

Blockprint, 12-3/16 x 13-9/16": *The New Yorker*, November 28, 1925: Collection of Mrs. John Held Jr.

HER BEAUTY SHE SOLD FOR AN OLD MAN'S GOLD
SHE'S A BIRD IN A GILDED CAGE
BY JOHN HELD JR THE PIONEER ENGRAVER

Blockprint, 13-5/8 x 11-5/8″: *The New Yorker*, October 27, 1928: Collection of Mrs. John Held Jr.

The DEAR DEAD DAYS
THE MILLINER AND THE CITY DRUMMER—OUT FOR NO GOOD
BY JOHN HELD, JR. A SENTIMENTAL ENGRAVER

Blockprint, 15-3/8 x 11-3/16″: *The New Yorker*, October 8, 1927: Collection of Mrs. John Held Jr.

STUDIO ON HILL WITH GOATS [*ca.* 1923]   Watercolor, 8-3/4 x 11-13/16″: Collection of Mrs. John Held Jr.

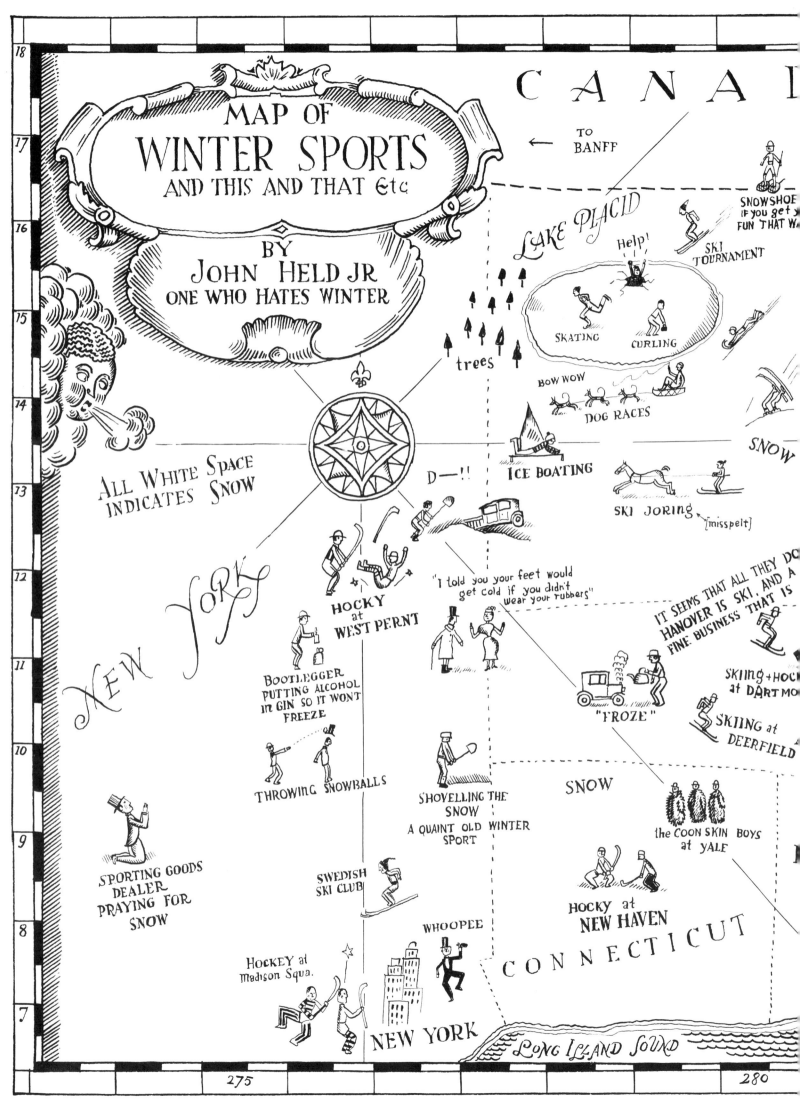

MAP OF WINTER SPORTS [Late 1920's]   Pen and ink, 24-3/16 x 15-3/16": Collection of Mrs. John Held Jr.

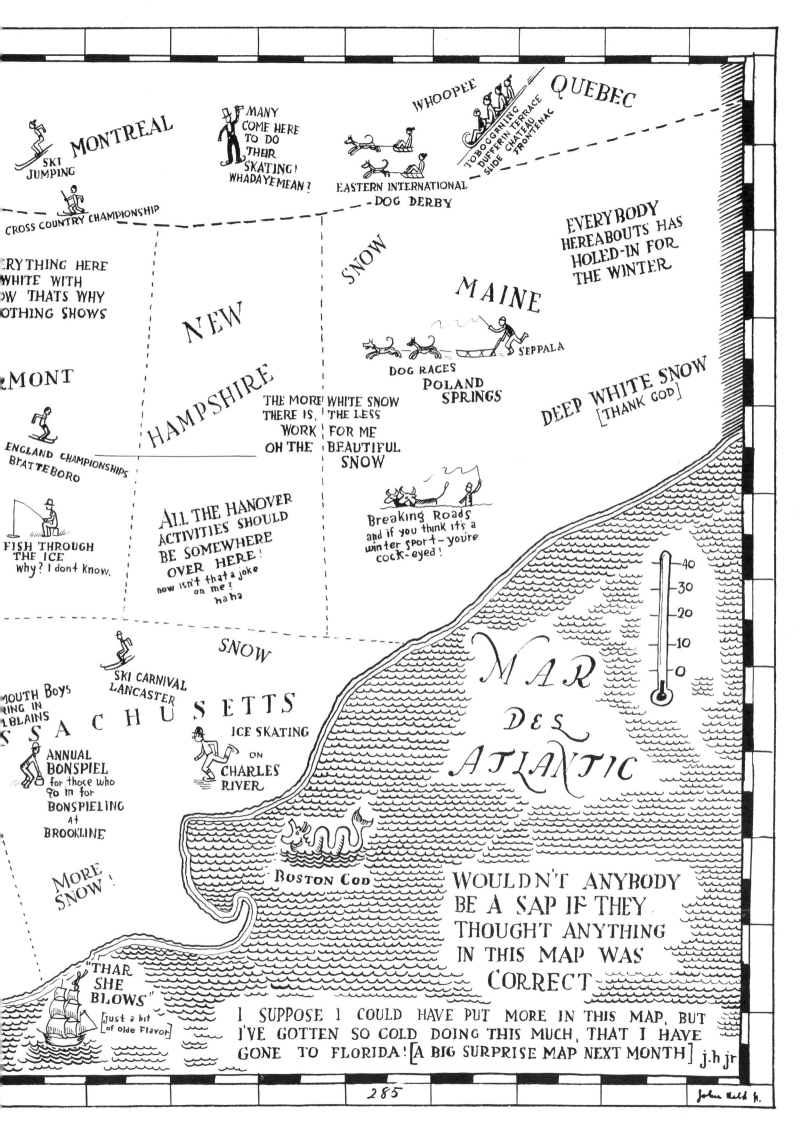

SKI JUMPING

MONTREAL

MANY COME HERE TO DO THEIR SKATING! WHADAYEMEAN?

WHOOPEE

TOBOGGANING
DUFFERIN TERRACE
CHATEAU FRONTENAC
SLIDE

QUEBEC

CROSS COUNTRY CHAMPIONSHIP

EASTERN INTERNATIONAL
-DOG DERBY

EVERYBODY HEREABOUTS HAS HOLED-IN FOR THE WINTER

ERYTHING HERE WHITE WITH OW THATS WHY OTHING SHOWS

NEW HAMPSHIRE

SNOW

MAINE

SEPPALA

DOG RACES
POLAND SPRINGS

DEEP WHITE SNOW
[THANK GOD]

RMONT

ENGLAND CHAMPIONSHIPS BRATTEBORO

THE MORE THERE IS WORK OH THE

WHITE SNOW THE LESS FOR ME BEAUTIFUL SNOW

FISH THROUGH THE ICE
why? I dont Know.

ALL THE HANOVER ACTIVITIES SHOULD BE SOMEWHERE OVER HERE!
now isn't that a joke on me?
ha ha

Breaking Roads
and if you think it's a winter sport - you're cock-eyed!

SNOW

SKI CARNIVAL LANCASTER

MOUTH Boys RING IN LBLAINS

SACHUSETTS

ICE SKATING
ON
CHARLES RIVER

MAR
DES
ATLANTIC

40
30
20
10
0

ANNUAL BONSPIEL
for those who go in for
BONSPIELING
At
BROOKLINE

MORE SNOW

BOSTON COD

WOULDN'T ANYBODY BE A SAP IF THEY THOUGHT ANYTHING IN THIS MAP WAS CORRECT

"THAR SHE BLOWS"
[Just a bit of olde Flavor]

I SUPPOSE I COULD HAVE PUT MORE IN THIS MAP, BUT I'VE GOTTEN SO COLD DOING THIS MUCH, THAT I HAVE GONE TO FLORIDA! [A BIG SURPRISE MAP NEXT MONTH] j.h jr

John Held jr.

BURLESQUE NUMBER   Watercolor, 10-5/8 x 13-13/16″: *Life* cover, April 19, 1928: Collection of Mrs. John Held Jr.

A SWELL MAP OF NEW YORK   Pen and ink, 12-7/8 x 18-1/4″: *The New Yorker*, December 31, 1927: Collection of Mrs. John Held Jr.

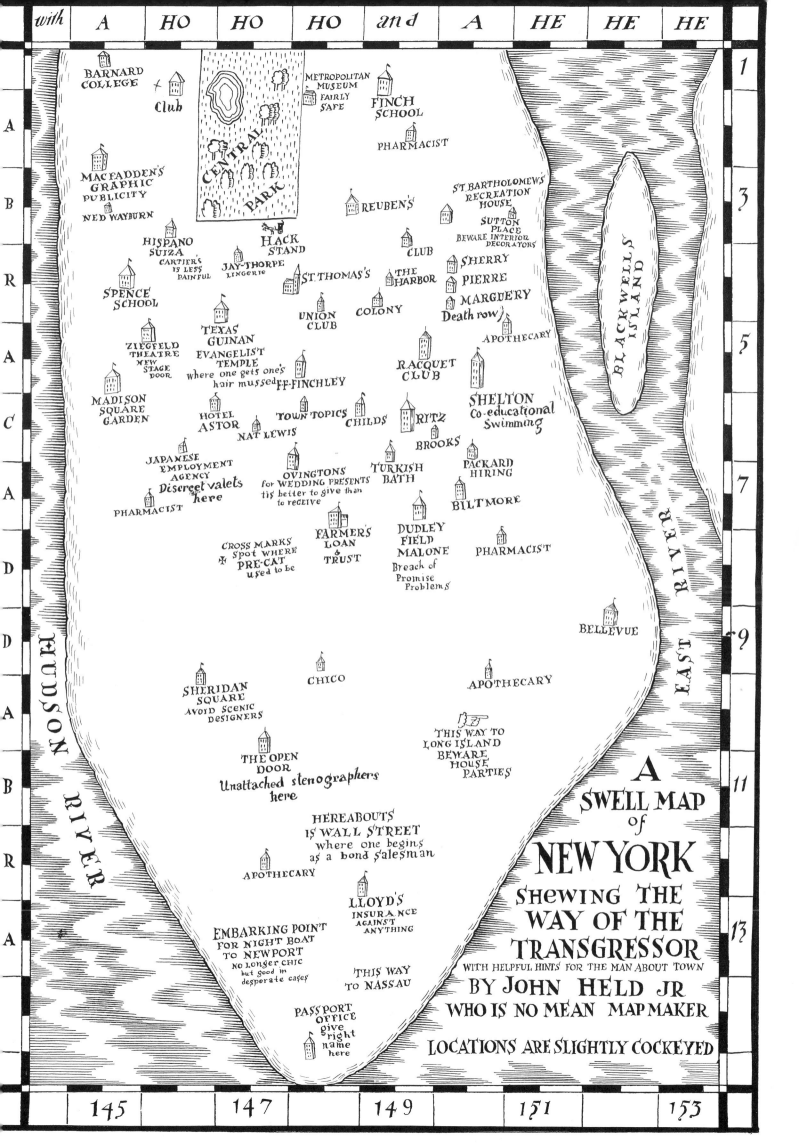

PINK STORMY LANDSCAPE [*ca.* 1923]   Watercolor, 7-1/16 x 9-1/2″, on folded sheet of brown wrapping paper: Collection of Mrs. John Held Jr.

THE DIVE   Pen and ink, 11-1/2 x 13-11/16″: Collection of Mrs. John Held Jr.

DAY-DREAMS OF SENTIMENTAL MEMORY

DANCING THE TURKEY TROT

ENGRAVED BY JOHN HELD JR AS HE SNAPS HIS FINGERS IN THE AIR

HEATHS SALT PALACE

DANCING TWO BITS

Scratchboard, 9-1/2 x 12-1/4″: *The New Yorker*, May 23, 1931: Collection of Mrs. John Held Jr.

**WHEN THE THEATRE WAS FRAUGHT WITH ROMANCE
ANNA HELD'S MILK BATH
ENGRAVED BY JOHN HELD JR WHO IS NO RELATION**

Scratchboard, 11-13/16 x 9-1/8″: *The New Yorker*, September 20, 1930: Collection of Mrs. John Held Jr.

For example, the wrists and hands of his people possess joints and knuckles, all accurately articulated and subtly indicated, the knees have kneecaps, where they show, and the girls' legs curve as the bones themselves bend in nature. At the same time, astute liberties enhance male and female characteristics: the heavy outsize masculine hand in contrast to the tense female one, like the taut strands of a spider web, define the mood and the moment experienced by the dancing couple [page 67] with truthful exaggeration.

SHE MISSED THE BOAT   Watercolor, 11-1/4 x 14-9/16″: *Life* cover, April 28, 1927: Collection of Mrs. John Held Jr.

March 31 1927

Price 15 cents

Life

John Held Jr.

SITTING PRETTY

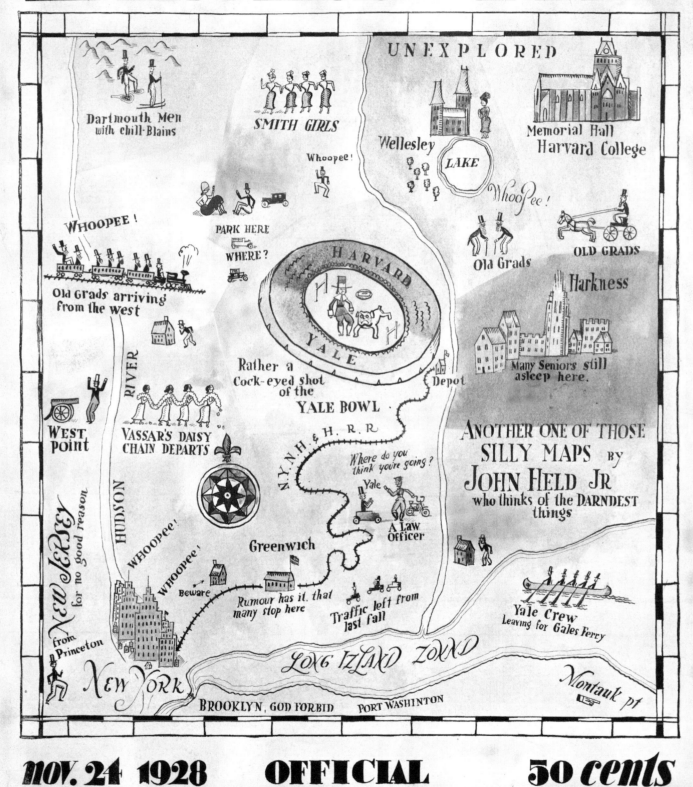

HARVARD vs YALE   Pen and ink, 12-1/2 x 16″: Football program cover, November 24, 1928: Collection of Mrs. John Held Jr.

Tangier

May – 1935

I Bet You Wish You Were Out in the Parkin' With a Girl, Maybe Kissin' Her   Pen and ink, 6-1/2 x 9-3/8":
From "Until the James Runs Dry" in *Grim Youth*, 1930: Courtesy Addison Gallery of American Art, Phillips Academy,
Andover, Massachusetts

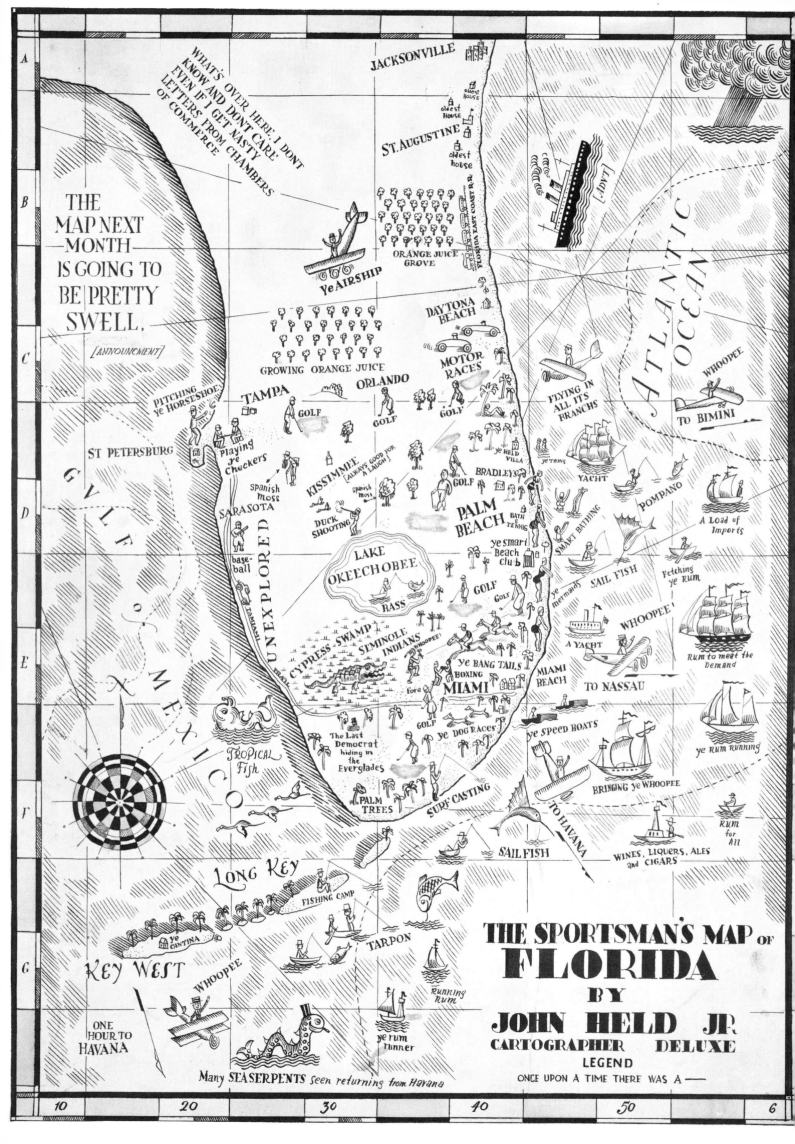

THE SPORTSMAN'S MAP OF
FLORIDA
BY
JOHN HELD JR.
CARTOGRAPHER DELUXE
LEGEND
ONCE UPON A TIME THERE WAS A——

BUT, MADAM, IT'S THE LATEST   Pen and ink, 12-3/8 x 8-3/16": *Liberty*, October 24, 1931: Collection of Mrs. John Held Jr.

SPORTSMAN'S MAP OF FLORIDA [Late 1920's]   Pen and ink, 13-3/8 x 18-1/16": Collection of Mrs. John Held Jr.

You've Opened Up a Bit of America I Wasn't Familiar With   Pen and ink, 6-11/16 x 10-7/8″: From "Miss Universe" in *Grim Youth*, 1930: Collection of Mrs. John Held Jr.

Afternoon Fantasy [mid-1920's]   Watercolor, 14-7/16 x 19-7/16″: Collection of Mrs. John He

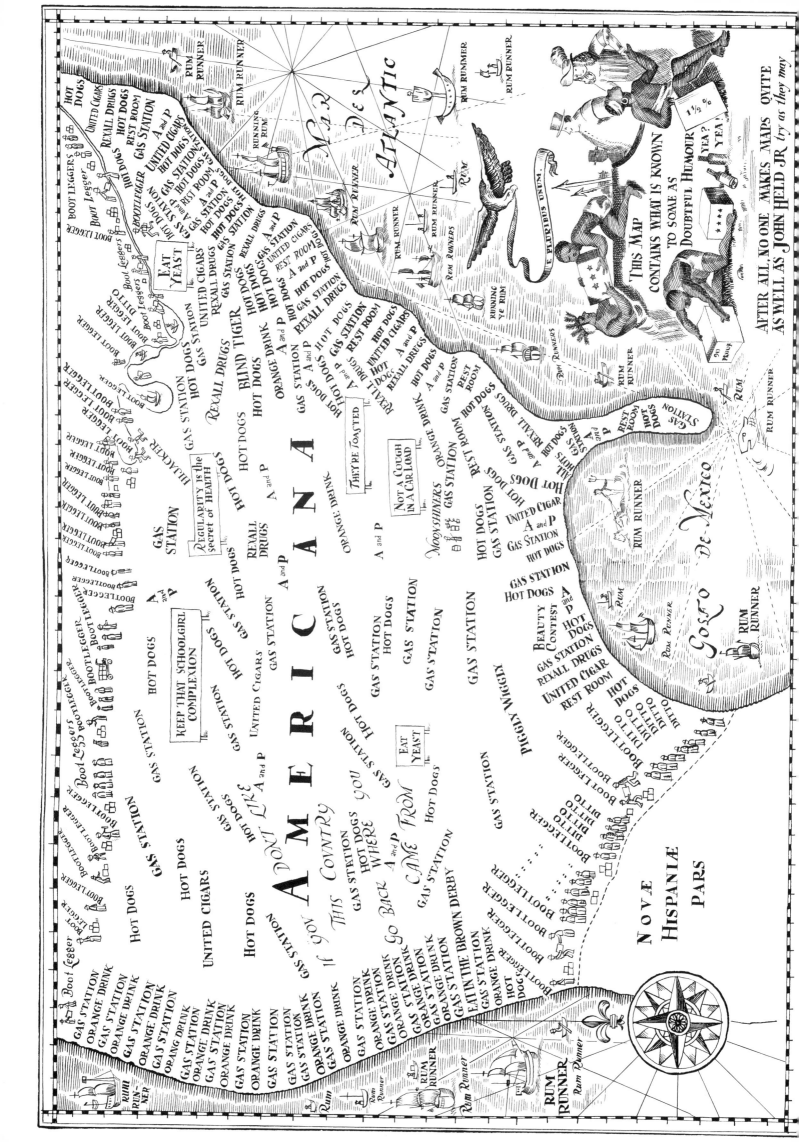

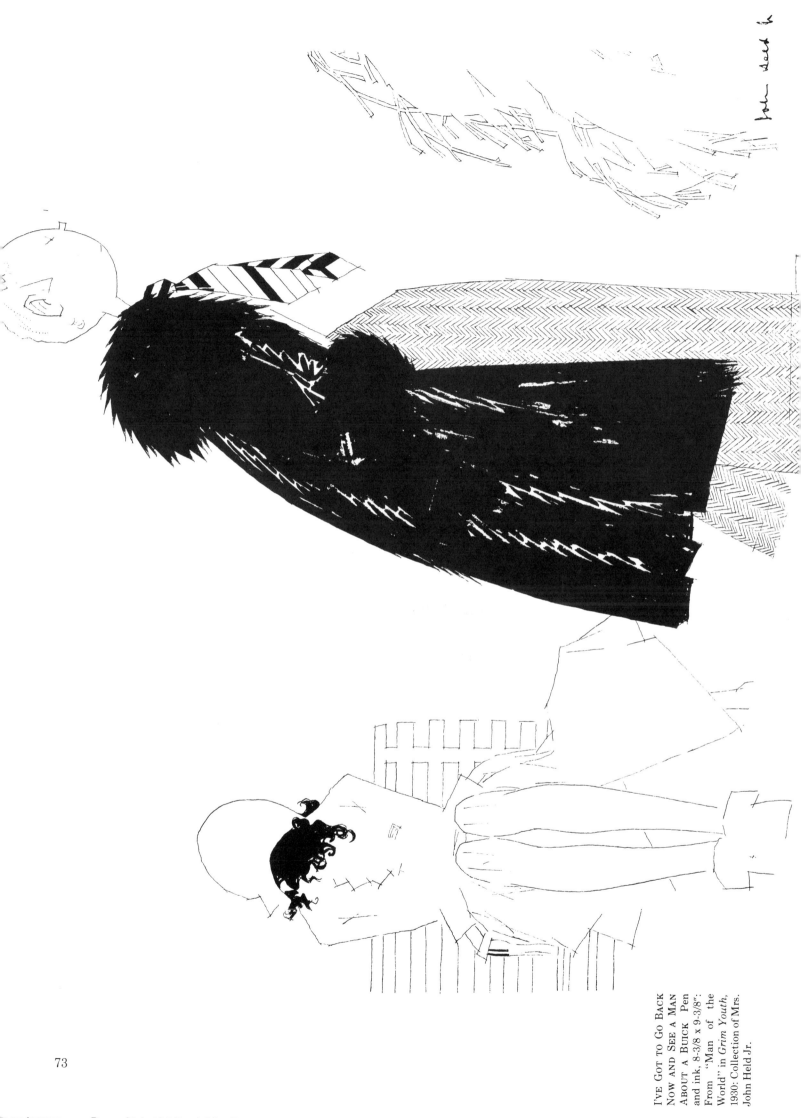

I'VE GOT TO GO BACK NOW AND SEE A MAN ABOUT A BUICK   Pen and ink, 8-3/8 x 9-3/8": From "Man of the World" in *Grim Youth*, 1930: Collection of Mrs. John Held Jr.

P OF AMERICANA   Pen and ink, 12-7/8 x 18-3/8": *The New Yorker*, August 18, 1928: Collection of Mrs. John Held Jr.

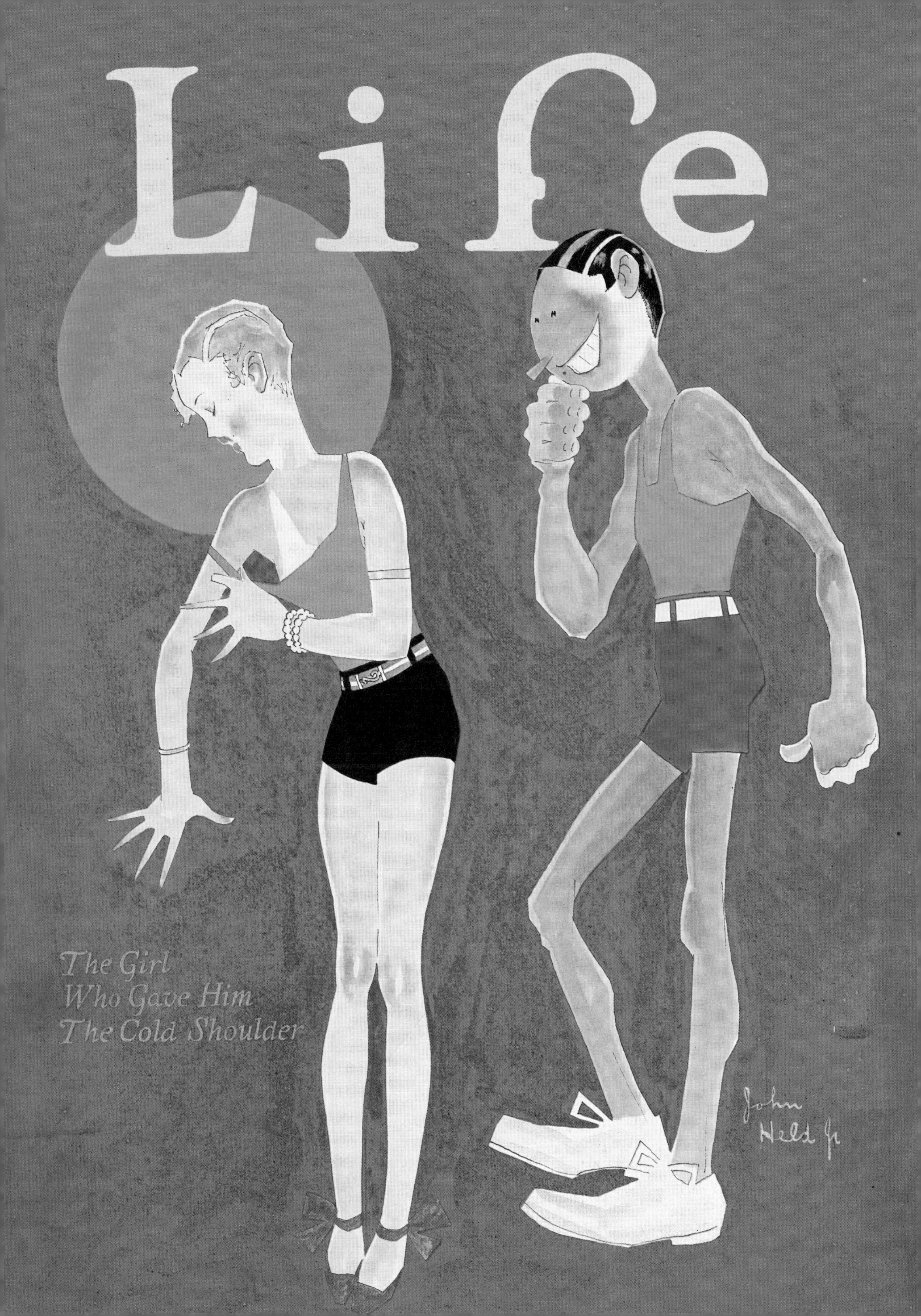

Life

The Girl
Who Gave Him
The Cold Shoulder

John Held Jr

THE BRONC. October, 1930   Bronze sculpture, height 14″: Photograph by Nicholas Muray: Collection of Mrs. John Held Jr.

His fondness for animals would rarely let him subject them to satire (although
there are exceptions, but even in such cases it is man who is the victim of his
derision, rather than the animals). In his drawing preparatory to sculpture and
in the sculpture itself, he observes his subject with a sedate, accurate eye.

THE GIRL WHO GAVE HIM THE COLD SHOULDER   Watercolor, 12-1/2 x 16-9/16″: *Life* cover [late 1920's]: Collection of Mrs. John Held Jr.

John Held Jr.

COLT Pen and ink, 10 x 5-3/4″: From *A Bowl of Cherries*, 1932: Collection of Mrs. John Held Jr.

RODEO

He knew how David felt
When he slew Goliath with a rock;
He knew how Bat Nelson felt
When he whipped Joe Gans,
Once he, too, had been a conqueror;
Between his knees had been
Hell in horsehide

When out of the chute
Came an untamed brute
Screaming and squealing
And bucking,

He had ridden Steamboat,
But that was long ago—
Before he got cracked up.
Now he sits up near the roof
And watches the youngsters
Top bronks.
He sits in silence
And hears the cheers
Echo in the canyon
Of his youth.

PORTRAIT OF A GANDER [*ca*. 1927]   Watercolor, 9-7/16 x 12″: Collection of Mrs. John Held Jr.

His things were in what was considered a new style and he was soon in demand to supply a fresh note in the jaded field of comic art, so-called. His dislike of social pretense made his wit biting and sardonic.

His artistic urge was toward higher planes than funny pictures. He wanted to paint, but his humorous drawings brought high prices and he was able to make a needed income from the magazines and the newspapers. He painted whenever he could spare time from his commercial art. He could now command larger sums from advertising agencies that planned campaigns "of the better sort."

Don't ever begin to believe that when you get to a certain point you're there. Don't ever put a limit to what you want to be, because when you get to that place, you're nowhere. Don't ever set yourself a stopping place, because maybe that's just the beginning. [Crosstown.]

I think there's a door in the back of everybody's head that lets out the dreams, or the creative instinct, or the mild madness or whatever you want to call it that makes us want to make our livings this way, and not sensibly. For the lucky ones, that door closes at puberty; the unfortunates go on all their lives fighting with publishers or art dealers. They never grow up, and don't say Peter Pan or I'll sock you. [From a 1934 interview.]

HERE WAS A CLASSICAL INTERLUDE COME TO LIFE   Pen and ink, 6-11/16 x 10-7/16″: From "An Afternoon" in *Grim Youth*, 1930: Courtesy Addison Gallery of American Art, Phillips Academy, Andover, Massachusetts

Peter sat at one end of the green davenport, with his feet tucked under him, seriously tooting on a saxophone that moaned its agony by changing register without warning. The room was warm and Peter's hair was tousled, a twisted curl stood out on each side of his forehead, and what with his ears being slightly pointed, he resembled the age-old symbol of youthful mischief. If one happened to have a turn of imagination, here was a classical interlude come to life. Peter was a faun, and the green davenport a grassy knoll, and the saxophone was a reed lute, and dryads were dancing to the music. This idyl could be seen only through the pink haze of imagination, as Peter was very real and the melody he was playing was hideously popular.

"All I need is time and less antagonism and I'll have this baby down hot. This is the way Rudy Vallee got his start." [**Grim Youth.**]

Figurative drawing is not always a matter of representing what can be seen by the naked eye, but sometimes by what is known and can be imagined. The youth and his saxophone are drawn as concrete images. The simple outline of the sofa and the frame on the wall provide an explicit setting. However, the mood which the wailing instrument induces is represented by dotted lines, much as an invisible but known edge is imagined in engineering drawing.

What can be observed as fact and what can be suggested as idea are distinctions which come only from visual training. The amateur will usually delineate complete contours even though in everyday experience the eye does not focus equally on them. The selectivity and economy of means is perhaps the most signal aspect of Held's artistry, and he learned this selective ability early in his career.

81

SEPT 9 — 31
Lac St Jean St Felix d otis

LAC ST. JEAN. September 4, 1931   Watercolor, 11-9/16 x 15-11/16″: Collection of Mrs. John Held Jr.

A Vision in a Pink Organdy Frock   Pen and ink, 6-1/2 x 9-3/8″: From "Waltz" in *The Flesh is Weak*, 1931: Collection of Mrs. John Held Jr.

Scratchboard, 12-1/4 x 11″: *The New Yorker*, January 24, 1931: Collection of Mrs. John Held Jr.

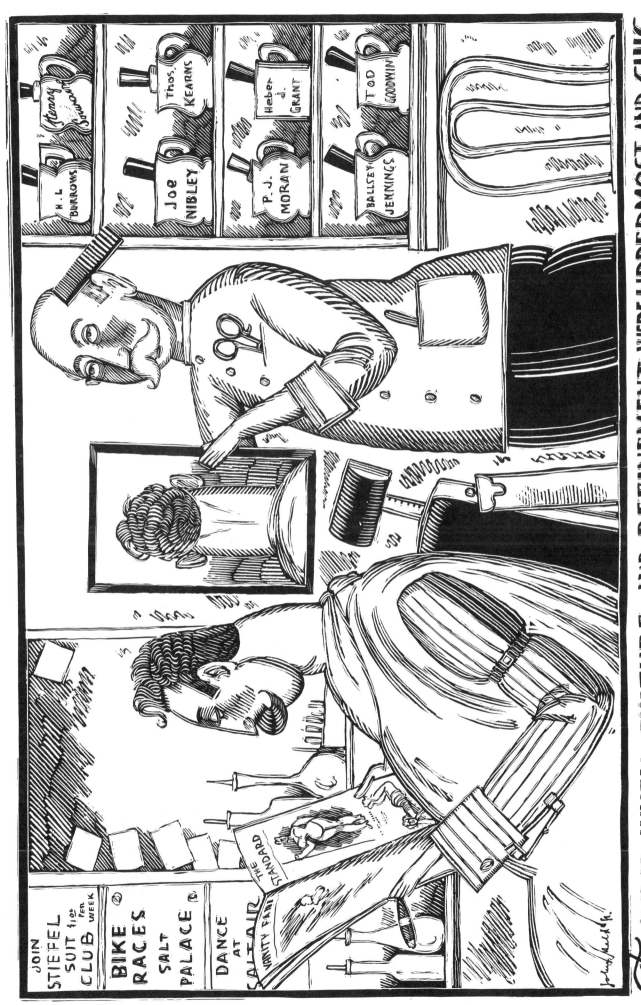

Scratchboard, 12-1/16 x 9-5/16": *The New Yorker*, June 6, 1931: Collection of Mrs. John Held Jr.

THE SUNSET [*ca.* 1938]   Watercolor, 15 x 19-9/16″: Courtesy Addison Gallery of American Art, Phillips Academy, Andover, Massachusetts

You Can Talk Softly: Your Mother Will Think I'm Making Love to You   Pen and ink, 11-1/4 x 15″: From "Ride of the Valkyries" in *Grim Youth*, 1930: Courtesy Addison Gallery of American Art, Phillips Academy, Andover, Massachusetts

MOTOR CAR

At most colleges, students are forbidden to have, use, or maintain motor cars. This rule can be gotten around by garaging the car in the nearest neighboring town. If the car is not furnished by the parents, it must be purchased by the student. A good "student car" is priced anywhere from fifteen dollars up. Sometimes these cars are not the very latest models, but if ingenuity is used, mechanical difficulties are overcome without much bother. I know of one car that was purchased for the astounding sum of seven dollars. It was a model T Ford. This car was held in equity by nine boys. It served its purpose very well until the engine fell out in the midst of traffic at a Harvard-Yale football game. This necessitated the New Haven police to detour the cars that were returning to New York. The motor car is an educational factor in college life. The chief study is, What on earth makes some of the cars run?

PARKING

Parking is a delightful evening's study. The student and female companion drive out to some lonely place on a little-used road. There the car is stopped and the lights turned out. If the young lady is adept at parking, there is no difficulty. But, if she is one that the student isn't very well acquainted with, it is always convenient to run out of gas at some dark spot. At this point, the young lady either walks back, or she doesn't. If a closed car is used, there is more room if one door is opened.

BUSHING

Bushing is, in some respects, the same as Parking. A car is not necessary for Bushing. A heavy dew is disastrous to really good Bushing. But on a dry moonlit night, with the windows of the club house sparkling with light, and the faint strain of a waltz floating out over the ornamental shrubbery, Bushing is very intriguing. If a bench is convenient, so much the better. If you do your Bushing at the country club, don't let the lady walk on the eighteenth green in French-heeled shoes.

THE RELUCTANT PARTNER   Pen and ink, 6-9/16 x 10-7/16″: From *The Dublin Letters*, 1931: Collection of Mrs. John Held Jr.

PAN AND THE SHEEP [1930's]   Watercolor, 14-13/16 x 19-3/4": Collection of Mrs. John Held Jr.

NORTHWARD   Travel poster for the New Haven Railroad [mid-1930's]: Collection of Mrs. John Held Jr.

THE GARTER [1930's]   Pen and ink, 6 x 8-7/16″: Collection of Mrs. John Held Jr.

AND HOW MANY CARBONS, SIR?   Pen and ink, 12-3/8 x 8-1/16″: *Liberty*, December 12, 1931: Collection of Mrs. John Held Jr.

"Gosh, He's Got a Hot Line," She Said   Pen and ink, 6-1/2 x 9-1/2": From "Waltz" in *The Flesh Is Weak,* 1931: Collection of Mrs. John Held Jr.

A Cowboy Saint Francis [*ca.* 1935]   Watercolor, 15 x 19-7/8″: Collection of Mrs. John Held Jr.

WHEN THE THEATRE WAS FRAUGHT WITH ROMANCE

· DOING THE SPLIT ·

ENGRAVED BY JOHN HELD JR MAN AND BOY

96

[STALKING] THE THANKSGIVING TURKEY   Pen and ink, 8-1/4 x 12-1/2": *Liberty*, November 28, 1931: Collection of Mrs. John Held Jr.

NAVAJO PAN [ca. 1938] Watercolor, 15-1/4 x 20"; Collection of Mrs. John Held, Jr.

UNCLE PIERRE AND THE HALCYON DAYS

Uncle Pierre was indeed a minor genius. He was one of the most versatile mechanics that I have ever known. He had no inventive side, but let someone else invent and he would improve to the extent of making the apparatus do many more things than it was intended to do. He was touched by the gods.

It was in his ascendancy that electricity was harnessed and put to use. Uncle Pierre seemed to understand this miracle and he tamed it from the start.

In his day the pioneer engineers of the mid-Rockies had utilized the water power in the mountain streams and had electrified the sovereign city of Zion in Deseret. Uncle Pierre was the city's trouble shooter. The most difficult electrical contrivance was child's play to him because he always, somehow, managed to make it tick.

Not only any electrical problem, but any mechanical poser was his meat. If a machine would not perform, Uncle Pierre would either make it accomplish its original function or would make it do something different. But right or wrong, he always managed to make it work.

When my father was working out the construction of his embossing presses and the complicated mechanics of printing copper plates, it was Uncle Pierre who supervised the precision castings and the adjustment of the delicate bearings. For all this machinery they made the irregular wooden forms, did the castings from the illustrations in a manufacturer's catalogue of that type of press, and, by the great Jehovah, it worked, and was in operation for many years. I operated these presses in my apprenticeship of the copper-plate and steel-die printing of visiting cards and embossed stationery.

Outside interests other than those of the Mormon Church crept in to the thriving hub metropolis of Zion, and later the name of the town was Anglicized to Salt Lake City. With coming of statehood, the Territory of Deseret became the State of Utah.

Salt Lake was a booming place and a wide-open city, a mining and cattle center. The miner of gold and silver and copper came in with pockets burning with money to spend on a high time, and the night life knew no bounds.

In every saloon, bar or public place were slot machines—not the nickel variety, but the two-bit, four-bit and dollar wheels of chance. These complicated gambling devices had to be kept in repair, and the man to do that job, and do it with mastery, was Uncle Pierre. Whenever one of these machines became unruly and paid off too large a percentage, Uncle Pierre would appear, and with a few expert touches of his screwdriver or pliers, the machine would go back into line and make a larger profit for the owner.

In this service Uncle Pierre widened his acquaintance in the half-world, or the nocturnal civilization, of Salt Lake. He knew and was a friend of every saloonkeeper, bartender, gambler, and lady of the evening. He was a personal friend of every madam in established houses of delight, of which there were none more delightful or elegant between Denver and San Francisco. It was said that the elegance of these palaces surpassed the lavishness of even New Orleans or Omaha. This was probably hearsay, as a gold or silver miner's or a cattle or sheep man's idea of elegance was moot in the extreme.

Uncle Pierre picked up a tidy income by installing electric bells in these abodes of pastime. His account book read like a *Who's Who in the Underworld.*

In those days the hot spots of Salt Lake were located in a tidy manner on a street that ran between First and Second South and Main and State.

This thoroughfare was called, without any attempt at grim humor, Commercial Street. Within the street were saloons, cafés and parlor houses, and cribs that were rented nightly to the itinerate Ladies of The Calling. Soliciting was taboo, so these ladies sat at the top of the stairs and called their invitation to "come on up, kid."

The parlor houses allowed no such publicity. There was no outward display to gain entrants to a parlor house. One pushed an electric bell (installed by Uncle Pierre) and was admitted by a uniformed maid or an attendant. The luxury of these houses always included a "Professor" at the piano. There was none of the brashness of the mechanical piano; those were heard in the saloons and shooting galleries of the street.

The names of two of the madams are engraved on my memory, just as they were cut on the copper plates that Dad made for printing the ladies' personal cards. In Dad's engraving shop an order for cards from the madams was always welcome. They demanded the finest and most expensive engraving, and the cards were of the finest stock, pure rag vellum. The dimensions of these cards were different from the accepted social standard: they were always about one-half inch by one and one-half inches. This size was very difficult to print by hand from the copper plate, and the order was in most cases for five hundred or more. This was a long run, but the money was fresh and there was no quibbling about price.

One of the madams called herself Miss Ada Wilson. Hers was a lavish house on Commercial Street. Another gave her name as Miss Helen Blazes. Her establishment catered to the big money, and in it only wine was served. In other houses, beer was the popular refreshment—at one dollar a bottle, served to the guests in small whiskey glasses. These were mere token drinks, on which the house made a good, substantial profit.

It was a familiar sight in the streets of Salt Lake

to see Miss Wilson take her afternoon drive in a smart dogcart with a shiny chestnut Hackney pony. Her companion was usually a rather handsome mulattto, supposedly her personal maid. Miss Blazes, however, made no such ostentatious display, as hers was a very conservative house.

There were many other houses of repute—ill, that is—in the town, but the names of these others are gone from my memory. I do remember vividly that the decorations ran to mirrored ballrooms and red plush.

In my introduction to these spots, Uncle Pierre was my mentor. His purpose was purely social the first time I went with him as his guest, and my pleasure was short-lived. I was then around fifteen years old, and after a few dances and light beers I was one sick pigeon. So my baptism in the fleshpots was a dim grey puling celebration.

The orchard of Salt Lake's night life was bearing rich golden fruit, and it was easy pickings. Both Sodom and Gomorrah were paying high dividends. Many greedy eyes sparkled, many mouths watered, and hosts of palms itched for this bounty.

Then the hue and cry rose to "Clean up Salt Lake." Committees of decency were quickly formed and the fight was on. At the outset it was a moral issue. The newspaper opposing the current regime screamed its banner headlines, and "the decent people of the city" rose in protest against the system in power. There was a suggestion that control should be exercised over the dark side of the city's life—a subtle thought, but it worked; and the battle continued in its planned strategy.

By strange coincidence this crusade was at its height when, lo and behold, it was time for an election. Those in power had grown sleek, fat, and lazy as the golden crop ripened and fell into their laps, and when the votes were counted, virtue had triumphed over evil and the opposition was in. There was a complete housecleaning in the city administration. Most important of all was a new police department, which went right to work making a reality of the campaign slogan to "Clean up Salt Lake." Actually, the old regime had begun cleaning up; but now there was a new broom, and what a new broom does is traditional. The opposition had won on a virtue program, so virtue must be enforced.

Soon it was hinted that the oldest profession was a necessary evil, after all: since it was impossible to do away with this trade, the best way out was to control it, and segregation was the only solution to the problem. Just by chance there was a lady going by the name of Belle London in the town of Ogden, forty-odd miles north of Salt Lake, who was an expert on this sort of quandary. Fortunately she could be persuaded by the new city government to come to Salt Lake and take charge of the entire perplexing situation. She dealt with it by closing all the gilded ballrooms and the cribs of Commercial Street, and the occupants were denied their trade.

The new city administration was again in luck by being able to secure a tract of real estate down near the Rio Grande Western Railroad depot where a walled "Stockade" was erected. Inside, buildings were provided, some large and some merely a series of small rooms that opened on the streets and passageways. All this complex was to be operated by Miss London under license from the police. Here was perfect control under one management—and an arrangement that made the pickings much easier.

In Commerical Street all the red lights were extinguished. The street became respectable: it now sheltered only saloons, gambling houses, shooting galleries and opium dens; the old familiar feminine faces were seen there no more. And the Held Engraving Company lost the lucrative business of engraving and printing the madams'—shall we say, business?—cards, because Miss Belle London had *her* cards done in Denver.

Of course in all moral groups there are some fanatics, so while the Stockade was operating satisfactorily for the new police force and Miss London, there was a demand every so often for a clean-up. This demand was met by a police raid on the area, attended with sufficient publicity.

To make these raids painless to the occupants of the Stockade, a system of alarm bells was installed inside its enclosure, for use in case a raid came without previous warning. It was Uncle Pierre who installed this warning system.

At the entrance to the walled city of sin there was stationed a gatekeeper, there to guard the inmates from undesirable clientele, so to speak. All he ever did was to keep the kids out and sound the alarm bell in the event of a so-called necessary raid.

On the face of things this was the only entrance to the Stockade, but there were several secret openings in the walled enclosure, known to the inmates and most of the incorrigible young males of the fair city.

Saturday night was the big night all over town, and also, of course, within the Stockade. It was payday, and after a man had mucked all week in the bowels of a mine or worked for six days on a railroad construction gang, his appetite was for a high old time with money no object.

On the particular Saturday night I have in mind, while the lights were bright and the fleshpots were boiling, the alarm-bell system went wrong, and Uncle Pierre was called to make repairs. I had been watching him install some lighting fixtures in one of the showcases in Dad's shop, marveling at the miracle that he brought forth from electricity. Naturally I went with him to help carry his bag of tools to repair the Stockade alarm bell.

The festivities and joys were in high crescendo when we arrived. Uncle Pierre, upon making his investigation as to what was wrong with the alarm bell, touched

Blockprint, 14 x 11-3/4": *The New Yorker*, September 29, 1928: Collection of Mrs. John Held Jr.

a connection in the wiring and the bell sounded its alarm with a great to-do. Whereupon all joy ceased, the music was quieted, and all inmates and clients silently stole away through the secret exits that led to darkness in the underbrush—leaving Uncle Pierre, the gatekeeper and me alone in the building. Uncle Pierre calmly went about making the repairs. Just as he finished, there came the police, accompanied by a Moral Committeeman, in a surprise raid.

Upon the approach of the raiding party, the gatekeeper disappeared in the fog of coal smoke from the switch engines in the railroad yards.

Uncle Pierre and I were the sole occupants of the half-world. The Committeeman demanded action in the cause of Purity.

The chief of police winked at Uncle Pierre and me, then shouted: "I arrest you in the name of the Law!" This seemed to satisfy the Committeeman and he saw us safely aboard the horse-drawn Black Maria. Then Uncle Pierre excused himself for a minute, went back to the entrance and sounded the All Clear on the alarm system. Then we rode off uptown.

The police let us out of the paddy wagon at the city's center. It was a nice ride, and it saved us streetcar fare.

ANGEL OVER SAINT PATRICK'S [Mid- 1930's]   Watercolor, 14-1/2 x 19-1/2″: Collection of Mrs. John Held Jr.   102

COWBOY CENTAURS [*ca.* 1938]   Watercolor, 15-3/16 x 20″: Collection of Mrs. John Held Jr.

STANDING COWBOY [1930's]   Bronze sculpture, height 9-1/2″: Photograph by Nicholas Muray: Collection of Mrs. John Held Jr.

HER COSTUME WAS TOPPED OFF WITH A PAIR OF LONG, WHITE SAILOR PANTS   Pen and ink, 8-1/4 x 11-13/16″: From "Penitentiary Bait" in *The Flesh Is Weak*, 1931: Collection of Mrs. John Held Jr.

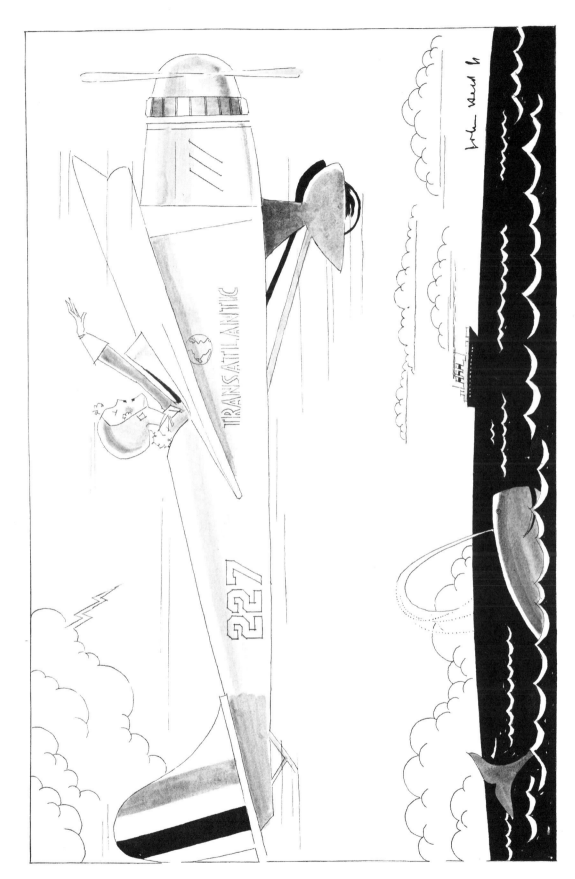

FLYING HIGH Pen and ink, 12-7/16 x 8-1/8"; *Liberty*, September 12, 1931; Collection of Mrs. John Held Jr.

A SCENE from the SENTIMENTAL PAST THAT ROMANTIC SPOT KNOWN AS THE "BACK ROOM" "AH-ME!" ENGRAVED BY JOHN HELD JR. WHO IS FAMED IN SONG AND STORY

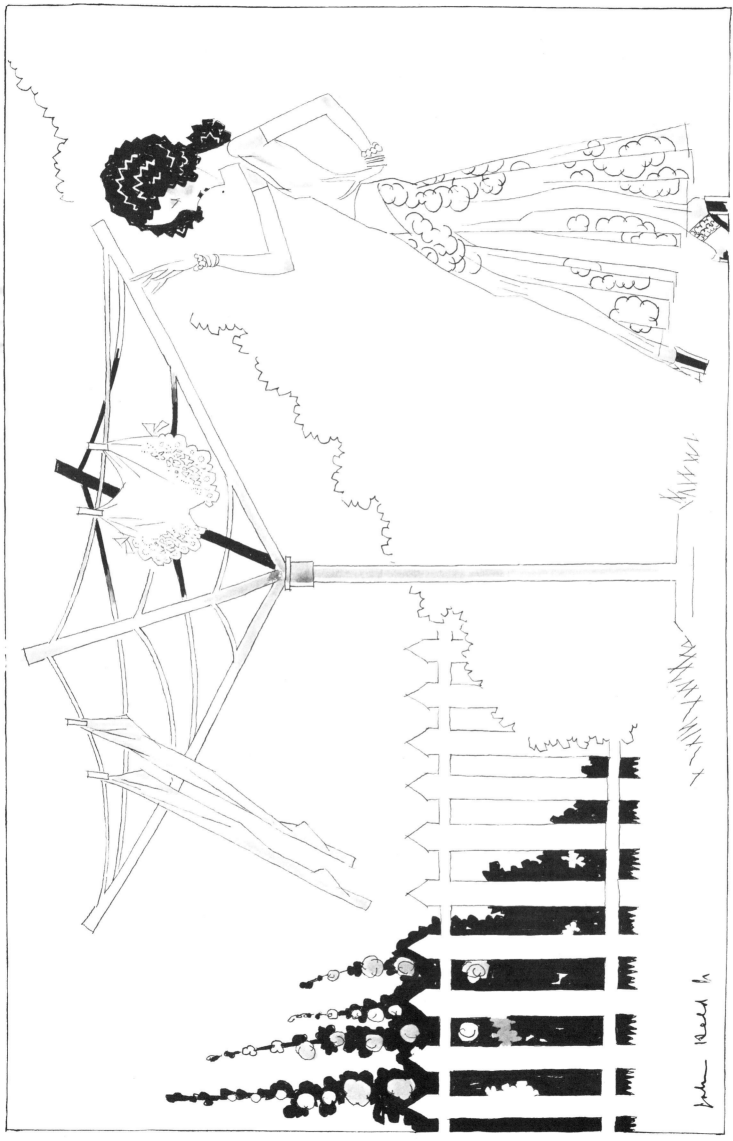

A SUMMER BREEZE   Pen and ink, 8-1/4 x 12-1/2": *Liberty*, October 31, 1931: Collection of Mrs. John Held Jr.

HE WOULD KEEP US IN THE AIR FOR HOURS   Pen and ink, 6-1/4 x 9-3/4″: From "The Pigeon of St. Patrick's" in *The Flesh Is Weak*, 1931: Collection of Mrs. John Held Jr.

RED MANHATTAN [*ca*. 1936]   Watercolor, 14 x 10": Collection of Mrs. John Held Jr.

To fly high and look down on the great city with its deep traffic lanes, surging with thousands of motor cars and millions of people and all the tall skyscrapers pointing up at me; to see the curling smoke make dancing shadows on the roof tops; to watch the light change and make lovely colors in the dim canyons; to see the wide rivers on each side of the city with the queer-shaped boats cutting silver streaks in the water; to fly high and see all this at a glance is romantic, and don't let anyone tell you different. [The Flesh Is Weak.]

111

OKAY, MEET ME AT THE CORNER   Pen and ink, 6-5/8 x 9-3/16″: From "Sax and Sex" in *The Flesh Is Weak*, 1931: Collection of Mrs. John Held Jr.

"You know, Baby, I've been thinking lately. It's funny how a man will get thinking, isn't it? I've been thinking about life. There's more in it than appears on the surface. You know, life is very complex," Spug went on, without looking at the girl by his side. "I've been trying to figure out a lot of problems. Now, take me. When I look back at what I was two years ago, I must've been terrible. I didn't know what the right thing was then. I didn't know the right kind of clothes from the wrong kind; I didn't know about manners, except the wrong steer that Dad and Mother tried to give me. I must have been terrible then. These last two years have made a big difference in my life. I was terribly narrow-minded.

"You wouldn't believe it, but two years ago I actually wore a hat—sounds silly to you, knowing me now, doesn't it?"
[Grim Youth.]

Held's art, as we have now come to think of it, subjectively diagrammed the foibles as well as the innocent and not so innocent virtues of contemporary youth. The virtue was an uncompromising honesty regarding a youthful society's self-determined behavior. A social code was emerging which was both absurd and dignified, and therein lies the humor and historical value that form the content of his keen observation and deft draftsmanship. The revival of the coonskin coat today, as well as the coincidental elongation of the female leg in response to the mini-skirt, are points of fashion which contribute to the vivid enjoyment of his art and retrieve it from what might otherwise be merely quaint.

Over the balustrade a view of New York's skyline presented itself. The towers and shafts of the skyscraper city rose in the distance across the space of the lower buildings that had been older New York. The outlines of the structures cut the sky and made a pattern against the sunset.

The faint music of a hurdy-gurdy rose from the tenement street near the river. To the south were more fantastic designs of set-back buildings and smokestacks. Deep below on the east flowed the dark waters of the East River—the surface cut in shimmering ribbons by tugs with barges in tow, and flickering lights of water traffic, and the bridges that stretched thin spans and joined the island with another island. The prison roofs and walls and grass plots appeared attractive from the heights. [Crosstown.]

The ability to see objects in their exact relation one to the other, and to separate the important details from the mass are the first requisite of the artist. The second requisite is the power to re-create the image so that the many may also see through the artist's eyes. The multitude looks, but does not see. The average man, even if he saw, could not reproduce the scene with brush or pen.

114

MANHATTAN DAWN. March, 1936   Watercolor, 14 x 12″: Collection of Mrs. John Held Jr

THE TRAIN   Pen and ink, 12-3/8 x 8-1/8": *Liberty*, December 19, 1931: Collection of Mrs. John Held Jr.

116

Now There Are Four   Pen and ink, 8-1/8 x 12-3/8": *Liberty*, December 26, 1931: Collection of Mrs. John Held Jr.

MORNING [*ca.* 1936]   Watercolor, 10 x 14″: Collection of Mrs. John Held Jr.

Mazie was fond of lying in the shade of the chimneys and watching the clouds. On windy days the clouds would race fast and their movement seemed to animate the skyline. "It's fun to just lay here and watch the buildings move," she said to Buddy. "If you kind of close your eyes it seems like the big smokestacks of the slaughterhouse are falling."

She would lie for hours and watch the flocks of circling pigeons as they winged to heights until they were small dots in the sky. They would disappear from sight as they turned, and it was a great game to locate them by the flashes of light on their beating wings. She would watch the flocks merge and then will in her mind which room they should return to at the signals of the keepers, who waved flags of rags attached to long bamboo fish poles. The pigeon-flyers were on the roofs from morning until darkness drove them in and the birds to roost.

This morning was perfect. The sky was deep blue and the fleecy clouds were tinted opalescent as they moved at different speeds in their heights.

Mazie, tiring of the clouds and pigeons, stretched herself, stomach down, on the coping and watched the street below. A slight giddiness added to the attraction. A gang of boys played baseball between the passing traffic. The blatant music of the German bands had been stilled by the War and had not as yet attempted re-appearance. The music was furnished this morning by a cracked-voiced soloist, who sang in an adjoining airshaft, and by a hurdy-gurdy that ground "There's a Long, Long Trail a-Winding" in the next street.

A wagonload of gay growing plants turned the corner into the street and came to a stop beneath her. Buddy had joined his mistress in watching the bird's-eye view. He barked at the horse and at the wagon's cargo of bloom.

"Don't bark at my garden," said Mazie. "It's beautiful."
[Crosstown.]

119

Beulah spent her days from eight to five at the Athens Candy factory. She was, among others, a wrapper of U-Wanta Nut bars. She was eighteen. After one year of Junior High School, she had started to work steady. In the three years since leaving school, there had been no need for education, except that it enabled her to read the moving-picture magazines, and these she devoured.

She was the Greta Garbo type. That is, she wore her ash blonde hair the same way as the movie star. There the likeness ceased. She was thin; she lacked grace; her face was much too small in proportion to her height. She was pretty but cheap. She used too much perfume. Her voice was husky and her manner of speaking was monotonous. She was attired in a very short, high-waisted, black satin skirt, worn shiny; a rayon shirtwaist, elaborate but faded; a white knitted beret was her millinery. Her long thin legs were sheathed in silk hose. There was a mended run down the back of the right calf. On the left was a run unmended. Her stockings were rolled down to the hem of her skirt. A blue garter on each leg could be glimpsed from the rear as she walked. There was a dark spot on each ankle where her black silk pumps rubbed at each step. A horseman would say that she interfered. The heel of one pump was slightly run over. [The Flesh Is Weak.]

AL AND BEULAH   Pen and ink, 6-3/4 x 8-13/16″: From "The Holy Bonds" in *The Flesh Is Weak*, 1931: Collection of Mrs. John Held Jr.

UNICORN LEADING A HERD OF WILD MARES [ca. 1938]   Watercolor, 17-9/16 x 20": Collection of Mrs. John Held Jr.

COWBOY'S CHRISTMAS [*ca.* 1938] Watercolor, 19-3/8 x 10-5/16". Collection of Mrs. John Held Jr.

COWBOY TIGHTENING GIRTH [1930's]   Bronze sculpture, height 9-1/2″: Photograph by Joseph Szaszfai: Collection of Mrs. John Held Jr.

A still more important aspect of drawing in general is what, for want of a better term, may be called visual weight—one visual attraction balanced by a different sort of visual attraction. For example, the dark opening of the trees through which the forest is defined lift the "wrestling match" out of a setting which could be almost anywhere. But by *not* drawing actual trees the artist constructs his stage. The zig-zag lines to the upper right of the drawing provide a three-dimensional sense of space and also a counter-balance to the linear lightness of the "babe," whose black-gloved hands, incidentally, are entangled with the marcelled male hair, both figuratively and as a compositional unit.

I Figure a Little Wrestling Was the Least I Could Do for Her   Pen and ink, 10-3/4 x 14-3/4″: From "Lochinvar" in *The Flesh Is Weak*, 1931: Collection of Mrs. John Held Jr.

MIDTOWN MORNING. March 25, 1936   Watercolor, 14 x 20″: Collection of Mrs. John Held Jr.

"ARE YOU A VIRGIN?" HE ASKED COLDLY   Pen and ink, 6-1/2 x 9-7/8″: From "Nocturne" in *The Flesh Is Weak*, 1931: Collection of Mrs. John Held Jr.

127

FIVE MINUTES MORE   Pen and ink, 6-9/16 x 10-3/8″: From *The Dublin Letters*, 1931: Collection of Mrs. John Held Jr.

"Yeah, It's Cooler Here," She Answered As She Crossed Her Legs   Pen and ink, 6-1/4 x 8-5/8": From "Penitentiary Bait" in *The Flesh Is Weak*, 1931: Collection of Mrs. John Held Jr.

When I arrived at Cambridge for the beginning of Harvard's 1940 Spring term, I was set upon by a crowd of Boston newspaper men. They asked me what the title of Artist in Residence meant, and what my duties were. I answered, "You know just as much about it as I do, Chum."

. . . I got going very well with the sculpture. I started to do a Percheron stallion, having had the idea in my mind for some time. The starting of this created a bit of interest, and several of the boys started dropping in to watch me. The particular boys, two of them Chemistry majors and one in Military Science, had never come in contact with Art and its doings.

Even with all the lack of art students seeking my help, life in Adams House was very pleasant. The house members were a very pleasant crowd. I was particularly impressed with the civilization of it all. An agreeable interlude each week were the dinners every Thursday with the **Lampoon** staff, to which they cordially invited me. I had a regular place at the table, and they made me and Honorary Editor. Several members of the staff were sons of several of my old friends, and they were upholding the traditions that had been maintained by their fathers. The dinners were always great sport. At first I couldn't quite make out if the occasion was a cocktail party with lamb chops and mashed potatoes for hors d'oeuvres or if the cocktails were served all during dinner. The evenings spent with the **Lampoon** boys will always be a rosy memory to me. As luck would have it, my quarters were only across the street from the **Lampoon** building. This was very handy indeed. The parties always ended early, so on Thursday nights I was always early to bed.

The boys on the **Lampoon** did a very sweet thing just before I left. They presented me with one of their pewter drinking mugs, inscribed with my name.

. . . I began to feel that my work, and my being there, was becoming of wider interest in the house. I began to have more visitors. I had what I called my regular callers. Their ranks began to swell. It made me feel that, if I wasn't really teaching art to any of them, I was, in a way, opening up facets that had been dimmed, and was implanting some slight appreciation.

I had completed the sculpture of the stallion, and was working daily on the rabbit. He proved to be a good model, and was content to abide in the studio hutch as long as I would go to market each day and provide him with carrots and cabbage. The only trouble was, he became very belligerent, and took to snapping his teeth at visitors' fingers. This was the first time in my experience that I ever saw a mean and vicious rabbit. I don't know how he got on later with his conjuring owner.

I finished the small sculpture of the rabbit, and needed to supply my model with cabbage no more, as I returned him —a fatter, but more independent, Belgian hare—to his owner.

I started a small statuette of a calf. I had made a preliminary sketch on a dairy farm the summer before, but had never gotten around to modeling the subject. I finished the calf as my daily droppers-inners watched me with ever-increasing interest.

My next beginning was a life-sized portrait bust of Heywood Broun. Heywood had been a Harvard student, and the doing of this increased the interest in my work. On this I worked from drawings I had made before his death, and my photographs that I had gathered.

Smog. March 1936   Watercolor, 13-7/8 x 20": Collection of Mrs. John Held Jr.

There was a Dark Form at the Other End of the Bench   Pen and ink, 6-9/16 x 10″: From "The Awakening" in *Grim Youth*, 1930:
Collection of Mrs. John Held Jr.

THESE TWO RABBITS MET FOR LUNCH EVERY DAY   Pen and ink, 6-5/16 x 9-1/8″: From "Dumb Bunny" in *The Flesh Is Weak*, 1931: Collection of Mrs. John Held Jr.

GOLDEN EMPIRE STATE. March 1936   Watercolor, 13-7/8 x 20″: Collection of Mrs. John Held Jr.

MAGNOLIA. Athens, Georgia, 1940   Pen and ink, 9-7/8 x 13-5/8″: Collection of Mrs. John Held Jr.

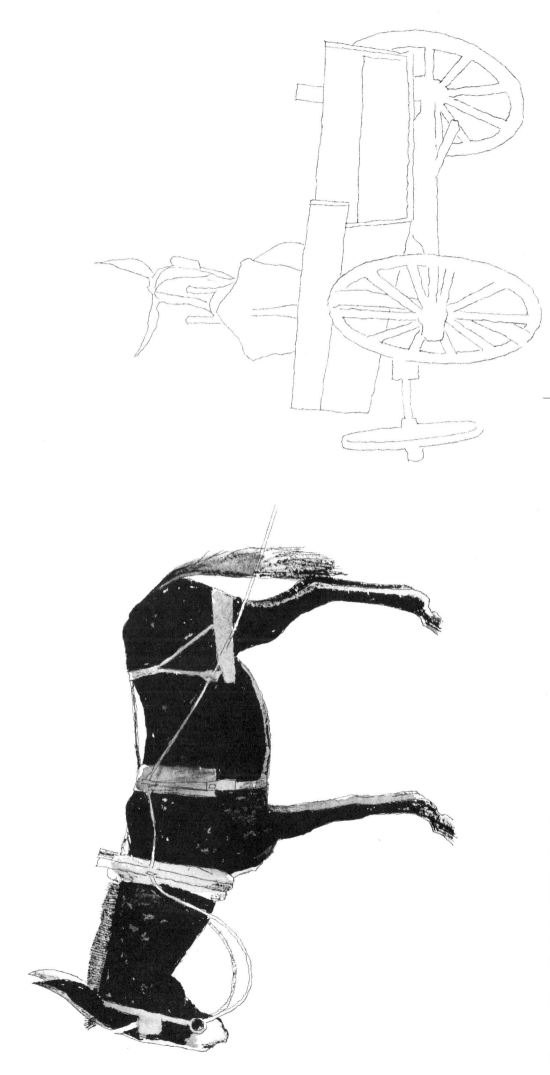

Mule and Wagon (Study) [April 1941] Watercolor, 5 x 10-3/4": Collection of Mrs. John Held Jr.

136

BLACKSMITH SHOP. Athens, Georgia, April 1941   Watercolor, 7-7/8 x 11-3/4": Collection of Mrs. John Held Jr.

We lived high on the North Bench, and our house was usually the first visited by the braves and their families as they came off the Reservation, and Mother would present them with a cornucopia of sugar or coffee.

There was a silent old Ute chief with three wives and countless children, who visited us regularly every fortnight. The chief would leave the children of our same age to amuse themselves at play with my brother and myself. So Jumbo, my brother, and I were the cynosure of all the other kids in the Twentieth Ward because we played at Indians-and-Cowboys with genuine Indians.

The small fry today are armed with imaginary Garand rifles and bazookas and fast vocal firing of machine guns, while then we fought with muzzle-loading rifles, and bow and arrow, and tomahawks. We made the mountains ring with our war whoops, at which the Indians were experts. Many a rousing re-enactment of the Mountain Meadow Massacre took place in the dry Mormon afternoons.

As Autumn approached and the hills were dry and parched, and the time neared for us to abandon our vacation sports and go back to school, the Indian children staged a rebellion. They refused to play our game. They took the stand that they were sick and tired of always having to play the part of Indians. They thought it only fair that their side be allowed to win once in a while.

The sublety of John Held Jr.'s perception was dependent upon, although in contrast with, two other elements of his personality: one was the serious side which took the world around him at face, yet lyrical, value. This is to be seen in several resplendent watercolor landscapes—documents of nature, as he found special pleasure in it.

In the early drawing of the balloonist [page 20]—Held was then about a dozen years old—the crowd is recorded studiously and sensitively, and is observed as a crowd, not as individuals. His exploring outlook on the world was too important to be taken lightly. As years passed, however, the more he observed it, the more he saw this outward world through his innate humor—the second, but no less important element of his personality. His humor was frequently puckish, occasionally witty; he often depended on punning, a temperament which commended him to the editors of the light-hearted, yet often pungent, magazines of the time.

DRUMMER   Pen and ink, 8 x 6-11/16″: From *Held's Angels*, 1952: Collection of Mrs. John Held Jr.

YELL Pen and ink, 7-1/2 x 9″: *The New York Times Magazine*, January 16, 1954: Courtesy Addison Gallery of American Art, Phillips Academy, Andover, Massachusetts.

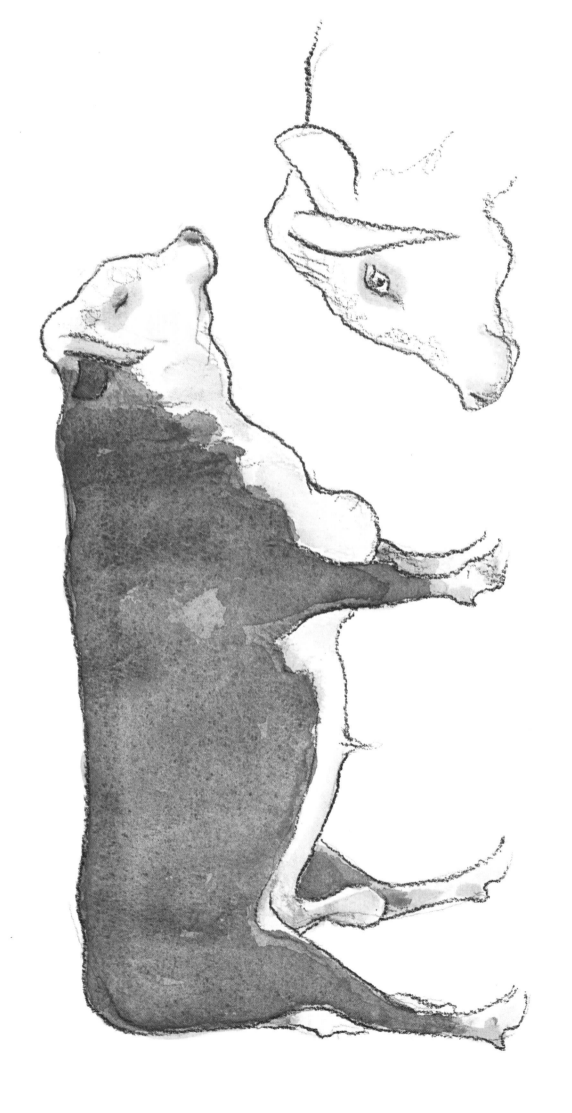

Herford Bull
Georgia aghy
May 41

STANDING HEREFORD (Study). 1941   Watercolor, 11-3/16 x 6-3/4": Collection of Mrs. John Held Jr.

142

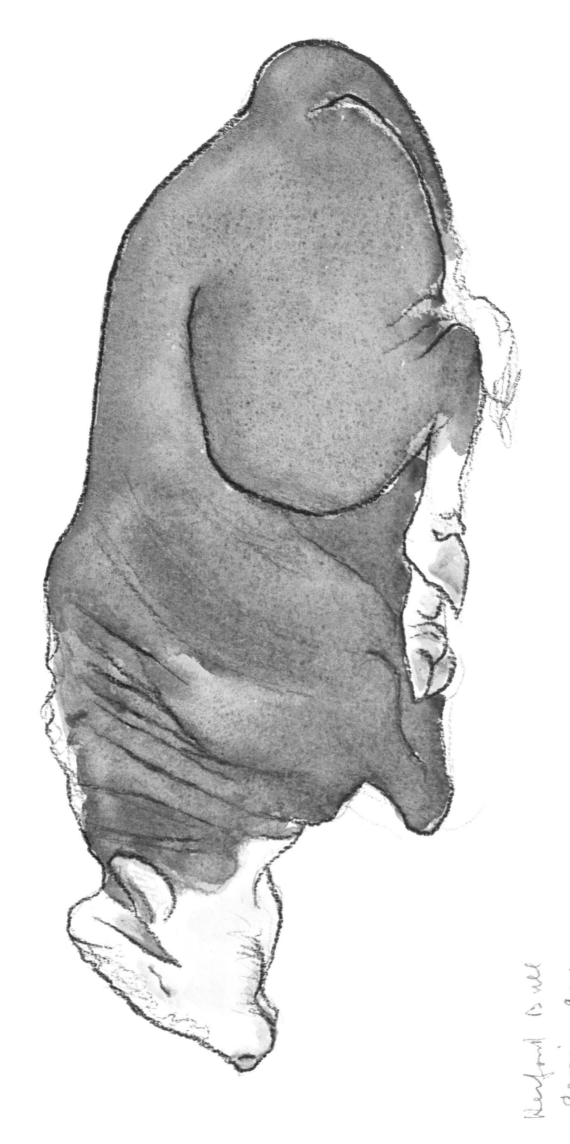

HEREFORD LYING DOWN. 1941   Watercolor, 11-1/4 x 6-1/4": Collection of Mrs. John Held Jr.

OLD SCHUYLER FARMHOUSE [1940's]   Pen and ink, 7-1/2 x 13-7/16″: Collection of Mrs. John Held Jr.

Chronology

"I didn't do my best work till I got kicked in the head by a horse."

Jan. 10, 1889 Born in Salt Lake City, the son of Annie Evans Held and John Held Sr.

1898 Sold his first art for $9.00.

1904 Sold his first cartoon to *Life* magazine.

1905 Was sports cartoonist for the *Salt Lake City Tribune*. Began his blockprints.

Early 1900's First and only art training with Mahonri Young, well-known sculptor and grandson of Brigham Young.

1910 Married Myrtle Jennings, society editor for the *Salt Lake City Tribune.*

1912 Went to New York, worked for Colliers Street Railway Advertising Co., designing display cards, doing ads for Wanamaker's, etc.

1914 Returned to linoleum blockprints.

1915/16 Drawings began appearing in *Vanity Fair*, all signed "Myrtle Held." Style stiff.

Early 1917 Drawings appeared signed by him. Toured Central America in dual role of artist/intelligence officer.

1918 Married Ada "Johnny" Johnson after divorce. Style changed to roundheaded, big-footed, one-eyed girl who later evolved into the famous Flapper of the 20's.

1919 Purchased first Grindstone Hill Farm, Westport-Weston, Connecticut. Art appeared regularly in the *New York Times Sunday Magazine.*

1925 Designed costumes and scenery for a number of Broadway musical revues.

1925 Accident with horse.

By 1927 He was featured in *Life, Judge, Smart Set, Vanity Fair, The New Yorker*, and had own syndicated cartoon strips, *Margie* and *Rah Rah Rosalie*. He had run for Congress and lost (he never made a speech or left his home), adopted three children, and was fantasti-

cally successful, often naming his own price.

1930 Publication of the limited edition of *The Saga of Frankie and Johnny* (blockprints).

Early 1930's Lost his money in the Ivar Kreuger, Swedish Match King, swindle. He wrote and illustrated many books, the most notable being *Grim Youth* (1930) and *The Flesh Is Weak* (1931).

1931 Had a nervous breakdown. Divorced.

1932 Married "Miss New Orleans" and had a daughter.

1937 Produced Tops Variety Show—promoting collegiate talent. Did the sets for the enormously successful comedy hit *Hellzapoppin.*

1939 Seriously turned to sculpture and had a successful one-man show of bronze horses at the Bland Gallery.

1940 Artist-in-residence at Harvard University and later that same year at the University of Georgia.

1942 Married Margaret Schuyler Janes. During W.W. II he and his wife worked as civilians for the Signal Corps, painting pictures of radar apparatus which was at that time in process of design.

1943 Purchased Old Schuyler Farm and worked as a free lance, writing and illustrating children's stories among other activities.

1950's "Rediscovery" of John Held Jr. First issue of *Playboy* carried a reprint of his linocuts for "Frankie and Johnny."

1958 John Held Jr. died on March 2, having lived a vigorous, productive life.

1967 October-November: Art Association of Indianapolis's exhibition "John Held Jr."

1968 November-December: Rhode Island School of Design's exhibition "The Jazz Age," featuring Held and two other artists.

1969-1972 Smithsonian Institution's nation-wide traveling exhibition of "The Art of John Held Jr."

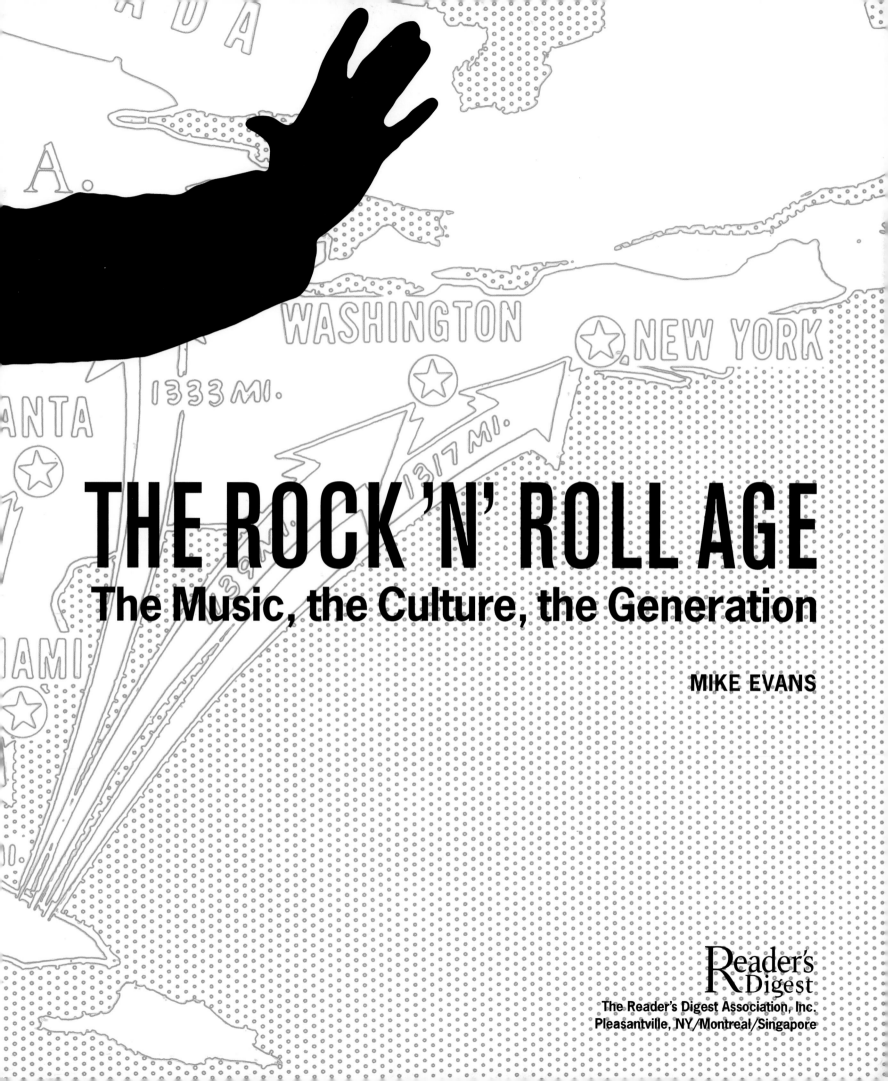

THE ROCK 'N' ROLL AGE
The Music, the Culture, the Generation

MIKE EVANS

Reader's
Digest

The Reader's Digest Association, Inc.
Pleasantville, NY/Montreal/Singapore

A READER'S DIGEST BOOK

This edition published by The Reader's Digest
Association, Inc., by arrangement with Essential
Works Limited.

Copyright 2007 Essential Works Limited
www.essentialworks.co.uk

Library of Congress Cataloging-in-Publication Data

Evans, Mike, 1941 Oct. 30-
   The Rock and Roll Age : The Music, the Culture,
the Generation / Mike Evans.
        p. cm.
   Includes index.
   ISBN 13: 978–0–7621–0820–6
   ISBN 10: 0–7621–0820–7
   1. Rock music–United States–History and criticism.
2. Rock music–Social aspects–United States.
I. Title.
   ML3534.E983 2007
   781.6609- -dc22   2006050424

FOR ESSENTIAL WORKS
Editors: Mal Peachey, Rod Green
Designer: Kate Ward

FOR READER'S DIGEST
U.S. Project Editor: Kimberly Casey
Editor: Amy Boaz
Canadian Project Editor: Pamela Johnson
Associate Art Director: George McKeon
Executive Editor, Trade Publishing: Dolores York
Associate Publisher, Trade Publishing: Rosanne McManus
President and Publisher, Trade Publishing: Harold Clarke

We are committed to both the quality of our products
and the service we provide to our customers. We value
your comments, so please feel free to contact us.
    The Reader's Digest Association, Inc.
    Adult Trade Publishing
    Reader's Digest Road
    Pleasantville, NY 10570-7000

For more Reader's Digest products
and information, visit our website:
    www.rd.com (in the United States)
    www.readersdigest.ca (in Canada)
    www.rdasia.com (in Singapore)

Printed in Singapore

1 3 5 7 9 10 8 6 4 2

CONTENTS

INTRODUCTION

When rock 'n' roll made its noisy debut via Bill Haley, Little Richard, and Elvis Presley, the mainstream adult world simply didn't know what had hit it. Popular music up until then had been characterized by smooth singers and slick dance bands, with songs written to order in Tin Pan Alley—but the new music the kids were listening to was something that sounded far more earthy and far sexier—it sounded dangerous.

Despite John Lennon famously once having said that before Elvis "there was nothing," rock 'n' roll—which has dominated popular music in one way or another for the last 50 years and more—didn't simply start when it hit the charts in the midfifties.

It had its roots in blues, hillbilly, and jazz music that stretched way, way back to the twenties and thirties and first came together after World War II, when the boom in big band swing began to wane. The rock 'n' roll age began right then, heralding a period of total transformation—not just in music but in the social attitudes that the new music would, in many ways, reflect. For 20 years, from the declaration of peace in 1945 to the start of a new, more liberated era in the midsixties, the rock 'n' roll revolution provided the soundtrack to unprecedented change in both its birthplace of America and the rest of the world.

For America, the late forties and early fifties were a time of previously unimaginable affluence. Industry boomed, the neat-lawned suburbs expanded, gas-guzzling cars grew bigger and bigger, and every family soon had the wonder of the age right there in their home—a TV set.

With its great wealth, mainstream America was largely insulated from the rest of the world and, as a consequence, was deeply conservative. It was an inward-looking society with an ever-present fear—the atomic bomb. The mushroom-cloud shadow of nuclear war fed a paranoia that gripped the United States in the early fifties, with radical attitudes and "un-American" ideas persecuted in anti-Communist witch hunts.

This material well-being also created a new generation of young people with money to spend for the first time, representing a whole new market for clothes, fast food, movies—and music. The media soon found a new name for them, too—teenagers—though to a lot of adults the word just spelled trouble from the start.

Dire warnings about juvenile delinquency abounded, and the first widely publicized "teenage" movies featured rebellious antiheroes—Marlon Brando's *Wild One* and James Dean's *Rebel Without a Cause*. *The Blackboard Jungle*, a film about young hoodlums in school, created the first rock 'n' roll million-seller "Rock Around the Clock." It also prompted teenage riots wherever it was screened.

Walk a Lonely Street

Any concern about Bill Haley's perceived influence on the young was nothing compared with the furor when a young Elvis Presley lasciviously wiggled his hips on nationwide

In the space of two short years in the midfifties, Elvis Presley went from being an unknown truck driver to the first—and eternal—King of Rock 'n' Roll after a string of hit singles.

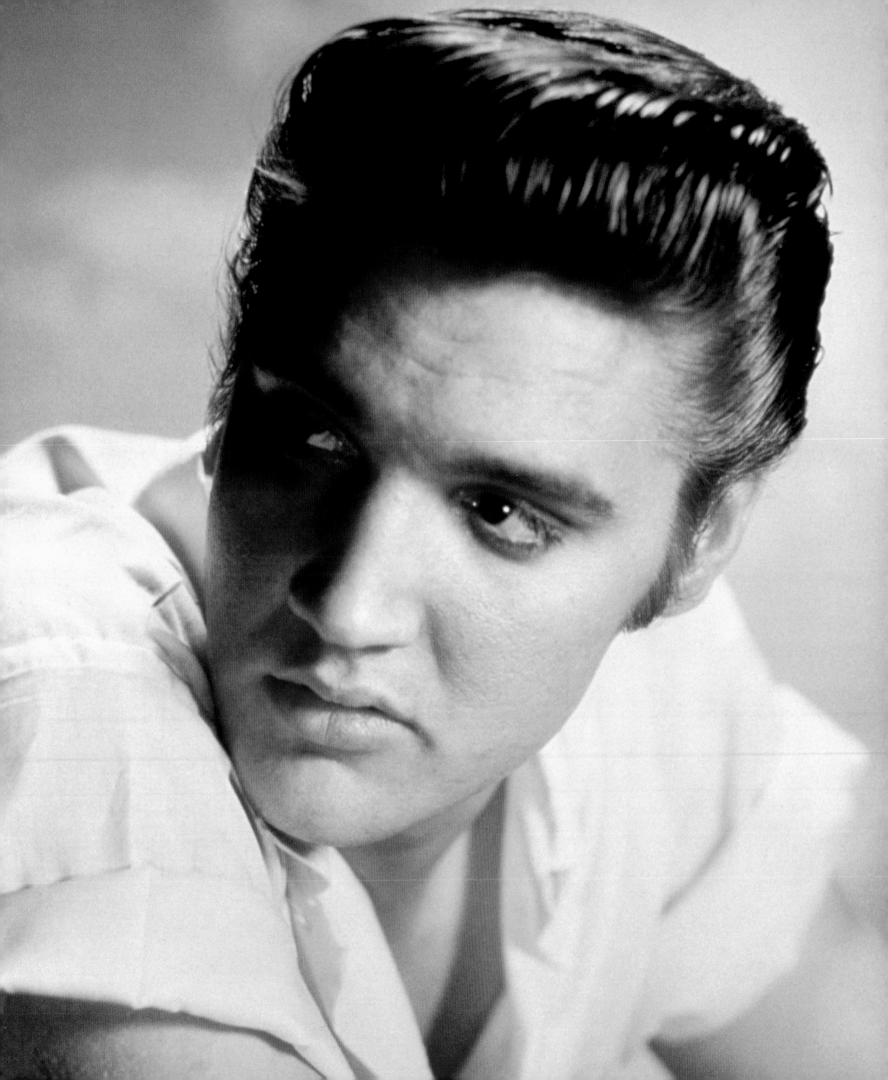

TV for the first time. Now the preachers and teachers just knew that rock 'n' roll was the work of the devil: It was all about sex.

Such notions gradually became a thing of the past, however, as society adopted a generally more liberal stance. From Brigitte Bardot's provocatively baring all in *And God Created Woman* in 1956, the sexual revolution progressed as far as the introduction of the contraceptive pill by the early sixties.

Other traditional values challenged included the no-questions-asked respect for authority, which was born of a "never again" attitude on the part of young people toward war, and a rejection of the "red scare" paranoia fostered by certain politicians. In an era in which Hungarians confronted Soviet tanks in the streets and bearded revolutionaries ousted an American-backed dictator in Cuba, it seemed that power was to be questioned on every front, whether it was the Oval Office of the White House or racially bigoted law enforcers in the Deep South.

And race was a major issue, specifically in the struggle for civil rights for African Americans, which dominated U.S. domestic politics throughout the fifties. Birmingham and Montgomery, Alabama; Little Rock, Arkansas; and Oxford, Mississippi, were among the places that played witness to scenes of heroic confrontations between African-American schoolchildren, bus passengers, students, lunch-counter customers, and the advocates of continuing white supremacy.

Race was very much a factor in the early bias against rock 'n' roll itself. One thing that shocked many white Americans about Elvis, apart from his overt sexuality, was the fact that he sounded like an African-American man. The biggest objection encountered by pioneering disc jockeys and record producers in the early promotion of rock 'n' roll was that it was, by and large, "African-American" music. In fact, its first crusader, Alan Freed, actually coined the term rock 'n' roll to shortcut the latent prejudice against black-associated rhythm and blues.

New Generation

Overall, the rock 'n' roll age was the era of the new. In every area, radical innovations were taking place.

In literature, the Beat writers broke every rule in the book. Allen Ginsberg's *Howl* and Jack Kerouac's *On the Road* became the bibles of a generation. Previously inadmissible books such as *Lady Chatterley's Lover* and *Lolita* were seen fit for publication, eroding the censorship of decades. On the stage, and more significantly on the screen, the Method actors—such as Marlon Brando, Paul Newman, and Rod Steiger—brought a stark reality to dramatic performance. In visual art, the Abstract Expressionists, such as Jackson Pollock, extended the boundaries of painting. And the world of science took great leaps forward, most spectacularly into space, where the first astronauts were circling the Earth by the early sixties.

Keep on Rocking

"If you're looking for youth, you're looking for longevity. Just take a dose of rock 'n' roll. It keeps you going." So said rock 'n' roll veteran Hank Ballard, who died in 2003 at the age of 76.

When it was conceived and nurtured during the 20 years after World War II that are discussed in this book, rock 'n' roll was indeed the music of youth. But like a lot of the ideas and events of that era, its influence has continued ever since.

Martin Luther King Jr. is arrested in Montgomery, Alabama, in 1958 for "loitering" outside a courtroom while one of his integration activists stood trial inside. He claimed that the officers beat and choked him during his arrest. They denied it and no charges were filed.

BIKINI THRILL!

When America carried out its atomic bomb tests on Bikini Atoll in the South Pacific on June 30, 1946, little did anyone know that the name would be synonymous with an event that sent just as many shock waves around an unsuspecting world—the birth of the bikini bathing suit.

During World War II, the U.S. government actually had a hand in promoting two-piece bathing suits. In 1943, as part of its wartime austerity measures, the government ordered that fabric used in women's swimwear should be reduced by 10 percent. Swimwear designers decided that the most stylish way to achieve this was to remove the midriff.

But it took a Frenchman—in fact, two Frenchmen—to seize the public imagination with the skimpiest beachwear yet seen. A Parisian designer, Jacques Heim, had fashioned a teeny-weeny two-piece and called it, in the spirit of the times, the atome; but it was fellow countryman Louis Réard who dubbed his own similar creation after the nuclear test site.

The minimalist swimsuit was first modeled in public on July 5, 1946. It was an immediate sensation worldwide, and bikini became a part of the international vocabulary. It was the earliest hint of a sexual and social revolution that, along with the threat of nuclear annihilation, would be part of the chemistry involved in the birth of rock 'n' roll.

ROOTS OF ROCK 'N' ROLL—THE BIG BANDS

Up to the end of World War II, swing was truly king. In the late thirties, musicians like trumpet virtuoso Harry James, or clarinet stars Benny Goodman and Artie Shaw, were the pop stars of their time. Fronting 18-piece bands in ballrooms across America, they had female bobby-soxer fans entranced—and they sold records by the million.

Even during the war, bands like the Glenn Miller Orchestra entertained the troops and the folks back home—as well as listeners worldwide—with their hit records and radio broadcasts. The foremost names in the jazz world fronted big bands, including Count Basie, Duke Ellington, and flamboyant showmen like Cab Calloway.

But the end of the war was the beginning of the end for the big swing bands. Touring with a large group of musicians was growing more expensive, and even the most famous musicians could barely afford to keep their shows on the road anymore. Many bands broke up during the conflict when their members were called into the service, and getting the band back together again was often so problematic that it simply didn't happen. Small combos became the order of the day.

Among the big lineups that did survive, many owed their continued existence to the fact that they had a featured vocalist who would front the band for certain numbers. It soon became clear that the records featuring the vocalists were the ones that sold the most. Singers like Ella Fitzgerald (with the Chick Webb orchestra), Frank Sinatra with Tommy Dorsey, and (before her movie stardom) Doris Day fronting Les Brown all rose to fame in a big band environment—the era of the individual pop star had arrived.

Bebop

The demise of the big bands coincided with the arrival of young, mainly African-American jazz musicians who were frustrated by the way that they felt jazz was heading down a dead-end street. Looking for new ways of playing what jazz musicians had always played—a mix of standards and blues-based originals—the new experimenters shocked critics and amazed fans and fellow musicians with a daring assault on the chord structures and time signatures that had been the music's solid base.

The new music—the pioneers of which included alto sax player Charlie Parker, trumpeter Dizzy Gillespie, pianist Bud Powell, and drummer Max Roach—grew out of the hothouse atmosphere of late-night jam sessions in clubs like those centered around New York's 52nd Street. It soon acquired a name, taken from the scat singing of the few vocalists (among them Slim Gaillard and King Pleasure) who attempted the style. It was dubbed bebop.

But bebop was basically listening music. Sure, its audiences became energized when things heated up but, unlike the sound of the swing bands, bebop was not designed as dance music.

Jump and Jive

To fill the gap, especially for audiences who'd jitterbugged and jived to the wilder, blues-based big bands such as that of Lionel Hampton, a new style of "jump-jive" jazz evolved. Initially aimed at African-American audiences as far as the record industry was concerned, it was released as part of their race records catalogs—in fact, it wasn't until June 1949 that *Billboard* magazine changed the name of its "Race Music" chart to "Rhythm and Blues."

As far back as 1939, Hampton had hinted at things to come, with his no-holds-barred hit "Flying Home," which featured the screaming

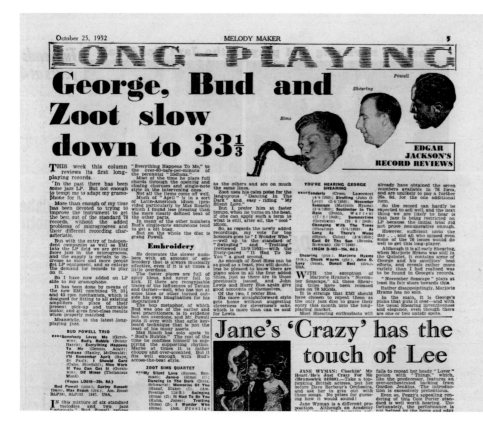

tenor sax of Illinois Jacquet. Throughout the decade, sax-led outfits dominated the "chitlin'" circuit of dance halls and clubs across African-American America, mainly small bands under the leadership of players like Arnett Cobb, Red Prysock, and Big Jay McNeely. These were a new breed of sax player, zoot-suited wild men of the horn who drove the crowds crazy as they jumped, jived, and wailed—often ending their frenetic solos atop the piano or flat on their backs, squeezing notes out of their instruments that only dogs were supposed to hear.

The most successful saxophone star was alto player Earl Bostic, who crossed into the

mainstream market with a string of hits including the million-selling "Flamingo" in 1951. Alto man Louis Jordan similarly cracked the pop charts with jumping vocal hits like 1945's "Caldonia" and 1946's "Choo Choo Ch'Boogie." And the fact that Jordan also sang prefigured big changes, as the instrumental hits gave way to vocal acts in the rhythm and blues charts of the early fifties. These were the direct forerunners of rock music. But the very earliest hint of what subsequently became rock 'n' roll had come from those tough tenor sax men of the forties whose red-hot, blues-wailin' combos succeeded the big band era.

OPPOSITE: A 1952 music paper in which long-playing records are reviewed for the first time. They were all jazz records at the time, and it wasn't until 1956 that rock 'n' roll long-playing records were released.

Above: Harry James and his orchestra appear in the 20th Century Fox film, *I'll Get By*, 1950. James gave Frank Sinatra his first big break when he hired the 20-year-old singer to front the Harry James Big Band when it toured America. Frank's crooning supplied the slow spots between the jump-and-jive numbers that kept America's teenagers dancing during the war years.

BIKER GANGS AND BOBBY-SOXERS

At the end of World War II, America was one of the world's only two superpowers, on the verge of an age of unprecedented affluence. Unlike war-torn Europe, including Britain, where food rationing and other austerities persisted into the early fifties, most of America began to enjoy an economic boom almost immediately.

Most people … but not all. Ironically, one group that found it difficult to adjust to the peace was returning servicemen, newly demobilized GIs who had gone to war in their teens and were now unprepared for civilian life. They came home to the reality of jobs they were unqualified to fill, quickly becoming bored and disillusioned. A large number of these men ended their service in sunny California and chose to settle there. As servicemen, they had been used to regular pay, but had little to spend it on—now many spent their savings on motorcycles.

In the years immediately following the war, these veterans formed motorcycle clubs across California, with names like the Jackrabbits or the 13 Rebels. The members wore club sweaters, rode, and partied together, organizing informal motorcycle meets with other clubs.

Hollister

Through the thirties, the small central-California town of Hollister was the site of July 4 weekend motorcycle races, which were suspended during the war. In 1947, the event was reinstated, and local businesses welcomed the potential revenue. But they hadn't expected the new breed of ex-Army motorcyclists, their capacity for alcohol, and their sheer numbers.

One Friday, thousands of the bikers poured into town from San Francisco, Los Angeles, San Diego, and places as far away as Florida and Connecticut. By evening, the main street was choked with motorcycles. To contain the "threat" to public safety, the seven-man Hollister Police Department set up roadblocks at both ends of the road.

From there on, the street was virtually a "no-go" zone for all but the bikers, who drank nonstop and were welcomed by bar owners — despite the fact that bikes were ridden right into one of the bars! The vets staged wheelies, drag races and other impromptu displays on the main street, taking no notice of the official races being held in the local park. About 50 bikers were arrested for minor offenses, such as drunkenness and reckless driving.

When the highway patrol arrived on Sunday and threatened to break things up with tear gas, the revelers went their separate ways. But the myth of the rebellious "Hell's Angel" biker was born, subsequently aided by the 1954 Marlon Brando film *The Wild One*, which was based on the events at Hollister.

Teenagers!

For most young people, however, the newly created affluence brought spending power. Recognizing that they were an economic group in their own right, either via increased allowances from financially comfortable parents or as workers in the new job market, they were specifically targeted as part of the consumer boom, as customers with their own taste in clothes, movies, and music. It was the birth of the teenager.

OPPOSITE: In the early fifties, teenagers became an economic group in their own right.

ABOVE: The popular magazine *Photoplay* clearly targeted teenagers toward the end of 1953.

PHOTOPLAY (1954) will
be better than ever …

"IT ISN'T

JUST THE DUST THAT IS SETTLING IN KOREA ... IT IS AMERICAN BLOOD."

DOUGLAS MacARTHUR, 1951

When the war in Korea broke out in June 1950, with United Nations troops supporting the South and the invading forces of North Korea backed by Communist China, many regarded the Cold War-era conflict as a war by proxy between the United States and its allies, and the Communist bloc. Although the fighting ended with a cease-fire three years later, the war was never declared officially over.

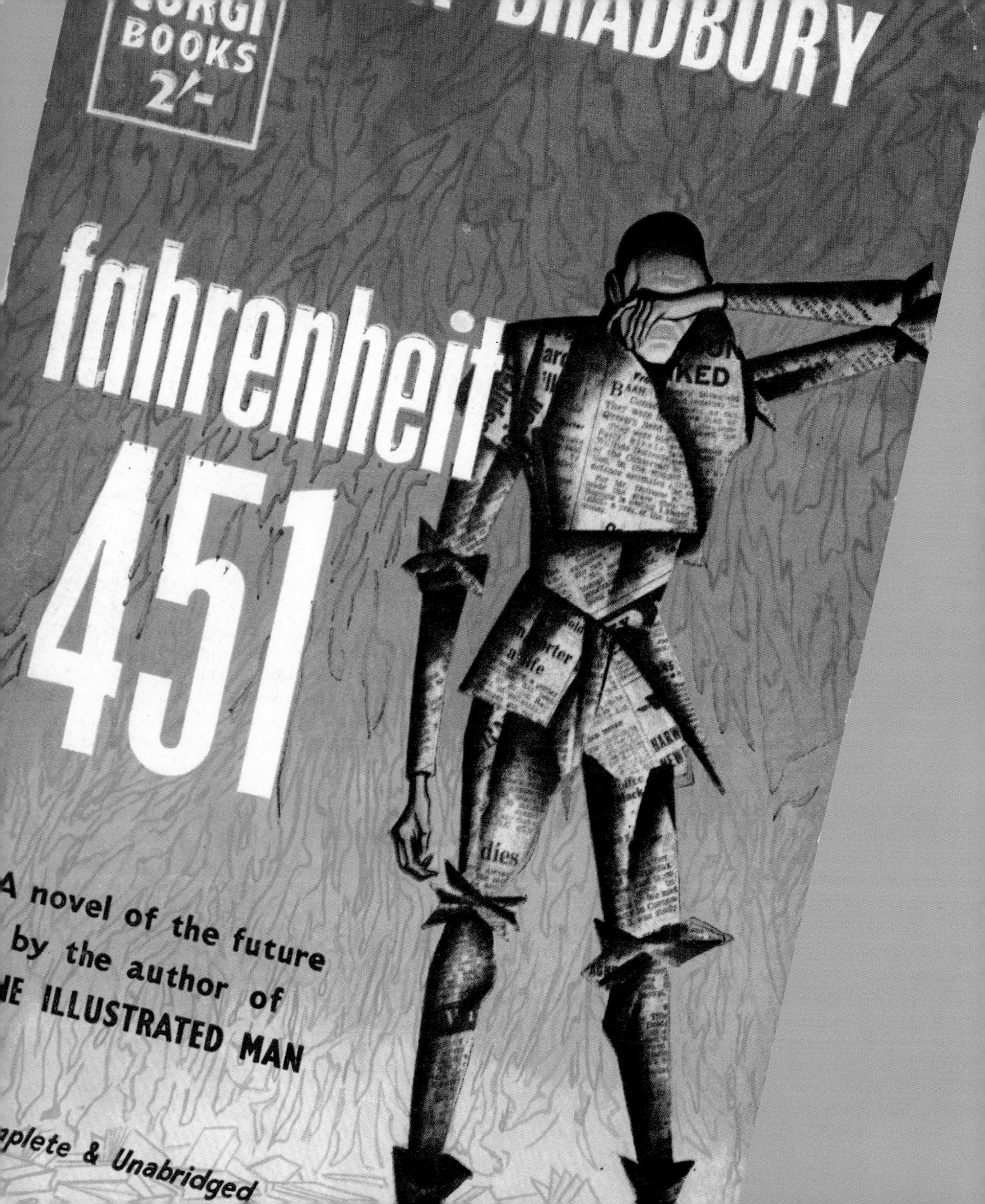

BRADBURY

CORGI
BOOKS
2/-

fahrenheit
451

A novel of the future
by the author of
THE ILLUSTRATED MAN

Complete & Unabridged

BIG BROTHER, BOMBS, AND ROBOTS

ABOVE: Norman Mailer's war novel had a huge impact.

LEFT: Ray Bradbury looked forward to troubled times in Farenheit 451.

As in other areas, the shock waves of change reverberated through the literary world of the postwar years. A number of key works had a huge and lasting impact, heralding new attitudes in society, especially among the young.

The war was a very recent memory, and the shadow of The Bomb was omnipresent as Cold War politicians on both sides of the Iron Curtain diced with global death. There was a growing mood that questioned authority and the status quo in a way that previous generations had simply never done.

Some of the new writing came straight from experiences in the war; Norman Mailer's The Naked and the Dead, published in 1948, was based on his own period in combat. Set in the South Pacific, it deals with the relationships and tensions between the men of a single rifle platoon, focusing on the lieutenant and how he deals both with the men under him and with his commanders. The book's impact was immediate and profound, throwing a harsh light on the realities of war and the often unheroic effect on its participants.

The same year saw Irwin Shaw's first novel, The Young Lions, based on his wartime service in Europe. It was followed in 1951 by The Troubled Air, chronicling the rise of McCarthyism, to which Shaw himself fell victim, moving permanently to Europe as a consequence.

English writer George Orwell's disillusionment with the politics of power resulted in one of the most powerful works in twentieth century literature, 1984, a political satire that warned of the dangers of doctrinaire thinking leading to totalitarianism. Its notions such as

"Big Brother" and "the thought police" subsequently became part of the language of the generation growing up in the early fifties. First published in 1949, the novel was grimly prophetic—particularly in the context of the McCarthy assault on media freedom, which was gaining pace in the United States.

Also timely was J. D. Salinger's Catcher in the Rye, which encapsulated the traumas of youthful angst before the term teenager had even been invented. It first appeared in serial form in America through 1945 and 1946, and as a book in 1951. Its first-person protagonist, Holden Caulfield, describes his adventures over a few days in New York City, after he was expelled from boarding school. His contempt for the "phonies" of the adult world he's about to enter would resonate with generations of young readers from the fifties onward.

Science fiction writing, previously regarded as merely a part of "pulp fiction" publishing, came into its own as "serious" literature in the forties and fifties. Along with the space adventures and alien-invasion thrillers of the kind that fed the appetite of B-movie audiences in the early fifties, there were prophetic works that captured the imagination of a new generation of readers, written by critically acclaimed authors such as Theodore Sturgeon, Richard Matheson, Isaac Asimov, and Ray Bradbury.

Among these, Isaac Asimov's I, Robot, published in 1950, predicted a not-too-distant world where android machines served mankind, while Ray Bradbury's 1953 novel Fahrenheit 451 foresaw a society in which books were banned in favor of a bland diet of "harmless" television that stifled dissent.

ROOTS OF ROCK 'N' ROLL—RHYTHM AND BLUES

As early as 1938, at the famous "Spirituals to Swing" concerts at New York's Carnegie Hall, blues-shouting vocalist Big Joe Turner created a prototype for rhythm and blues when he stormed through "Roll 'Em Pete" accompanied by the boogie-woogie pianist Pete Johnson. Justifiably, Joe was nicknamed the "Boss of the Blues" by the early fifties, as he rolled out hit after hit, including "Honey Hush" (1953), "Flip Flop and Fly" (1955), and, most significantly, in 1954, the original version of "Shake, Rattle, and Roll"—which Bill Haley turned into a somewhat watered-down rock 'n' roll hit that same year.

And Turner wasn't alone in promoting the burgeoning rhythm and blues market through the postwar years. Among the biggest R&B hit makers were Roy Milton and his Solid Senders (who hit with "RM Blues" in 1946), Joe Liggins and the Honeydrippers ("Pink Champagne," 1950), and Big Mama Thornton with the original "Hound Dog" in 1953. These were the true precursors to rock 'n' roll, even down to some of the titles: Roy Brown smashed in 1947 with "Good Rockin' Tonight," the great blues shouter Wynonie Harris declared "All She Wants to Do Is Rock" in 1949, and the same year singer-saxophonist Wild Bill Moore released "Rock and Roll."

Jazz Turns to R&B

During his hit-making years of the early fifties, Joe Turner was with Atlantic Records, the New York label founded by Herb Abramson and Ahmet Ertegun in 1947. Initially recording only jazz, after its 1949 hit with Stick McGhee's "Drinkin' Wine Spo-Dee-O-Dee," it became the preeminent label in rhythm and blues. Between 1950 and 1953, hits on the label included "Teardrops from My Eyes," a 1950 R&B chart topper for Ruth Brown, as well as Ray Charles's "It Should've Been Me," Clyde McPhatter's "Seven Days," and the Drifters' debut "Money Honey," all in 1953.

Along with Atlantic, a number of other independent R&B labels across America can include themselves among the progenitors of rock 'n' roll. Chess Records was formed in Chicago in 1949 by the brothers Phil and Leonard Chess. It featured southern blues names including Howlin' Wolf, Little Walter, and Muddy Waters, who collectively evolved an electric big-city version of the country blues, providing a springboard for the label's biggest rock 'n' roll artists, Chuck Berry and Bo Diddley. Among the frequent appearances by Chess (and its subsidiary Checker) at the top of the R&B charts were "Juke" by Little Walter in 1952, Willie Mabon's "I'm Mad" in 1953, and what many consider the first "real" rock 'n' roll record, Jackie Brenston's (with Ike Turner) "Rocket 88," released in 1951.

More New Labels

Other labels among the pioneers of rock included King in Cincinnati (formed in 1943), which had its first R&B hit with Bullmoose Jackson's "I Love You Yes I Do" in 1947, and in Peacock, one of the few African American-owned companies, launched in Houston, Texas, in 1949. Out on the West Coast, there were a clutch of "indies," including two R&B labels that would impact directly on the genesis of rock 'n' roll, Specialty and Imperial.

Specialty Records was formed in 1945 by Art Rupe in Los Angeles and its R&B roster included Joe and Jimmie Liggins, Roy Milton, Lloyd Price, and Guitar Slim. Its part in the rock 'n' roll revolution was assured when it signed Little Richard in 1955. Lloyd Price had an R&B number 1 with "Lawdy Miss Clawdy" in 1952 (later to be covered by Elvis Presley) and, like Guitar Slim, he was based in New Orleans, as was Imperial's biggest R&B star, Fats Domino.

Domino was probably the best example of an R&B artist who moved effortlessly into the rock 'n' roll arena without changing his style one iota. After his 1949 debut, "The Fat Man," he sold over a million records by 1953 and became a fifties superstar with his undiluted version of New Orleans rhythm and blues. Lew Chudd's Imperial label had started life in 1947 in L.A., and its R&B catalog also included Smiley Lewis. Lewis was best known for "I Hear You Knockin' " (1955) and 1956's "One Night of Sin," which Elvis Presley covered in 1957 as a cleaned-up version chastely titled "One Night."

Sam Phillips's Memphis Recording Service produced numerous R&B hits that it leased to other labels, including records by B. B. King and Rosco Gordon and Jackie Brenston's historic Chess release, "Rocket 88." When Phillips formed Sun Records in 1952, southern rhythm and blues formed the backbone of the label's output, with artists like Rufus Thomas and Junior Parker, but it was when African-American R&B fused with the sound of white country music that Sun Records became a major catalyst in the birth of rock 'n' roll.

Fats Domino's brand of R&B had made him a household name by the time this album was released.

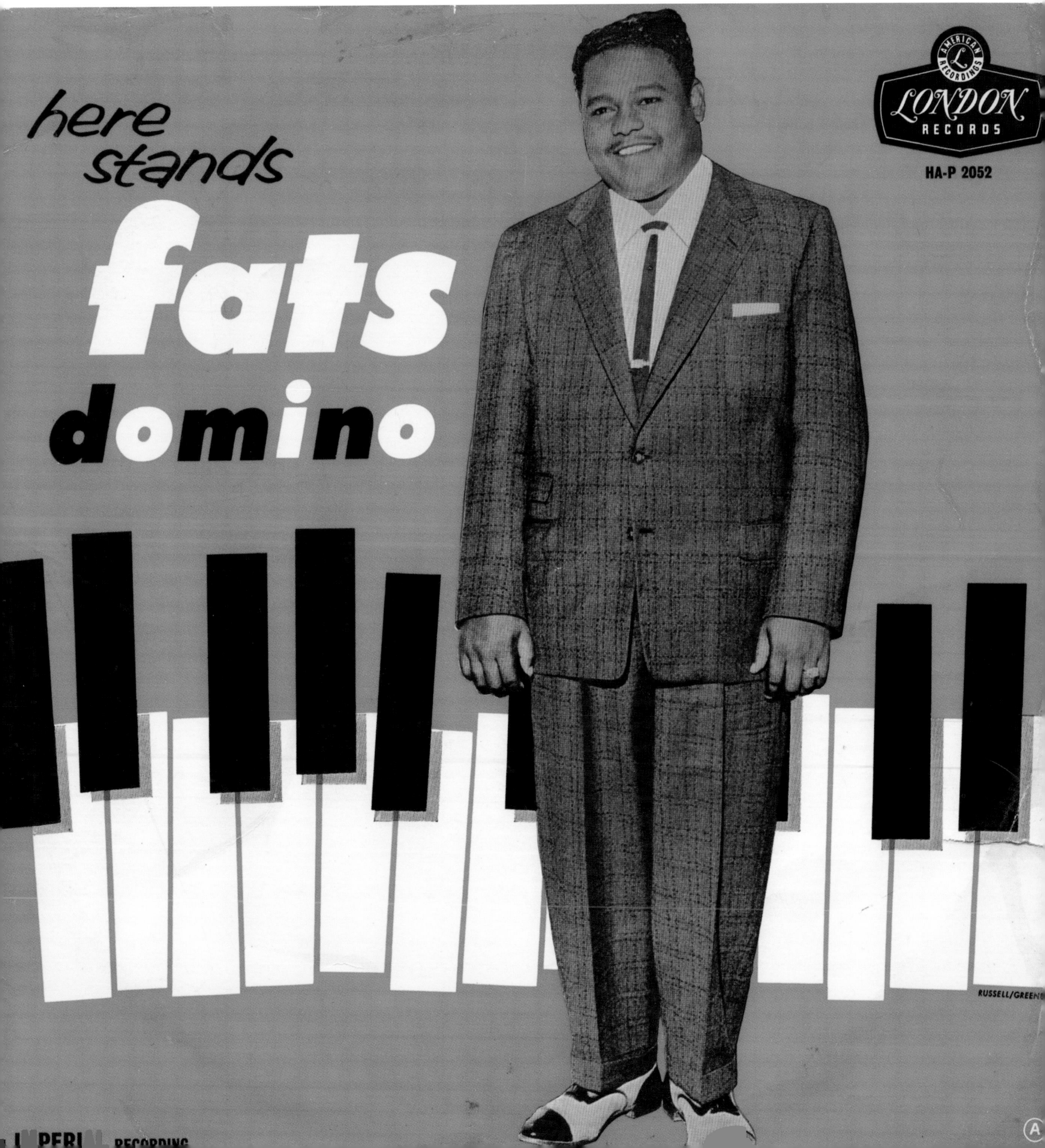

here
stands
fats
domino

LONDON
RECORDS

AMERICAN RECORDINGS

HA-P 2052

RUSSELL/GREEN

IMPERIAL RECORDING

ROOTS OF ROCK 'N' ROLL—COUNTRY MUSIC

Country music, like rhythm and blues, played a key part in the birth of rock 'n' roll. The music of rural America, "hillbilly" music, had thrived through the Depression years. But in the forties, more urban country impacted on the wider mainstream market in the form of western swing and honky-tonk.

Emanating from Texas and Oklahoma during the big band era, western swing was hot country dance music performed by large swing-style bands. Country instruments such as steel guitars and fiddles were augmented by jazz-oriented saxophones and brass, all played with a strong blues feel. The most popular and influential western swing group was Bob Wills and his Texas Playboys, while other big names included Milton Brown, Spade Cooley, and Cliff Bruner's Texas Wanderers.

It was with smaller groups, however, in the work of musicians such as Freddie Slack and Bill Haley, that western swing became one of the early ingredients of rock 'n' roll. With vocalist Ella Mae Morse, pianist Slack had a huge hit in 1946 with the boogie-based "House of Blue Lights," a harbinger of rock if ever there was one.

Cowboy Jive

In 1951, Bill Haley recorded with the Saddlemen, whose R&B take on country had them billed as the Cowboy Jive Band. They covered Jackie Brenston's seminal "Rocket 88," followed by the jive-talking "Rock the Joint" in 1952. Finally, in 1953, Haley threw away his cowboy hat, changed the band's name to the Comets, and had his first Top 20 hit with "Crazy Man Crazy."

Honky-tonk was originally a term used to describe speakeasy music joints selling alcohol during the Prohibition era, but by the forties honky-tonk had come to refer to the first truly urban form of country music. Like western swing it originated out of Texas, where the oil boom that preceded America's industrial recovery had seen an upsurge in dance halls and nightclubs.

Following the example of the western swing bands, honky-tonk saw the introduction of electric instruments to country music. Ernest Tubb is credited as being the first country artist to employ an electric guitar in his lineup when he recorded "Walkin' the Floor Over You" in 1941. It was an early hint of rock 'n' roll instrumentation to come. "Tennessee" Ernie Ford was a country music superstar whose 1950 hit "Shotgun Boogie" was a true forerunner of rock 'n' roll.

But the biggest name to emerge from the honky-tonk scene was Hank Williams. With songs such as "Lovesick Blues" and "Hey Good Lookin'," he sold millions of records between 1949 and his untimely death in 1953—a demise precipitated by the kind of drink-and-drugs lifestyle associated with the stars of rock 'n' roll years later.

ABOVE: The popularity of country music was exploited by stars like Gene Autry, who were singing their way through cowboy movies.

RIGHT: Perhaps the most famous singing gunslinger of them all—Roy Rogers, with his equally famous horse, Trigger.

"BACK THEN THERE WASN'T MANY ALBUMS. YOU SOLD SINGLES."

MEL TILLIS

The advent of rock 'n' roll coincided with the introduction of vinyl records in the form of the long-playing album and 7-inch 45-rpm single—a great advance over bulky (and easily breakable) shellac 10-inch 78s. Most important, the 45, which first appeared in 1949 but really took off in the midfifties, meant that new high-tech jukeboxes could hold up to 100 songs rather than the previous dozen or so. And with the new lightweight records came portable record players that teenagers could afford; now they could play music in their bedrooms, on the beach, or wherever they liked, without being tied to the domestic phonograph that was so much a part of the family furniture.

"THE SO-CALLED BEAT GENERATION

. . . CAME TO THE CONCLUSION THAT SOCIETY SUCKED."

AMIRI BARAKA, AMERICAN WRITER AND ACTIVIST

Postwar America saw the beginnings of a movement whose work and lifestyle had a huge influence on the art and attitudes of the late fifties, into the sixties and beyond—the so-called Beat Generation.

The phenomenon began in the midforties, when the movement's three major literary figures—Jack Kerouac (1922–1969), William Burroughs (1914–1997), and Allen Ginsberg (1926–1997)—met in 1944 as part of a bohemian circle centered at New York's Columbia University. The group, which also included Lucien Carr, Herbert Huncke, Carl Solomon, and Joan Vollmer (and, in 1946, Neal Cassady), theorized about a new vision of artistic creativity through the liberation of the senses. It was the launchpad for radical literary evolution and a general attitude that was completely at odds with the conformism of postwar American society.

The Beat philosophy deplored consumerism, denounced the Cold War, and encouraged sexual freedom and hedonism as a means to self-expression. The new bohemia also identified with the underside of Eisenhower's bland, conservative America—the alternative late-night world of jazz with its bebop heroes like Charlie Parker and West Coast "cool school" players, such as Gerry Mulligan. Burroughs, Kerouac, and Ginsberg all adopted aspects of jazz's spontaneity and "jive talk" in their writing (just as Abstract Expressionist artists like Jackson Pollack sought to evoke the improvised quality of jazz in their paintings). The emergence of the Beats also saw the birth of the archetypal "hipster," who like the writers assimilated the jazz (African-American) vernacular into everyday language. Outside the jazz world, it was the first time white Americans were to be heard addressing each other as "man."

Between 1947 and 1950, Jack Kerouac crisscrossed America in a series of journeys by automobile, bus, and hitchhiking, working his experiences into a novel as he traveled. By April 1951, he'd completed what would be the most influential book to emerge from the Beat scene, On the Road, eventually published in 1957. The thinly disguised hero of On the Road, Dean Moriarty, was based on Neal Cassady, who was central to the Beats and to Jack Kerouac's work in particular.

Through the early fifties, the first Beat writings were published. Kerouac's The Town and the City appeared in 1950, based on his move to New York from his hometown of Lowell, Massachusetts. It was followed in 1952 by John Clellon Holmes's seminal portrait of the Beat scene, Go! and William Burroughs's Junkie in 1953. An introspective vision of Burroughs's experiences as a drug user, Junkie was certainly the most shocking of the three books—as were his works later in the decade, including the initially banned Naked Lunch.

Holmes's Go! was the first book to talk about the Beat Generation phenomenon. Three years earlier, in 1948, Holmes had pressed Jack Kerouac to describe the unique qualities of his generation, and Kerouac apparently invented the term on the spot. The book was quickly picked up by the press, resulting in a landmark article by Holmes in the New York Times, in November 1952, "This Is the Beat Generation."

In California, meanwhile, a parallel Beat scene had developed, involving figures such as Kenneth Rexroth, Philip Whalen, Gary Snyder, and Lawrence Ferlinghetti. In July 1953, Ferlinghetti and Peter D. Martin opened America's first paperback bookstore, City Lights, at 261 Columbus Avenue, San Francisco. In August 1955, City Lights Press published its first book, Ferlinghetti's sensational Pictures of the Gone World. On October 13, 1955, Ginsberg astounded a San Francisco audience when he first read his marathon poem "Howl" in public, and exactly a year later, City Lights published Howl and Other Poems, which, second only to On the Road, became the most celebrated and most quoted work in Beat literature.

The Beats were constantly on the move, seeking new insights and experiences, physically and spiritually. Eastern religion—especially Zen Buddhism—influenced Ginsberg, Kerouac, Snyder, and Gregory Corso in particular.

Burroughs went to live in Mexico City and then (after a trip to southern Mexico in search of the hallucinogenic yage) to Tangiers. The others followed, with Beat colonies developing in Mexico and Tangiers. Later in the decade, Paris also became a center. All of the leading figures located there for a time, living and writing at the now legendary Beat Hotel.

In an America overshadowed by the specter of the atomic bomb and increasingly paranoid about the "red menace" of Communism, the Beat Generation anticipated a seismic shift in social attitudes that would reverberate through Western culture in the years that followed.

A Beat gathering in Morocco. Standing from left to right are Ian Sommerville, Gregory Corso, Alan Ansen, Allen Ginsberg, and William Burroughs. Paul Bowles and Peter Orlovsky are seated.

JOE McCARTHY AND THE RED MENACE

As the Cold War heated up, with the Soviet Union blockading Berlin in 1948 and testing its first atomic bomb in 1949—some of its nuclear technology developed courtesy of espionage in America—a "red menace" paranoia in the form of McCarthyism swept the United States. Named after Joseph McCarthy (1909–1957), a Republican senator for Wisconsin, McCarthyism manifested itself as a series of witch hunts instigated by the senator and involved notorious hearings in front of the House Un-American Activities Committee (HUAC) in the early fifties.

The HUAC, which was formed in 1938, first reared its head before McCarthy rose to prominence in 1950, and by the late forties it had focused on Hollywood and the broadcasting media as a potential hotbed of Communist subversion. In October 1947, it began hearings to investigate the "Hollywood Ten," nine screenwriters and one director (Edward Dmytryk)

who refused to answer any questions or name colleagues with left-wing sympathies, claiming their constitutional rights under the Fifth or First Amendments. At the same hearings, stars Gary Cooper, Robert Taylor, and future president Ronald Reagan appeared as "friendly" witnesses, denying association with anything (or anybody) deemed un-American.

Four days later, Humphrey Bogart and his wife, Lauren Bacall, headed a contingent of 50 Hollywood celebrities who flew to Washington to challenge HUAC's investigations. Among them were Danny Kaye, John Huston, Gene Kelly, Frank Sinatra, and Groucho Marx. The Hollywood Ten, however, were cited for contempt of Congress and sent to prison.

McCarthy himself came to the fore when he made a six-hour speech on the floor of the Senate on February 20, 1950. He called attention to over 200 people who had worked in the State Department or wartime agencies such

as the Office of War Information and the Board of Economic Warfare, implying that a Soviet-inspired espionage ring was operating within the government and the Truman administration was doing nothing about it.

As the senator wielded increasing power over the committee, its influence was felt more drastically in the movie industry. Eventually some of the most prominent Hollywood names of the era (including Orson Welles, Lucille Ball, Dashiell Hammett, and Lillian Hellman) were subpoenaed before the HUAC. In total more than 300 artists—including directors, actors, and screenwriters—were boycotted by the studios. Some, like Charlie Chaplin, left the country to continue their work. Others resumed their careers in the 1960s. And some, inevitably, "named names"—as in the case of actor Sterling Hayden and director Elia Kazan—then were haunted by it for the rest of their lives.

At the same time, between 1947 and 1954, almost 40 explicitly propagandistic anti-Communist films were made in Hollywood. These sensationally lurid "red menace" movies included *The Iron Curtain* (1948), the Howard Hughes production *I Married a Communist* (1949), *I Was a Communist for the FBI* (1951), and *The Red Menace* (1949)—the poster for which declared solemnly, "So shocking it was filmed behind locked studio doors." And there was the now-almost-forgotten television series, *I Led Three Lives*, which ran from 1953 to 1956, featuring Richard Carlson as an undercover FBI agent who was a "plant" in a Communist spy ring—while also maintaining his cover by holding a day job as an advertising executive. Another product of the general paranoia was the "flying saucer" scare that gripped the U.S. media in the early fifties, and the "alien invasion" movies of the period such as *The War of the Worlds* (1953) and *Invasion of the Body Snatchers* (1955).

COMMUNIST PARTY ORGANIZATION U.S.A—FEB. 9, 1950

It was amid this atmosphere of suspicion throughout American society that Julius Rosenberg and his wife, Ethel, were tried, convicted, and executed in 1953 for spying for the Soviet Union. Specifically, the couple were charged with conspiracy to commit espionage and accused of passing nuclear weapons secrets to Russian agents. Both of them were American citizens and members of the Communist party and, although evidence published decades later indicated that Julius Rosenberg was active in espionage, there was no direct evidence that he performed the specific acts for which he was convicted, or that Ethel Rosenberg was involved.

McCarthy's influence began to wane in 1954, when the distinguished CBS news broadcaster Edward R. Murrow aired the *Report on Joseph R. McCarthy*, which used actual footage of the senator to demonstrate dishonesty in his speeches and his abusive tactics toward witnesses. While some of the more outrageous accusations—such as the claim that President Eisenhower was a Communist—now appear laughable, at the time the "red scare" witch hunts wrecked careers and ruined lives.

OPPOSITE: The Communist threat was reflected in the topics of popular fiction and films.

ABOVE: Joe McCarthy demonstrates the extent of Communist party influence using a map of America.

...EAD!

GLAMOROUS NEW FUTURAMICS !

BRILLIANT "ROCKET" ENGINES !

W WHIRLAWAY HYDRA-MATIC DRIVE !

Hydra-Matic Drive, at new reduced price, now optional on all Olds

Meet Oldsmobile's New Futuramic Fleet! See the Futuramic
Oldsmobile's glamor star! "Rocket" Engine! New Whirlawa
Hydra-Matic! Lowest, widest Fisher Body in Oldsmobile history!
the newly-styled Futuramic "88"—Oldsmobile's *action* star!
"Rocket" performance now even *smoother* with new Whirlaway
Hydra-Matic! See the Futuramic "76"—Oldsmobile's *value* star!
It's the lowest-priced Futuramic car! Take your choice! Futurami
"Rockets!" Hydra-Matics! Finest Oldsmobiles ever!

"STEP IN MY ROCKET AND DON'T BE LATE . . ."

"Rocket 88," recorded in 1951 by Jackie Brenston and his Delta Cats—usually cited as the first rock 'n' roll record—served as inspiration for streamlined car design. The car industry was starting to be influenced by the sleek lines of sci-fi and space travel, and that year the eight-cylinder Oldsmobile 88 was reckoned to be the fastest machine on the road—magazine ads for the car even featured a man and woman astride a space rocket.

"ROCKET"! HYDRA-MATIC!

"88"

Oldsmobile has both!

The famous high-compression "Rocket" Engine—plus new Oldsmobile Hydra-Matic Drive*! Try this thrilling combination at your nearest Oldsmobile dealer's!

*Above, Oldsmobile "88" Holiday Coupé. *Hydra-Matic Drive optional at extra cost on all Oldsmobile models.*

OLDSMOBILE

A GENERAL MOTORS VALUE

I LIKE IKE

"I Like Ike" was one of the most memorable presidential campaign slogans of all time, and when Dwight D. Eisenhower swept to power in a landslide victory in 1952, it seemed that most of America agreed.

Retiring from active service in the U.S. Army to enter politics in 1952, Eisenhower was a president waiting to happen. He was appointed chief of staff of the U.S. Army in November 1945 and returned to the United States as a popular

hero, soon coming under great pressure to run for public office. The antithesis of a career politician, it was not even immediately apparent which party he would choose to join, but he finally opted for the Republicans and was nominated as their candidate for the 1952 presidential election.

The contest for the Republican nomination became a struggle between Ike, representing the moderate wing of the party, and Senator Robert

A. Taft of Ohio, standing for the conservative element. Eisenhower won the nomination on the strength of his popularity in the country at large, and to placate the conservatives, he chose Senator Richard Nixon of California as his running mate.

It was a bad time for the incumbent Democratic President, Harry S. Truman. The war in Korea had been dragging on for two years, Senator Joe McCarthy's "red menace" witch hunts were spreading suspicion of liberals everywhere, and disclosure of widespread corruption among federal employees rocked the administration. Before the Democratic Party nominations, Truman decided not to run, and the party nominated Governor Adlai Stevenson of Illinois, a far from charismatic candidate when compared with the war hero, Ike.

Televised Elections

The election campaign by both parties was the first to make major use of TV advertising. One of Eisenhower's ads featured an animated cartoon with a song, written by Irving Berlin, called "I Like Ike." And Ike's running mate, Nixon, skillfully used TV to defend himself after being accused of financial misconduct involving campaign contributions.

The speech was highlighted by a mawkish sentimentality, with Nixon even claiming that his wife, Pat, didn't wear mink, preferring what he termed "a respectable Republican cloth coat." He admitted that, among his other campaign contributions, he had been given a cocker spaniel named Checkers but said he was not going to give it back because his daughters loved it. The speech subsequently became known as the "Checkers speech" and resulted in a flood of support, prompting Eisenhower to keep Nixon on the ticket.

It wasn't the first controversy attached to "Tricky Dick," as he was dubbed later in his career. Nixon had played a dubious role in

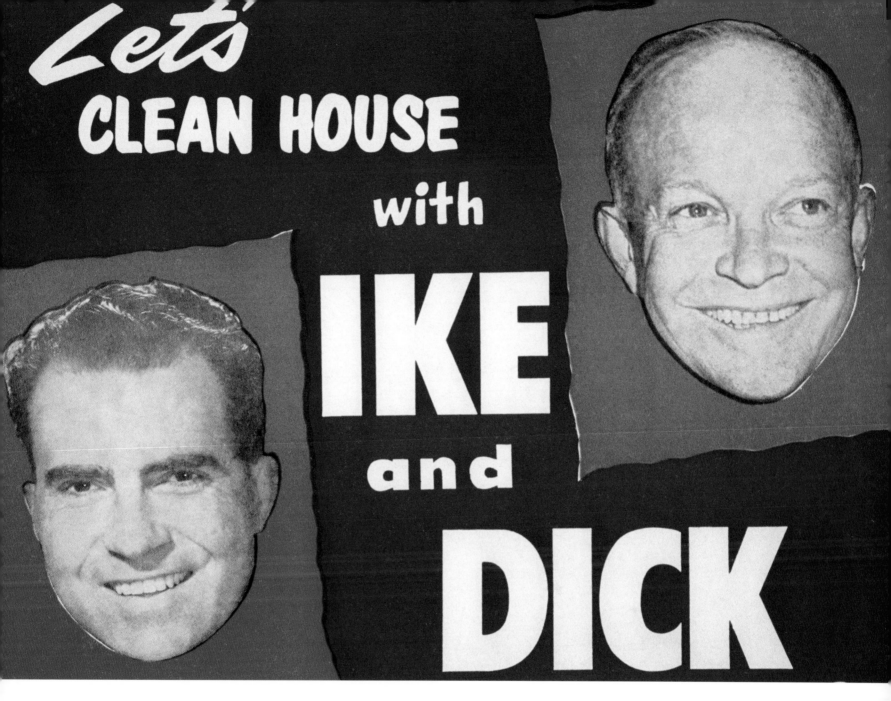

Let's **CLEAN HOUSE** with **IKE and DICK**

pressing for the House Un-American Activities Committee to act against United Nations diplomat Alger Hiss in 1948 (accusing Hiss of being a Communist spy), based on information received secretly from various sources, including the FBI and a notorious "Commie hunting" Catholic priest, Father John Francis Cronin. Hiss was jailed for five years but protested his innocence right up to his death in 1996.

CIA Interference

After a decisive election victory, Eisenhower initiated a policy of covert action abroad, using the newly created Central Intelligence Agency (CIA) to meddle in foreign affairs, generally succeeding only in raising the temperature of the Cold War. An early example occurred when the Iranian army, with American and British help, removed Prime Minister

Mohammad Mossadegh, replacing him with the western-friendly Shah, Mohammad Reza Pahlavi. Ike also achieved a cease-fire in the conflict in Korea after issuing a direct threat to use nuclear weapons, and formed an anti-Communist alliance with Asian and Pacific countries, SEATO (the Southeast Asia Treaty Organization).

At home, Eisenhower addressed what was perceived as a rising tide of juvenile delinquency. In the forties and fifties, there was a huge increase in the teenage population (between 1946 and 1960, U.S. teenagers increased from 5.6 million to 11.8 million), and the years 1948–1953 saw the number of juvenile delinquents charged with crimes increase by 45 percent.

Government commissions and the FBI (led by J. Edgar Hoover) were all warning of the

increasing threat of this adolescent crime wave. In what amounted to panic measures in some areas, cities passed new ordinances, including a number of local curfews for youths under 18. While these measures inevitably led to some increase in juvenile crime, the actual percentage of such offenses as part of the overall crime figures was no higher than in the previous decade. Nevertheless, the fear of juvenile delinquency became a national obsession in the early fifties.

OPPOSITE: Motorists could demonstrate their support for the Republican presidential candidate with bumper stickers.

ABOVE: An Eisenhower/Nixon campaign poster from 1952.

"WHAT'RE YOU REBELLING AGAINST

Marlon Brando in *The Wild One* in 1953, an
instant icon in his Schott Perfecto motorcycle
jacket for generations of would-be rockers,
rebels, and romantics.

1954

America, and the rest of the planet, was on the edge of something big, but no one was quite sure what. It was an age of unprecedented affluence, as prices on the New York Stock Exchange reached the highest point since 1927. The first shopping mall opened in Southfield, Michigan; pizza chains made their first appearance; and Davy Crockett debuted on TV—sparking a $100 million industry in coonskin caps. Screen goddess Marilyn Monroe married baseball hero Joe DiMaggio (only to divorce him nine months later). Americans took part in the first nationwide civil defense test against an atomic attack, and the mambo was the hottest dance craze since the Lindy Hop in the thirties.

The first generation of teenagers was flexing its muscles in all types of ways, from gum-chewing jive talk and hot-rod cars to cool clothes and gang warfare. Pioneering disc jockeys and radical record producers were about to give the youngsters their own music, too, as the birth pangs of rock 'n' roll crackled across the airwaves. It was the spark that would ignite a revolution.

SH'BOOM
DOO-WOP

When the Canadian vocal group the Crew Cuts made it to the number 1 position in the charts with "Sh'Boom" in 1954, it was one of several portends that year of the rock 'n' roll explosion to come. The group was initially inspired by the smooth close-harmony singing of the Four Lads (who came from the same high school in Toronto) but soon caught on to the doo-wop style sung by teenagers on the streets of New York since the late forties. "Sh'boom" was originally a hit for doo-wop group the Chords, who made number 3 in the R&B chart and the pop Top 10 in mid-1954. The Crew Cuts' 1955 follow-up smash, "Earth Angel," was also a cover of a doo-wop classic, an R&B chart topper for the Penguins in late 1954.

Doo-wop had developed as an a cappella style group vocalizing among African-American and Italian-American youths, usually featuring four-part harmonies of high tenor, mellower second tenor, baritone, and bass voices. It was a do-it-yourself form of R&B that involved thousands of amateur groups, hundreds of which got as far as cutting a record—a few even having hits.

Among those that did find fame, albeit usually only briefly, were the "bird" groups—the Crows, the Penguins, the Ravens, the Orioles, and so on—and the groups named after cars, like the Cadillacs and the Coupe De Villes. Cool-sounding musical names were also popular, from the Chords and the Cleftones to the Vibraharps and the Vocaleers.

The Crows hit the pop Top 20 as well as the R&B chart with "Gee" in 1954—the first record by an African-American group to be played on white radio stations. Meanwhile, the Clovers had achieved 13 consecutive hits in the R&B Top 10 between 1951 and 1954 before cracking the pop chart (with "Love, Love, Love" in 1956) as the first rock 'n' roll vocal group.

The Platters were the first doo-wop group to top the pop charts, with "The Great Pretender"

in December 1955. And it was a sure sign of the times when Frankie Lymon's group, the Premiers, were renamed the Teenagers before their 1955 hit "Why Do Fools Fall in Love," followed by the topically titled "I'm Not a Juvenile Delinquent."

The Cry Guy

Vocalist Johnnie Ray took his inspiration from rhythm and blues singers like Ivory Joe Hunter and LaVern Baker (who helped Ray in his early career). He developed a quasi-R&B approach that represented a stylistic link between the different branches of popular music—between Frank Sinatra and Elvis Presley.

Johnnie Ray's style struck gold in 1951 with the double-sided hit "Cry" and "The Little White Cloud That Cried." What struck a chord

with teenagers was his emotional delivery and onstage theatrics—breaking down in tears and writhing on the floor—which earned him such nicknames as "The Cry Guy," "The Nabob of Sob," and "The Prince of Wails." Once rock 'n' roll broke for real in 1954, however, he was dismissed as just another part of outmoded showbiz, although a sensational cover of the Drifters' "Such a Night" topped the U.K. charts that year despite being banned by the BBC for its sexual suggestiveness.

OPPOSITE: The Crew Cuts' origins as a high-school band shine through on this early album cover.

ABOVE: Doo-wop first topped the pop charts with the Platters.

"WE STEER COMPLETELY CLEAR OF ANYTHING SUGGESTIVE."

BILL HALEY

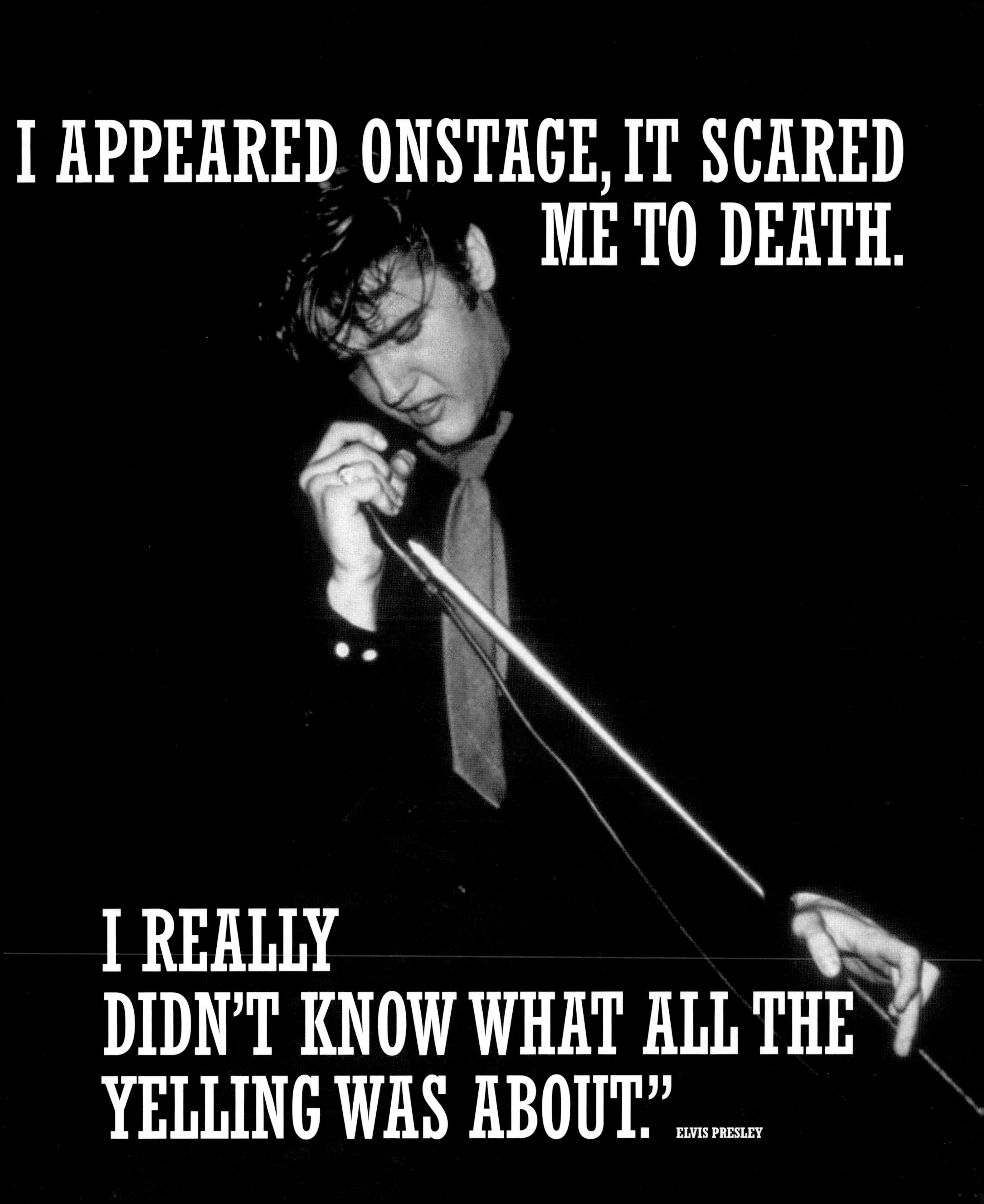

"I APPEARED ONSTAGE, IT SCARED ME TO DEATH.

I REALLY DIDN'T KNOW WHAT ALL THE YELLING WAS ABOUT."

ELVIS PRESLEY

THE ORIGINAL DYLAN

The year 1954 saw the publication and first broadcast of the celebrated radio play by Welsh poet Dylan Thomas, Under Milk Wood. Sadly, the poet, having collapsed and died after a drinking binge in New York's White Horse Tavern in November 1953, was no longer around to witness this landmark event. The year's other notable literary works included William Golding's novel Lord of the Flies, the story of a group of children stranded on a desert island. This was not to be confused with J. R. R. Tolkien's Lord of the Rings trilogy, which was also published during 1954 and 1955. Two other books published that year epitomized the taboo breaking that would proliferate through the early rock 'n' roll years—one book concerned sex, the other drugs.

The Story of O, by Pauline Réage, was published in its original French as Histoire d'O in 1954. The first English edition did not appear until 1965. The book, a fantasy about a female Paris fashion photographer—O—who is blindfolded, chained, whipped, and sexually abused, is now considered a classic of sadomasochistic literature. It won a French literature prize, the Prix des Deux Magots, in 1955, even though authorities had tried unsuccessfully to have it banned.

With a title taken from The Marriage of Heaven and Hell by the visionary writer William Blake, Aldous Huxley's The Doors of Perception described the author's experiences under the influence of the hallucinogenic drug mescaline. Highly influential, the book predated the "psychedelia" that would permeate rock in the late sixties—the Doors rock band took their name from the title.

ABOVE: Just as Under Milk Wood appeared only after Dylan Thomas's death, the unfinished work Adventures in the Skin Trade followed a few months later. Aldous Huxley's drug-inspired work predated rock's psychedelic era by over a decade.

RIGHT: Dylan Thomas, the son of a Welsh schoolmaster, photographed in 1946. He was 39 years old when he died in New York in 1953.

"THE NUCLEAR ARMS RACE HAS NO MILITARY PURPOSE. WARS CANNOT BE FOUGHT

The Cold War escalated dramatically on March 1, 1954, when the United States tested a hydrogen bomb at its Bikini Atoll test site in the Pacific, producing the biggest man-made explosion ever.

The bomb was 1,000 times more powerful than the atomic weapon that destroyed Hiroshima and was the equivalent of 20 million tons (20 megatons) of TNT. One of the atolls in the Bikini archipelago was totally vaporized, disappearing into a gigantic mushroom cloud that spread at least 100 miles wide before dropping back to the sea as radioactive fallout.

It was not the first time America had tested an H-bomb. At Enewatak Atoll, west of Bikini, initial H-bomb tests had been carried out on November 1, 1952. The explosion produced a light brighter than 1,000 suns and a heat wave that was felt more than 30 miles (50 kilometers) away.

That 10-megaton blast was part of a tit-for-tat response to the Soviet Union's testing an A-bomb in 1949. Predictably, the nuclear arms race did not end there, with the 1954 test conducted as a reply to the Soviets' detonation of their H-bomb the year before.

After nearly 18 months of construction, the world's first nuclear-powered submarine, the USS *Nautilus*, was launched on January 21, 1954. Although it didn't carry nuclear warheads, its ability to travel vast distances—including under the strategically important North Pole—raised the stakes even more. The arms race was on, and nobody was sure where it would end.

Domino Theory

A crucial element in President Eisenhower's foreign policy was his espousal of the domino theory, spelled out at a news conference on April 7, 1954. It warned of the dangers of Communism spreading across all of Southeast Asia should Indochina fall, and was used as a precursor to American intervention in Vietnam. If the Communists succeeded in Indochina (Vietnam, Laos, and Cambodia), Eisenhower argued, sympathetic local groups would have the encouragement and support to take over surrounding countries—Burma, Thailand, Malaya, and Indonesia. That, in turn, would put Japan, the Philippines, Australia, and New Zealand in the defensive front line. Eisenhower initially strengthened the French colonial presence in Indochina, then when France was defeated by Ho Chi Minh's Communist North, he assisted in the creation of South Vietnam as the "domino" the United States had to protect.

Chronicle of the Arms Race 1945–1954

July 16, 1945	U.S. tests first atomic bomb, Alamogordo, New Mexico
August 6, 1945	U.S. drops atomic bomb on Hiroshima, Japan
August 9, 1945	U.S. drops atomic bomb on Nagasaki, Japan
July 1, 1946	U.S. tests atomic bomb at Bikini Atoll
August 29, 1949	U.S.S.R. tests atomic bomb, Kazakhstan, U.S.S.R.
May 9, 1951	U.S. conducts first thermonuclear test
September 24, 1951	U.S.S.R. conducts second atomic bomb test
October 3, 1952	U.K. conducts first nuclear test, Monte Bello Islands, Australia
November 1, 1952	U.S. tests first hydrogen bomb at Enewetak Atoll
August 12, 1953	U.S.S.R. tests hydrogen bomb
March 1, 1954	U.S. tests 20-megaton hydrogen bomb at Bikini Atoll

WITH NUCLEAR WEAPONS." ADMIRAL EARL MOUNTBATTEN OF BURMA

WAR IN SOUTHEAST ASIA

Medal of Honor

Master Sergeant Travis Watkins, of Gladewater, Texas—Medal of Honor. On September 3, 1950, near Yongsan, Korea, Sergeant Watkins was wounded and paralyzed from the waist down. Ordering his squad to pull out and leave him, he stayed behind and died covering their withdrawal.

Sergeant Watkins gave his life for freedom. What can you do?

This. You can begin today to do your full share in defense of the country *he* defended so far "above and beyond the call of duty" by buying more . . . and more . . . and more United States Defense* Bonds.

For your Defense Bonds strengthen America. And if you will make our country strong enough now, American boys may never have to give their lives again. Defense is *your* job, too.

The war in what was still known as French Indochina was precipitated by the end of World War II, when Japanese forces—who had occupied the region during the war—pulled out. The French had tried to reassert their influence in the area but now found themselves up against the Viet Minh, Communist Vietnamese nationalists led by Ho Chi Minh. Supported by the United States against the Japanese during World War II, the Viet Minh controlled most of the country and when Ho Chi Minh declared (as its president) independence for the Democratic Republic of Vietnam in September 1945, it was only with the help of British and Indian troops that the French regained control.

In 1950, Ho Chi Minh again declared an independent Democratic Republic of Vietnam— which was now recognized by China and the Soviet Union—resulting in a bitter war between the Viet Minh forces and the French, which lasted until 1954. By then, the Viet Minh controlled the north of the country, and a decisive battle at Dien Bien Phu brought things to a head. The battle started on March 13, 1954, and within 10 days the French were on the defensive after the Vietnamese took control of the town's airstrip. The French were finally defeated at the beginning of May, leading to the country's partition at the Geneva Conference in July. Participants in the conference consisted of the United States, the Soviet Union, the United Kingdom, France, and the People's Republic of China. Agreements reached at the conference resulted in France's giving up any claim to territory in the Indochina region of Vietnam, Laos, and Cambodia.

The partition of Vietnam saw the Democratic Republic of Vietnam in the North controlled by the Viet Minh, and supported by China and the Soviet Union; while the State of Vietnam in the South was backed by the United States, the United Kingdom, and France. Despite the fact that President Eisenhower had

warned in February against U.S. intervention in Vietnam concerning the French conflict, America was now being inexorably drawn into that country's affairs.

In April, the president put forward his domino theory and, in direct response to the Communists' securing of North Vietnam at Geneva, formed the Southeast Asia Treaty Organization (SEATO) in September 1954.

Like NATO in Europe, SEATO—consisting of the United States, United Kingdom, France, Australia, New Zealand, Pakistan, Philippines, and Thailand—was conceived as a buffer

against Communist expansion among new and emerging nations. Both Laos and Cambodia gained independence by the end of 1954 after the breakup of French Indochina, immediately becoming the focus for U.S. concern about the perceived Communist threat to the region. But it was the newly created state of South Vietnam where the front line was to be drawn in the forthcoming conflagration. As the Communist North embarked on a relentless war of attrition against the South, the prospect of America's becoming embroiled in an armed conflict in Vietnam was already very real.

OPPOSITE: The U.S. government encouraged citizens to buy war bonds to support the military just as they had done in World Wars I and II.

ABOVE: Repatriated Chinese prisoners of war preferred to go to Taiwan rather than home to Communist China, some even carrying the flag of Taiwan's Nationalist government.

CONSPICUOUS CONSUMPTION

The automobile was *the* status symbol of the affluent society. In the midfifties, U.S. auto sales accounted for one-fifth of the gross national product. Superhighways were built to accommodate the new gas-guzzlers and, at 25 cents a gallon, millions of Americans were guzzling more gas than ever before. Whole new enterprises sprang up along America's highways, from motel chains like Holiday Inn to Howard Johnson's ubiquitous roadside restaurants.

Not only was the motor industry booming, but consumerism was evolving at an alarming rate. The first credit card had appeared in 1950, heralding a "buy now, pay later" ethos fueled by high-powered advertising—most potently via television.

Every home had a TV, and increasingly, every U.S. family owned their own home—preferably in the expanding suburbs. Public opinion polls found that three out of every four Americans considered themselves middle class, with the house, car, and TV set to prove it. Television promoted the American dream in feel-good sitcoms like *I Love Lucy*, while big-money quiz shows fed the worship of wealth even further.

As the whole family was seemingly glued to the TV set—including previously kitchen-bound Mom—the time was ripe for the emergence of the TV dinner. Introduced in 1954, the first TV dinner (turkey, corn bread dressing and gravy, buttered peas, and sweet potatoes) cost 98 cents and came in a box shaped like a TV. Ten million were sold by the end of the year.

If they didn't want to sit with the rest of the family, teenagers now had portable record players and the transistor radio, another innovation in 1954. In many families, they also had use of the second car. And, with the advent of rock 'n' roll, they had their own music as well.

A family gathers around their TV set in New Jersey in 1954.

TARANTULA

Aimed mostly at the new teenage audience, the monster movie craze started in 1953, when The Beast from 20,000 Fathoms rampaged through New York. The awakened dinosaur was followed in 1954 by The Creature from the Black Lagoon (in 3-D!), the giant ants of Them! and many, many more. In the United Kingdom, 1953's The Quatermass Experiment was the first of three TV serials that captured the nation's interest, while in Japan, Godzilla debuted on the big screen in November 1954. Before the end of the decade, there was even a magazine, Famous Monsters of Filmland, dedicated to the monster and horror film genre.

OPPOSITE: Tarantula! director Jack Arnold also made The Incredible Shrinking Man and It Came from Outer Space.

ABOVE: The Creature could also be seen in 3-D.

TEEN GANG WARFARE!

The fear of a rising wave of juvenile delinquency peaked in the midfifties, despite the fact that the actual proportion of teenagers who turned to crime had not risen since the end of World War II. What had increased, however, was the number of young offenders on America's streets, made more conspicuous by the rise in the teenage gang phenomenon.

There had always been street gangs in America's big cities, but by the fifties they had taken on a new, and often more violent, complexion. Before the mid-twentieth century, the majority of gangs in America were white, but after World War II, gangs from more diverse ethnic backgrounds began to appear.

Teenage gangs made their biggest impact in New York City with African Americans, Italians, Irish, Puerto Ricans, and countless other groups all contributing to the estimated 6,000 gang members and hundreds of gangs all staking a claim to their own territory. Most of the New York "gang wars" of the early

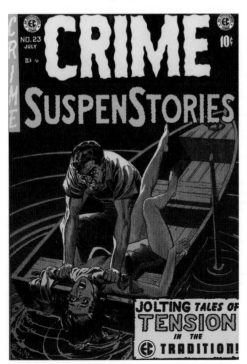

fifties—typically involving teenagers between 12 and 19 years old—were about territory, or "turf." As a rule, a gang would keep to its own turf unless it was out fighting its rivals. The turf borders were very clearly delineated, and often there would be a "no-mans'-land" between two areas. Big gang fights were known as "rumbles," where anything between 20 and 50 gang members on each side would meet at a prescribed battleground, often a park or school playground. Sometimes a rumble would be a spur-of-the-moment thing, but others were planned weeks in advance by the two gangs. The fight wouldn't last very long, but resulted in badly wounded, or even dead, youngsters.

Weapons among the gangs did not include the handguns that might be expected today, but the array of bicycle chains, switchblades, baseball bats, and car antennas gathered by police during their frequent gang roundups was lethal enough. The gangs, with brash names like Young Lords, Dragons, Egyptian Kings, and the Latin Gents, were a growing concern to law-abiding Americans, feeding public anxiety about juvenile delinquency. Benjamin Fine's 1955 book *1,000,000 Delinquents* predicted that, by the end of the decade, the United States would be home to one million teenage criminals.

Horror Comics

The mounting concern about teenage crime coincided with an increasingly hysterical campaign against "horror comics." The early fifties had seen a proliferation of comic books in America tackling often grisly subjects, with equally lurid cover illustrations to match. Titles like *Crime Suspense Stories*, *Tales from the Crypt*, and *The Vault of Horror* were on sale on every newsstand and hugely popular with a young readership.

The link between these publications and juvenile delinquency was forged by Dr. Fredric Wertham in 1953, when the *Ladies' Home*

Journal published a preview of his 1954 book, *The Seduction of the Innocent*. Wertham wrote that, in his studies with children, he found comic books to be a major cause of juvenile delinquency, but it was a theory based mainly on guilt by association. The vast majority of kids in those days read comic books, so that would inevitably include the minority who became delinquents. According to Wertham, however, the comics *caused* the children to become delinquents.

In June 1953, the Senate Subcommittee to Investigate Juvenile Delinquency in the United States was set up to ascertain the "possible influence of so-called crime comic books." Wertham seized upon the opportunity to further his crusade and he testified in April 1954. His general bias against comics was evident in one of his statements from the record: "I think Hitler was a beginner compared with the comic-book industry."

But the damage to the comic business was done, as public opinion rallied on the side of "decency"—and censorship. By October 1954, mainstream comics publishers formed the Comics Magazine Association of America, and all comics had to be submitted to an independent review panel before publication. Only those books that were deemed wholesome enough for the eyes of the nation's youth were allowed the "Comics Code Authority" stamp of approval.

LEFT: Horror comics and comics featuring violent crime were blamed for the rise in teenage delinquency.

RIGHT: Arrested for shooting another teenager, this 15-year-old member of the Bronx "Young Sinners" refuses to look at the weapon he used.

REBEL WITHOUT A CAUSE

In his red Harrington jacket and white T-shirt, James Dean was an instant symbol of "misunderstood" youth when Rebel Without a Cause was released in October 1955. His screen debut had occurred earlier that year in East of Eden, but before Rebel was released, Dean was dead—killed in a highway accident on September 30, 1955. Dean's brief period under the spotlight came in a year when radical changes were afoot in an otherwise conservative and insular world.

Entrepreneur Ray Kroc acquired the McDonald's chain of fast-food restaurants, a first step toward global domination by the burger brand. The Walt Disney empire expanded as never before, with The Mickey Mouse Club launched on nationwide TV and the first Disneyland opened in Anaheim, California. Another first to be aired on American TV, which by the midfifties had overtaken radio as the dominant broadcast medium, was the first televised presidential press conference.

Despite the great changes everyone was experiencing, mainstream society still simply did not know what to make of the new music erupting in its midst—the sound of the ghettos and hillbilly honky-tonks coming together in the name of teenagers, who'd found their own voice at last.

THE BLACKBOARD JUNGLE

The real breakthrough for rock 'n' roll came, some thought appropriately, via a controversial film about juvenile delinquency in America's schools, *The Blackboard Jungle*. The film—from a novel based on author Evan Hunter's own experiences as a teacher in New York's tough South Bronx—was directed by Richard Brooks and was never intended to exploit or glorify teen violence. Although advertisements for the picture sold it sensationally as "a shock story of today's high school hoodlums!" the movie began with a serious prologue identifying the problem of delinquency it was about to address. But what made the biggest impression came seconds later, as the credits rolled and the soundtrack crackled with "One, two, three o'clock, four o'clock rock," Bill Haley's opening lines to "Rock Around the Clock."

When the film opened on March 25, 1955, it caused a furor in the media with its graphic depiction of youthful violence. Crucial scenes included the attempted rape of one of the female teachers, and a telling episode in which a well-meaning tutor attempts to play his jazz records for the class, only to have them smashed by the hoodlum students.

But, more significantly, it soon had teenage audiences worldwide dancing in the aisles, slashing cinema seats and causing general mayhem in a fury of often copycat "riots" almost everywhere the film played. It also meant that 29-year-old Haley suddenly had a huge hit on his hands.

Rock Around the Clock

Although it was to be the first true anthem of rock 'n' roll, "Rock Around the Clock" almost didn't get made. Bill Haley had enjoyed minor hits in 1952 and 1953 with "Rock the Joint" and "Crazy Man Crazy" ("Rock the Joint" being credited with inspiring DJ Alan Freed to coin the phrase "rock 'n' roll") and he and his band the Comets were offered "Rock Around the Clock," a song in the same vein, allegedly written by James Myers (aka Jimmy De Knight) and Max Freedman. The boss of the Essex record company, however, didn't like it and tore up the sheet music in the studio after Haley had hopefully played through it a couple of times. Only when he moved to the Decca label in 1954 was Bill Haley actually able to record the number.

Even then, the song was relegated to the B-side of the next Bill Haley single, as producer Milt Gabler put one of his own compositions, "Thirteen Women," on the top side. "Thirteen Women," with its bizarre theme that the only survivors of an H-bomb blast are one man and 13 women, took Haley and the boys six takes

BLACKBOARD JUNGLE

IS THE MOST STARTLING PICTURE OF THE YEAR!

THE BLACKBOARD JUNGLE
By EVAN HUNTER

The sensational novel...now on the screen!

STARRING **GLENN FORD**
ANNE FRANCIS · LOUIS CALHERN
WITH **MARGARET HAYES** · SCREEN PLAY BY RICHARD BROOKS · BASED ON THE NOVEL BY EVAN HUNTER
DIRECTED BY RICHARD BROOKS · PRODUCED BY PANDRO S. BERMAN AN M·G·M PICTURE

to get right, leaving them only 40 minutes for "Rock Around the Clock." Released in May 1954, it did reasonably well, selling over 75,000 copies, but "Rock Around the Clock" composer Myers wasn't satisfied and sent copies of the B-side song to every producer in Hollywood.

Meanwhile, Bill Haley and his Comets were enjoying chart success with their hit cover of Joe Turner's "Shake, Rattle, and Roll," so they weren't too concerned about the fate of their previous flipside. But Myers doggedly campaigned for the song around the movie capital, and his persistence paid off when Richard Brooks decided to use it in *The Blackboard Jungle*. Apparently, the number was suggested to director Brooks by Peter Ford, the son of the film's lead, actor Glenn Ford.

Revolution

Taking note of the riotous reception the film was enjoying wherever it was shown, Decca re-released the single, this time with "Rock Around the Clock" as the A-side, and by mid-May 1955, it was topping the charts on both sides of the Atlantic. This triggered the worldwide rock 'n' roll revolution nearly a year before Elvis Presley first entered the charts. Haley went on to have another three Billboard chart hits in 1955, making six in all, followed by a best-selling album at the end of the year and another five hit singles in 1956.

While Bill Haley established rock 'n' roll as the new musical fabric, he was turning 30 and didn't really represent the teenage public his music had so galvanized. With his chubby face, trademark kiss curl, and tartan jacket stage

uniform, Haley was hardly a sex symbol, and as soon as Elvis burst onto the national scene in early 1956, Haley's days as the King of Rock 'n' Roll were truly numbered. For a few months through 1955, however, he was the music's chief ambassador, and certainly its very first superstar.

OPPOSITE: Rock 'n' roll fans caused controversy with their energetic appreciation of live shows and movies.

ABOVE: *The Blackboard Jungle*, with Bill Haley's "Rock Around the Clock" played over the opening titles, brought rock 'n' roll to a mass audience.

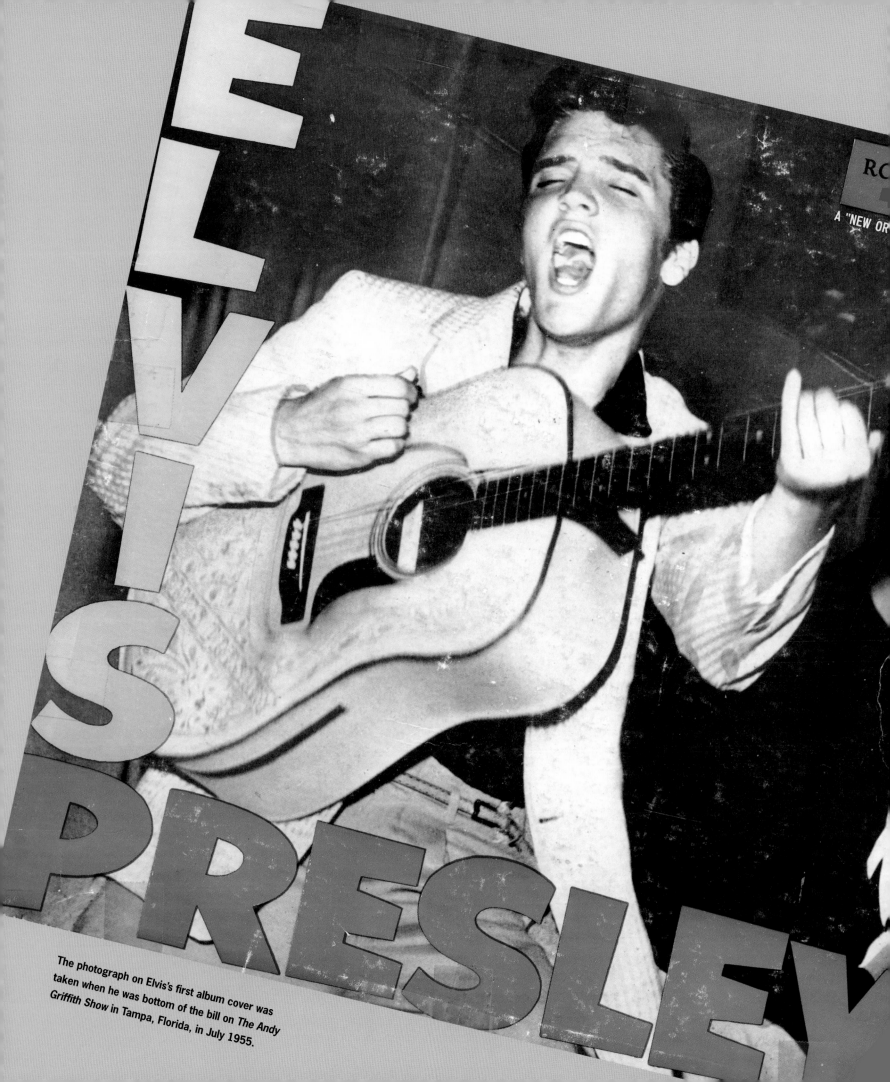

ELVIS PRESLEY

The photograph on Elvis's first album cover was taken when he was bottom of the bill on *The Andy Griffith Show* in Tampa, Florida, in July 1955.

ELVIS MEETS THE COLONEL

Barnstorming across the South through the summer of 1955 with his trio of guitarist Scotty Moore, bass player Bill Black, and drummer DJ Fontana, Elvis Presley—billed variously as the "Hillbilly Cat" and "Memphis Flash"— seemed ready to take on the world. He was signed to a management contract with a local promoter, Bob Neal, who had negotiated a weekly residency on the country-music radio show *Louisiana Hayride*, broadcast out of Shreveport, Louisiana, via 190 local stations across 13 states. The Hayride spot started in November 1954 and was crucial for two reasons: It gave Elvis a place in the Hayride live package shows that toured the South, and through those he met "Colonel" Tom Parker.

Parker claimed he was born in West Virginia in 1910, joining a traveling circus after being orphaned. But official records gave his real name as Andreas Van Kujik, who, it seems, had entered the United States from his native Holland illegally in the thirties. He drifted in and out of circus and fairground work until the end of the decade, when he began promoting country singers including Gene Autry and Roy Acuff.

After World War II, he went on to manage Eddy Arnold, securing him a record contract, Las Vegas engagements, and TV appearances. After splitting with Arnold, he teamed up with another country name, Hank Snow. Hank Snow Enterprises, partly owned by Parker, booked Snow and others into the Hayride shows. The Colonel's money-making instinct identified huge potential in the young Presley.

On August 15, 1955, Parker replaced Bob Neal as Elvis's manager, and so began the most famous (and some would say notorious) artist-management relationship in rock 'n' roll.

How the rising star would have fared without the Colonel's involvement is anybody's guess, but by November his Sun recording contract was sold to the major RCA label for an unprecedented $40,000. Within a few short months, his name and image would be the most famous in the world.

The Music Mafia

Wheeler-dealers like Tom Parker were, of course, nothing new in the music business. For years, the song-publishing world of Tin Pan Alley had been riddled with shady deals and sharp practices, while the rise of independent country and R&B record labels that preceded rock 'n' roll provided even more of a quagmire in which to conduct murky deals. Stories are legion about now-legendary singers and musicians receiving only a few dollars' fee for recording dates that produced million-selling discs, while song-writing credits were routinely signed away to the management or record company—often one and the same.

At the grassroots level, there was even more opportunity for corruption. The jukebox industry was, like radio, key in the promotion of records and was heavily infiltrated by organized crime, both in the provision of the boxes themselves (usually leased to a venue) and the distribution of the records.

And when the payola scandal broke in the late fifties, exposing the bribes that went to radio DJs to buy airplay for certain discs, *Billboard* magazine pointed out that it was nothing new. The practice had been rampant since the twenties, concluding that, "The cancer of payola cannot be pinned on rock 'n' roll."

ROUND AND ROUND WE GO

When New Orleans rhythm and blues singer Fats Domino entered the pop chart in July 1955 with "Ain't That a Shame," he was riding the start of a wave of African-American R&B artists who would break through into the mainstream charts as part of the rock 'n' roll explosion. Fats had been hot on the R&B charts since 1949, when "The Fat Man" was a million-seller, and his 1955 pop hit was the first of 37 Top 40 hits he would enjoy through to the early sixties.

A month after the pop-chart debut of Fats, Chicago-based Chess Records scored with Chuck Berry's first disc "Maybellene," hitting number 5. Like Domino, Berry would become one of the biggest and most influential names in rock 'n' roll through the latter half of the fifties and beyond, with teen-oriented anthems like "Roll Over Beethoven," "Rock & Roll Music,""Sweet Little Sixteen," and "Johnny B. Goode" that came to be regarded as part of the poetry of rock.

A label-mate of Berry, Bo Diddley didn't enjoy pop-chart success until later in the decade, though his 1955 debut release "Bo Diddley" backed with "I'm a Man" was a double-sided number 2 in the R&B charts. Similarly, songs like "Roadrunner" and "You Can't Judge a Book by the Cover" became instant R&B classics.

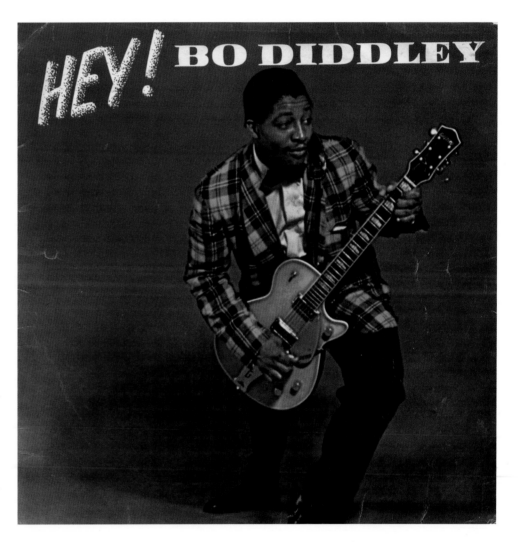

R&B Hits the Pop Charts

Other pop-chart entries by rhythm and blues artists included LaVern Baker with "Tweedle Dee" in January 1955; vocal group the Moonglows' "Sincerely" in March; the Platters with "Only You" (number 5 in October 1955) and chart topper "The Great Pretender" in December; and Frankie Lymon & the Teenagers with "Why Do Fools Fall in Love" right at the end of the year.

The end of 1955 also saw the R&B chart debut of Little Richard with "Tutti Frutti" when it hit the number 5 slot, before entering the pop Top 20 a month into 1956. Like Fats Domino's records, Richard's 1956 chartbusters—"Tutti Frutti," "Long Tall Sally," "Rip It Up," and "Slippin' and Slidin' (Peepin' and Hidin')"—were a form of rhythm and blues, albeit a much wilder version than Fats's melodic, laid-back style. R&B was now being marketed under the teen-friendly brand name of rock 'n' roll. Little Richard, more than anyone, represented the connecting point between the two genres.

Richard and Domino became household names, selling millions of records, appearing in rock exploitation films, and establishing African-American rhythm and blues as an essential part of the rock 'n' roll phenomenon. The days when R&B was by and large consigned to a cultural ghetto were truly over, with rock 'n' roll now being bought by teenagers of all races. This in itself was as revolutionary as anything manifest in the actual music.

OPPOSITE AND ABOVE: Both Chuck Berry and Bo Diddley were signed to Chicago's Chess Records, although Berry was first to see success in the pop charts.

ROCKABILLY REBELS

Following Elvis Presley's first recordings, Sun Records in Memphis became the artistic center of a brand of white "rebel rock" that was subsequently dubbed rockabilly. Artists signed by Sun manager Sam Phillips, including Johnny Cash, Carl Perkins, Jerry Lee Lewis, and Roy Orbison, created music with a potent mix of blues and country honky-tonk.

Sun's initial releases in the style included Malcolm Yelvington in October 1954 with a cover of Stick McGhee's "Drinkin' Wine Spo-Dee-O-Dee," Carl Perkins's debut "Movie Magg" in January 1955, Charlie Feathers's "Peepin' Eyes"

the following month, and Johnny Cash's debut in May 1955, "Hey Porter." Cash epitomized the tough no-nonsense country rocker with his early releases, including "Folsom Prison Blues" (inspired by the movie *Inside the Walls of Folsom Prison*) and his first pop-chart entry, "I Walk the Line" in 1956.

Carl Perkins's "Blue Suede Shoes," recorded at Sun in December 1955, was considered a classic of the genre. Encouraged by Johnny Cash to complete a song based on the line he'd written, "Don't step on my blue suede shoes," the number entered the Billboard pop chart on

March 10, 1956, climbing to number 2. On that day Elvis (who would hit with a cover of "Blue Suede Shoes" in April) also made his first appearance in the national charts, although by that time he'd left Sun for RCA.

The Rockabilly Boom

This was wild music, sung by white country boys with an aggressive fervor, anxious to prove that hillbillies could play the blues with a beat, alongside their African-American R&B counterparts on the label. And Sun wasn't the only rockabilly pioneer in the record industry. During 1955, Capitol released rockabilly discs by Ferlin Husky and Jimmy Heap; Imperial had Gene Henslee and Bill Mack; while Decca's Roy Hall gave fans sensational versions of "Whole Lotta Shakin' Goin' On" (later a hit for Jerry Lee Lewis), Fats Domino's "All By Myself," and Bill Haley's "See You Later Alligator."

With its emphasis on an insistent rhythm, electric guitars, and echo-enhanced vocals, this brand of raw rock 'n' roll had an appeal for teenagers that reached beyond the jump-jive lyrics of Bill Haley or romantic vocalizing of the doo-wop groups. It had an image, too—the pouting, leather-jacketed caricature of the rock 'n' roller had its roots in rockabilly with performers such as Gene Vincent and Eddie Cochran.

Musically, the influence of rockabilly was far-reaching, even featuring later in the repertoire of many sixties groups, including the Beatles, who recorded three Carl Perkins numbers ("Matchbox," "Honey Don't," and "Everybody's Trying to Be My Baby") in 1964.

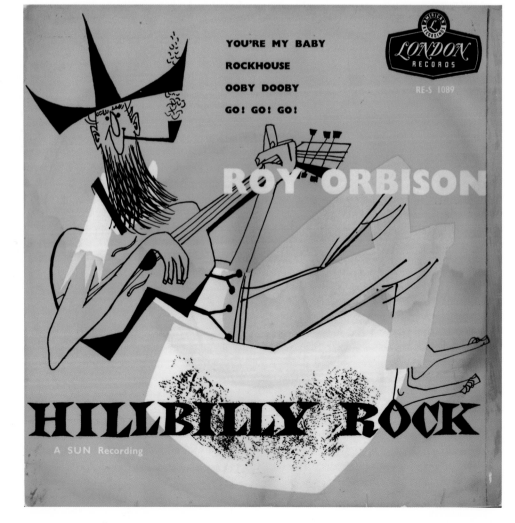

LEFT: Roy Orbison's early recordings for Sun were in the rockabilly style.

RIGHT: Johnny Cash backstage in White Plains, NY. He toured America constantly in the 1950s

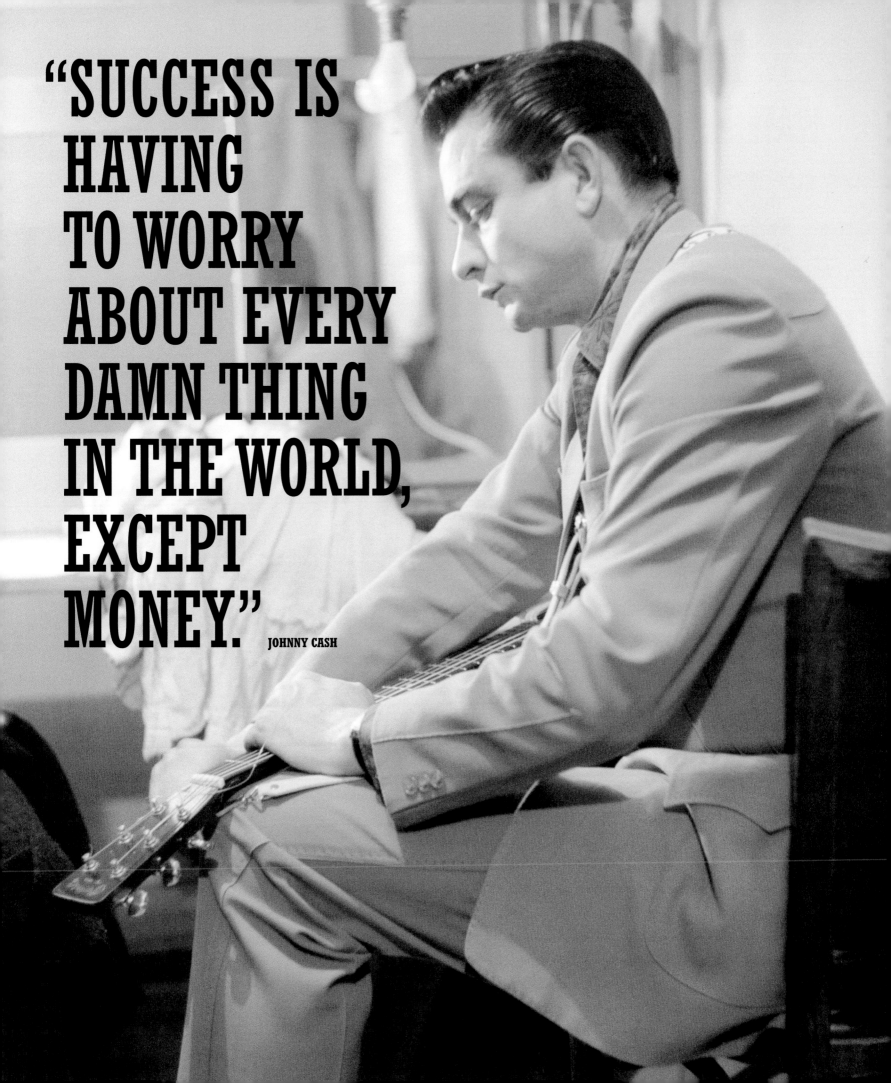

"SUCCESS IS HAVING TO WORRY ABOUT EVERY DAMN THING IN THE WORLD, EXCEPT MONEY." JOHNNY CASH

WATERED-DOWN ROCK

As soon as the record industry realized that rock 'n' roll—at least for the short term—was here to stay, it wasn't long before distinctly blander, less "threatening" records appeared, still aimed at the teenage market but at the same time acceptable to their parents.

The Canadian vocal group the Crew Cuts led the way with their hit cover of the Chords's doo-wop classic "Sh'boom" in 1954. Early in 1955, they followed that with a similar cover, this time of the Penguins's "Earth Angel," which reached number 3 in the pop charts. By February of the next year, the smooth-sounding Crew Cuts had scored no less than eight times in the *Billboard* Top 20.

In a similar vein, but with rather more sickly sentimentality, the female close-harmony group the Chordettes began a string of hits with "Mr. Sandman" in 1955, followed early in 1956 by "Eddie My Love," also a hit for the Fontaine Sisters and the aptly named Teen Queens.

Mainstream Rock 'n' Roll

The rest of the music industry seemed eager to jump onto the rock 'n' roll bandwagon by encouraging singers to tackle novelty rock items. Most successful of these was the former Glenn Miller vocalist Kay Starr, who topped the charts with "Rock and Roll Waltz." Recorded in late 1955, it was an early example of the mainstream already cashing in on what it saw as just a short-lived teen craze. Romantic crooner Alan Dale was another, his opportunistic "Rockin' the Cha Cha" even led to an appearance in the 1956 Bill Haley movie, *Don't Knock the Rock*. And bandleader Boyd Bennett adopted a Bill Haley style as he renamed his group the Rockets, hitting the charts twice in 1955 with "Seventeen" and "My Boy Flat Top."

Then there were the white singers who "made it" with drastically watered-down versions of R&B songs. Former big band vocalist Georgia Gibbs had hit the charts with the novelty "If I Knew You Were Comin' I'd've Baked a Cake" in 1950, but cracked the rock 'n' roll market with two innocuous covers of rhythm and blues hits in 1955, LaVern Baker's "Tweedle Dee" (which took Gibbs to the number 2 spot) and "Dance With Me, Henry," based on the overtly more sexual "Roll With Me, Henry" by Etta James.

The Clean-Cut Rocker

Pat Boone covered early rock 'n' roll classics in a similar way to the originals, but managed to make them sound less raucous in the process, making them even bigger hits as a consequence, starting with Fats Domino's "Ain't That a Shame" in 1955. Boone was noted for his clean-cut image, and it was said that he was so particular about grammar that he insisted on singing the line "Ain't that a shame" as "Isn't that a shame," until being persuaded otherwise. Boone's version went to number 1, the first of many hits.

Other watered-down covers of rock 'n' roll and R&B songs by Boone included Little Richard's "Tutti Frutti" and "Long Tall Sally," as well as Ivory Joe Hunter's "I Almost Lost My Mind." The pioneering DJ Alan Freed considered these bland versions of the real thing so reprehensible that he famously refused to play any Pat Boone records on his radio shows.

Pat Boone reviews the shooting script with Gale Storm prior to appearing with her on TV in *The Gale Storm Show*.

"THE SOVIETS FELT COMPELLED TO STRENGTHEN THEIR WESTERN DEFENSES BY ERECTING AN ALLIANCE UNDER THEIR OWN CONTROL."

MAJOR OLE MARTIN HOJEM, NORWEGIAN ARMY,

REPORTING ON THE WARSAW PACT

The Cold War became increasingly entrenched with the signing of the Warsaw Pact in the Polish capital in May 1955. Officially named the Treaty of Friendship, Co-operation, and Mutual Assistance, it was a military alliance between the Soviet Union, Poland, Czechoslovakia, Hungary, Romania, Bulgaria, Albania, and East Germany. The Russian delegates, led by Marshall Bulganin (front, third from left) landed in Poland on May 20 ready to lead the signing of the Warsaw Pact. It was seen as a response to the Western NATO alliance, which had been established in 1949 but had recently accepted into its fold the "remilitarized" West Germany.

PAUL NEWMAN
20TH CENTURY
See him in
"THE LONG HOT SUMMER"

Alongside the magical musicals and escapist adventures that traditionally sustained the cinema industry, the 1950s saw new, grittier "realistic" films start to emerge from Hollywood. Along with the new movies came a new breed of "Method" actors who would, as far as possible, avoid the straightjacket of the star system.

The Method style of acting developed initially from the teachings of the Russian actor and director Konstantin Stanislavski, and was taken up in New York by the Actors Studio, founded in 1947 by Cheryl Crawford, Robert Lewis, and Elia Kazan. Lee Strasberg became artistic director there in 1951.

The style required actors to immerse themselves in a character by bringing to bear their own personality, delving into their own emotional and psychological background in order to do so. With its insistence that an actor give all emotionally, the method found its best application in film—where a scene could be repeated until the "right" feel and expression was achieved.

The Actors Studio received the most media attention when Marilyn Monroe enrolled there early in 1955. But, as the training ground for a whole stable of new actors, it affected the world of theater and, more significantly, cinema. Names including Marlon Brando (who first demonstrated the method on-screen in 1951's A Streetcar Named Desire), Paul Newman, Rod Steiger, Shelley Winters, James Dean, Montgomery Clift, Karl Malden, and Steve McQueen were all products of the studio— names that were to change film acting forever.

OPPOSITE: Paul Newman was an early champion of Method acting.

ABOVE: Tennessee Williams's play inspired the movie in which Marlon Brando demonstrated the Method on-screen.

MONTGOMERY BUS BOYCOTTS

When 42-year-old Rosa Parks refused to give up her bus seat to a white man in Montgomery, Alabama, the incident triggered the civil rights protests that were to engulf the American South for the rest of the decade.

After finishing a day's work at a Montgomery department store on Thursday, December 1, 1955, the seamstress boarded the bus home, sitting in the first row of the backseats reserved for "colored" passengers. As the journey progressed, all the "white" seats at the front of the bus filled up and, as was normal practice in the segregated South, when more white folk boarded, African Americans were expected to give up their seats, stand if necessary, or even get off the bus if it became overcrowded.

Parks, like her fellow African Americans, had suffered indignation all her life as a result of "Jim Crow" regulations (named after a minstrel entertainment character who was popular when the first segregation laws were enacted) and refused to give up her seat. The bus driver called the police, who arrested Parks on the spot. She later said, "I only knew that, as I was being arrested, it was the very last time that I would ever ride in humiliation of this kind."

Disorderly Conduct

Four days later, on Monday, December 5, Rosa Parks was tried on charges of disorderly conduct and violating a local ordinance. She was found guilty and fined $10, plus $4 court costs. Parks appealed her conviction and challenged the legality of racial segregation, but most significantly, her case became the catalyst for the first mass mobilization of African-Americans against segregation in the South.

Immediately after her arrest, Parks's case was taken up by the Women's Political Council (WPC), which produced over 35,000 handbills announcing a bus boycott. On Sunday, plans for the boycott were announced at African-American churches in the area and in a front-page article in *The Montgomery Advertiser*. At a church rally that night, it was agreed to continue the boycott until African-American passengers were treated equally with whites, until African-American drivers were hired, and until seating in the middle of the bus was handled on a first-come, first-seated basis.

Despite heavy rain, the African-American community was unanimous in its support. Some rode in carpools, others traveled in African-American-operated cabs charging the same 10-cent fare as the bus, while the rest of the 40,000 African-American commuters walked, some as far as 20 miles. That evening, an organization was formed to run the boycott, the Montgomery Improvement Association (MIA), and it elected as its president a relative newcomer to Montgomery, the young minister Dr. Martin Luther King Jr.

White segregationists—many of them members of the Ku Klux Klan—retaliated with violence. Churches were burned and King's home was bombed in January 1956. But the boycott continued for a total of 382 days, leaving dozens of buses idle for months. Eventually, the loss of revenue and a decision by the Supreme Court forced the Montgomery Bus Company to accept integration. That was just the start—the bus boycott was the first of many similar protests in the civil rights battle that continued into the sixties with King at its forefront.

Rosa Parks sits in the front of a bus with a reporter in Montgomery, Alabama, following the Supreme Court ruling that made segregation illegal on the city bus system.

"I KNEW

SOMEONE HAD TO TAKE THE FIRST STEP AND I MADE UP MY MIND NOT TO MOVE."

ROSA PARKS

THE AFFLUENT SOCIETY

"Seventh heaven on wheels" was the way the advertisements described the 1955 Ford Thunderbird, and the sporty two-seater became an icon almost overnight. With its powerful V-8 engine, it was originally intended to compete with the Chevrolet Corvette, although it was never considered a full-blown sports car like the 'Vette. Ford described it as a "personal luxury car," creating a whole new market segment in the process. The advertisers saw it as the car of a new young "leisure class," a sleek (and sexy) symbol of the affluent society.

When it came to mobility, especially with respect to long-distance travel, the automobile was not alone as a venerated status symbol. More and more Americans were traveling by air, not just for overseas vacations but also for city-to-city business-meeting hops. And the railroad, long the transportation of choice for millions, was even more luxurious than ever, introducing leisure lounges, cocktail bars, and even small cinemas on its trains to compete with the proliferation of the car.

Back at home, it wasn't only the TV set in the corner (the latest ones could receive the color broadcasts launched in 1951) and the car in the garage that signaled prosperity on an unforeseen scale. All manner of laborsaving devices made life easier, from the power lawn mower and automatic air conditioner to a thousand household gadgets—refrigerator, freezer, food mixer, dishwasher, even the lowly electric toothbrush—that would have been considered the height of luxury in previous decades.

America accounted for just 6 percent of the world's population, but it owned 40 percent of radios, 58 percent of telephones, and 60 percent of the world's automobiles. And it was estimated that America's teenagers had an average of $400 a year each to spend on themselves. *Life* magazine figured they owned 1.5 million motor cars and spent $20 million on lipstick alone!

The most overt symbol of affluence in America in 1955 was the automobile and Ford's Thunderbird was even described by the company as a personal luxury car.

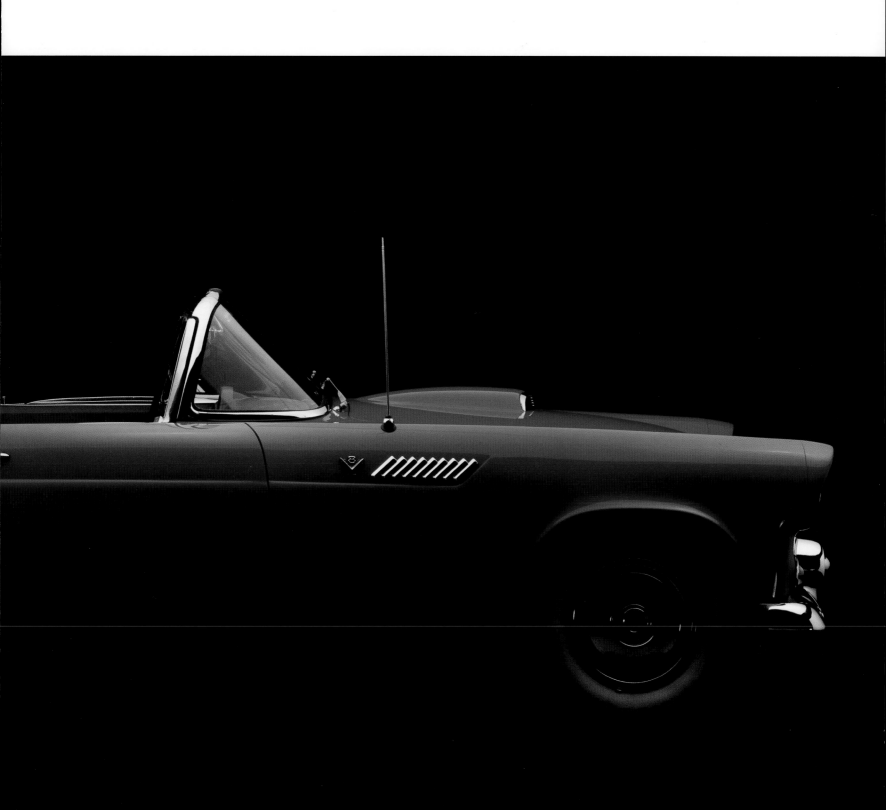

"IT'S BETTER FOR THE EVEN AS A SEX STAR, THAN NEVER

It was the era of the blonde bombshell in the movies, with Marilyn Monroe's sensational performance in The Seven Year Itch establishing her as the stereotypical platinum temptress. Others swiftly followed. Marilyn clone Jayne Mansfield was first noticed in *Pete Kelly's Blues* in 1955, and Kim Novak slunk seductively across the screen in the steamy Picnic while the queen of the B movies, Mamie Van Doren, appeared in an early teen-exploitation flick (her first of many), *Running Wild*.

WHOLE WORLD TO KNOW YOU, TO BE KNOWN AT ALL." MARILYN MONROE

1956

A-WOPBOPALOOBOP-A-WOPBAMBOOM

By the middle of 1956 it was obvious that (in the words of Danny and the Juniors) rock 'n' roll was here to stay. Elvis Presley had his first million-seller in the spring, and by summer was already starting to look less like a rock 'n' roll rebel and more a part of mainstream entertainment when he appeared on The Steve Allen Show wearing a tuxedo!

Teenage fashion was generally divided between the "weenies"—with white buckskin shoes, crew cuts, and back-buckled pants—and "greasers," who favored leather jackets, ducktail haircuts, and T-shirts. Bowling alleys became very popular, while more short-term crazes included the introduction of Silly Putty, and a fad in the pop charts for West Indian calypso music triggered by Harry Belafonte's hit "Jamaica Farewell."

In the wider world, meanwhile, the rumble of dissent could be heard on a number of fronts. In Britain, John Osborne's play Look Back in Anger spawned the disenchanted "angry young men," while in South Africa, Nelson Mandela and 156 other antiapartheid activists were arrested. On the other side of the world, the first stage of an epic struggle through the jungles and mountains of America's near-neighbor, Cuba, began on November 25 when Fidel Castro, Che Guevara, and 80 men set sail from Mexico in an old boat called the Granma.

ROCK 'N' ROLL MOVIES

No sooner had *The Blackboard Jungle* catapulted Bill Haley to fame, leaving a trail of trashed cinemas in its riot-torn wake, than the Hollywood movie machine started to feed rock 'n' roll through its processing system.

Columbia producer Sam Katzman, veteran of many a low-budget B movie, rushed out the 73-minute *Rock Around the Clock* in a matter of weeks early in 1956, with Bill Haley and His Comets getting top billing.

A wafer-thin plot concerned a small-time band manager who "discovers" Haley and, with the help of Alan Freed, launches rock 'n' roll as a national fad. Other musical appearances in the film included the Platters, Freddy Bell and the Bellboys, and an unlikely Latin American-style crooner, Tony Martinez.

Within days of the film's release, newspapers were full of stories of teenagers dancing in the aisles and ripping up cinema seats. Some towns in America and Britain had the film banned, but

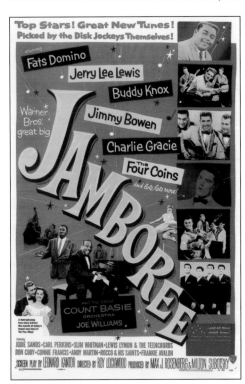

it was a box-office record breaker, with disc sales by Haley and the Platters rocketing into the millions as a result.

Columbia rushed out a quick follow-up, *Don't Knock the Rock*, with an equally flimsy plot still based around Haley and Freed, but this time with the musical support of Little Richard, the Treniers, and the now long-forgotten Dave Appell and his Applejacks. Not to be outdone, competitors in the budget-movie stakes, American International, put together another "rock 'n' roll vs. the squares" epic, *Shake, Rattle, and Rock*, with Fats Domino, Big Joe Turner, and Tommy Charles. From Universal International, *Rock, Pretty Baby*, billed as "The whole wonderful story of today's rock 'n' roll generation! … told the way they want it told!" had little rock to commend it, despite the title.

Elvis the Singing Cowboy

Released in mid-November 1956, Elvis Presley's first movie wasn't a rock 'n' roll film at all but a conventional western, *Love Me Tender*. Elvis had a dramatic role in which he flexed his thespian muscles, aspiring, it seems, to be a "serious" actor in the James Dean mold. But that was not to be; although his Hollywood career largely took over from his music in the sixties, he produced a string of mainly trite films in which feeble plotlines were usually matched by equally uninspiring songs.

Elvis did get to sing in *Love Me Tender*, of course, and the four musical items written into the plot had the girls screaming during what was an otherwise "straight" drama. The film was originally to have been called *The Reno Brothers*, but was changed to the name of the title song when the studio bosses decided that Elvis would be the big selling point. They were right; number 2 in *Variety* magazine's list of the week's top-grossing films, it was the only film in movie history to recoup its entire production cost in the first three days of release.

The Girl Can't Help It, released at the beginning of December 1956, was a different story entirely. Still acclaimed by many as the greatest rock 'n' roll movie ever, and certainly the best of its era, the full-color CinemaScope spectacular sported a strong cast, an amusingly satirical story line, and fine roster of rock 'n' roll cameo appearances. Starring the amply proportioned Jayne Mansfield in her first leading role (a part, apparently, originally earmarked for Marilyn Monroe), comic actor Tom Ewell (who'd played opposite Monroe in *The Seven Year Itch* the previous year), and tough guy Edmund O'Brien, the zany plot concerned a gangster's attempts to "buy" his girlfriend's success in the rock 'n' roll business.

From the opening sequence, as Mansfield sashays sexily down the street to the soundtrack accompaniment of Little Richard singing the title song, rock 'n' roll fans knew they were in for a treat. Little Richard appeared for another two numbers—"She's Got It" and "Reddy Teddy," Fats Domino delivered "Blue Monday," Gene Vincent and His Blue Caps premiered "Be Bop a Lula," and Eddie Cochran made a sensational debut singing "Twenty-Flight Rock." The Platters also put in an appearance, as did the sultry Julie London, with the ballad "Cry Me a River," plus lesser-known names including Eddie Fontaine, the Treniers, and the Chuckles. Edmund O'Brien's retired mobster even sang two spoof "penitentiary" rock numbers—"Rock Around the Rock Pile" and "Put No Lights on the Christmas Tree, Mother, I'll Be in the Electric Chair Tonight!"

LEFT: The music business love story *Jamboree* featured an impressive rock 'n' roll lineup as well as Count Basie and his orchestra.

RIGHT: Jayne Mansfield strikes a seductive pose in a promotional shot for *The Girl Can't Help It*.

ROCK 'N' ROLL INDIE LABELS

When rock 'n' roll burst onto the scene, the American recording industry was dominated by a handful of major companies, but there also existed scores of independent labels. Apart from Decca, which had fortuitously signed Bill Haley in 1954, and RCA-Victor, which had similarly acquired Elvis at the end of 1955, the other majors—Columbia, Capitol, MGM, Mercury, and ABC-Paramount—were little involved in rock until after it took off.

The major labels appeared to look upon the new music as a short-lived novelty. Even RCA and Decca didn't follow through with any other major rock 'n' roll signings, although the latter did represent Johnny Burnette and Buddy Holly via its autonomous subsidiary, Coral. Essentially, it was the "indie" labels that were largely responsible for the spread of rock 'n' roll.

Some of the indies were already in the vanguard of rock 'n' roll's earliest manifestations as well-established rhythm and blues labels. Atlantic Records in New York had the strongest R&B catalog in the industry, and it wasn't far from there to a string of rock 'n' roll hits with LaVern Baker, the Coasters, and Bobby Darin.

The Chess Players

Chicago-based Chess and its subsidiaries Checker and Argo, nerve center of the electric blues, was a natural environment for Chuck Berry, Bo Diddley, Dale Hawkins (of "Susie-Q" fame), and Clarence "Frogman" Henry. And on the West Coast, Specialty, home of wild rockers including Little Richard and Larry Williams, had been an R&B stronghold since its formation in 1945.

The most famous indie of them all, Sun Records in Memphis, had a blues-dominated roster before becoming the rockabilly label, launching Elvis Presley, Johnny Cash, Jerry Lee Lewis, Carl Perkins, and Roy Orbison.

Formed in Gallatin, Tennessee, in 1951, Dot Records started with a small list of country and R&B artists but really took off with rock 'n' roll hits by an eclectic mix of artists. These included Pat Boone (its biggest signing with 15 Top 10 hits between 1955 and 1958), hot female rocker Gale Storm, the eccentric Nervous Norvus (whose controversial "Transfusion" was a 1956 best seller), and the first mixed-race doo-wop group to make the charts, the Dell Vikings, with their 1957 smash "Come Go with Me."

Johnny Vincent founded Ace Records in 1955 in Jackson, Mississippi, and its relative proximity to New Orleans saw it signing some of the Crescent City's finest rockers like Huey Smith and the Clowns, Frankie Ford (who charted with "Sea Cruise"), Joe Tex, and Jimmy Clanton. The same year, Liberty opened for business in Hollywood, making its first rock 'n' roll signing in 1956 with Eddie Cochran.

Roulette Records' first rock chart busters were the Rhythm Orchids' duo from Texas, Jimmy Bowen and Buddy Knox, with two separate hits early in 1957. Later Roulette rockers included the Rock-a-Teens, whose "Woo-Hoo" made the Top 20 in 1959, and Ronnie Hawkins, whose group the Hawks later became the country-rock pioneers, the Band.

In New York, Cadence started in 1953 and was responsible for one of the biggest names in rock 'n' roll, the Everly Brothers, who had 12 Top 30 hits with the label from 1957 until leaving for Warner Brothers in 1960.

OPPOSITE: Recorded in October 1956 and released in 1957, the _Here's Little Richard_ album was on the independent Specialty label.

ABOVE: Eddie Cochran made his name with Hollywood's Liberty label.

ROCK 'N' ROLL WANNABES

Right from the start, rock 'n' roll was an international phenomenon. The cinema "riots" that had accompanied showings of *The Blackboard Jungle* and *Rock Around the Clock* were not restricted only to the United States, and were particularly evident in Britain. By the summer of 1956, with rockmania in full swing, the search was on across the United Kingdom for a genuine homegrown rock 'n' roll act.

The first groups were definitely bandwagon-jumpers, jazz musicians cashing in on what they saw as a mere craze. Tony Crombie & His Rockets were considered to be the very first British "rock" group, but ex-jazz drummer Crombie enjoyed a short-lived fame with his Bill Haley-derived records. What the record industry was really looking for was "Britain's Elvis" and they finally thought they'd found it in Tommy Steele.

Steele had been a seaman and, thanks to regular U.S. trips, was one of the first Britons to see Elvis perform. After leaving the merchant navy, he started performing at London's 2I's coffee bar, where he was spotted by his future manager John Kennedy. A recording contract was quickly secured with Decca Records, and Steele made the Top 20 with his debut "Rock with the Caveman" in October 1956, followed by a chart-topping cover of Guy Mitchell's "Singing the Blues" at the end of the year.

Tommy's toothy grin and bouncy blond hair hardly put him in the Elvis league image-wise, so he soon settled into the role of all-around entertainer. Other contenders followed, including Terry Dean, Marty Wilde, Billy Fury, and Cliff Richard—the last, like Steele, also achieving showbiz longevity over the years.

In France, despite the difference in language, they also had their own rock 'n' roll idol in Johnny Hallyday. Debuting in 1959 when he sparked France's first rock riots, his second record was a hit in 1960, and from then on he could do no wrong. Although he was not really a rock 'n' roll singer at all, the flamboyant showman Hallyday managed to convince many of his countrymen that he was, and he sold nearly 80 million discs.

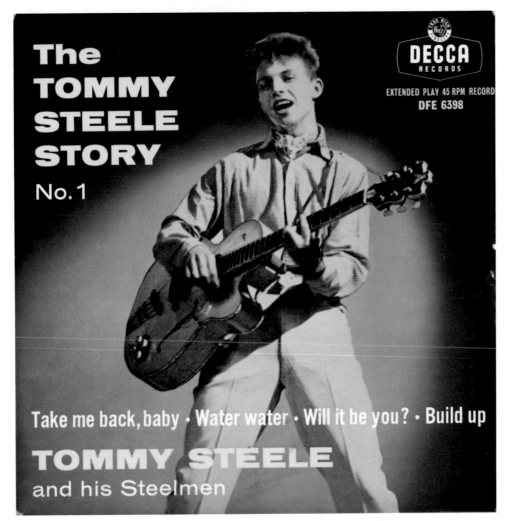

The TOMMY STEELE STORY
No. 1

DECCA
RECORDS

EXTENDED PLAY 45 RPM RECORD
DFE 6398

Take me back, baby • Water water • Will it be you? • Build up

TOMMY STEELE
and his Steelmen

OPPOSITE: Johnny Hallyday became France's own rock 'n' roll idol despite not really being a rock 'n' roll singer.

LEFT: Former merchant seaman Tommy Steele was one of the first British rockers to see Elvis perform live, then hit the charts after signing to Decca in 1956.

KHRUSHCHEV DENOUNCES STALIN

In a sensational speech to the 20th Congress of the Communist Party in February 1956, the Soviet leader Nikita Khrushchev denounced the former dictator Joseph Stalin, who had died three years earlier.

He said he wanted to put an end to the "Stalin cult" that had dominated Soviet society for the past 30 years, and described in detail the purges that Stalin had instigated against members of the party before World War II. These included the execution of leading figures in the ruling Politburo. Khrushchev revealed that in 1937 and 1938, 98 out of the 139 members of the Central Committee of the Communist Party were shot on Stalin's orders.

During the "Great Purge," Stalin also eliminated all his potential opponents in the army; 30,000 members of the armed forces were executed in the process, including 50 percent of all army officers. Finally, Stalin purged the NKVD, the dreaded secret police who had carried out his reign of terror. Khrushchev, claiming that such things would never be allowed to happen again, announced in his address that all the Soviet Union's political prisoners were to be released.

The speech also accused Stalin of virulent nationalism and anti-Semitism, and criticized his foreign policy at the beginning of World War II. As an ally of Adolf Hitler, Stalin had refused to believe that Germany would invade Russia, despite warnings from Winston Churchill and other Western diplomats. Khrushchev claimed that when Hitler's attack on Russia was launched, Stalin ordered the Red Army not to retaliate because the raid was merely a mistake on the part of some German army units.

In his speech, however, Khrushchev stressed to the delegates that these facts should be made known to the Soviet public only by degrees. It was clear that he was keeping an iron grip on things, as he'd demonstrated during the struggle for power that followed Stalin's death in 1953, and would again in his own purge of opponents just a few months after the Congress.

The policy of "de-Stalinization" that followed the speech encouraged Eastern European states to believe that they could now be more independent of the Soviet Union. This was a mistake for which the Hungarians would pay dearly when they flexed their democratic muscles later in the year.

Soviet Premier Nikita Khrushchev seemed ready to make great changes following his anti-Stalin stance, but by the time this photograph was taken when he arrived at Andrews Air Force Base on a visit to the United States three years later, relationships between America and the Soviets were fraught.

"IF YOU LIVE AMONG WOLVES, YOU HAVE TO ACT LIKE A WOLF." NIKITA KRUSHCHEV

"WE'RE NO LONGER COMRADES!"

CHANTS FROM 200,000 PROTESTORS IN PARLIAMENT SQUARE, BUDAPEST, OCTOBER 23, 1956

To crush a popular uprising in support of the liberal Communist leader Imre Nagy, the Soviet leader Nikita Khrushchev launched a massive armed offensive against the Hungarian capital, Budapest, in November 1956, overwhelming its defenders. The invasion, in which at least 25,000 Hungarians were killed overall, demonstrated to the world the USSR's domination of its Warsaw Pact "allies."

"HOW COULD WE POSSIBLY SUPPORT

BRITAIN AND FRANCE, IF IN DOING SO WE LOSE THE WHOLE ARAB WORLD?"

DWIGHT D. EISENHOWER

When President Nasser of Egypt nationalized the Suez Canal, Britain and France made a military alliance with Israel to regain control of the waterway, with Israel attacking Sinai while the European powers launched an attack on Egyptian bases. For the British soldiers (left), this meant celebrating Christmas under canvas in Egypt. Worldwide condemnation, including heavy criticism from both the United States and the USSR, forced Britain and France to withdraw, leading to the resignation of British Prime Minister Anthony Eden and signaling the end of the days of empire for Britain.

I LIKE IKE—AGAIN

Dwight D. Eisenhower was reelected president of the United States in November 1956 in a landslide victory even bigger than the one that had brought him to power four years earlier.

In September 1955, Eisenhower had suffered a heart attack but, having recovered by February, decided to run for reelection. His Democratic opposition tried to cast doubt on his physical ability to serve another term, but a thriving economy and his ending of the Korean War made him a popular figure and a strong candidate. The only question was whether the controversial Richard Nixon should run again for vice president, but Eisenhower eventually

decided to leave things as they were and not change running mates. In the Democratic camp, things were also much the same, with Adlai Stevenson once more securing the party's nomination.

Again "I Like Ike" became the Republican's slogan, but Eisenhower himself did little actual campaigning around the country because, he felt, the country was happy. It became very much a public relations exercise, with the actor Robert Montgomery hired to polish the presidential image. And it was even more of a TV election than the previous contest was, with prescheduled political broadcasts replaced

by spot ads dropped into regular programs—similar to sponsors' commercials. Eisenhower and his Republican campaign managers played on the female vote that had been crucial to his winning the 1952 election, with a succession of housewife-oriented TV ads.

The Winning Formula
Eisenhower's campaign message was a repeat of the 1952 formula, family and religion being presented as key elements in social cohesion and as a bastion against Communism. Juvenile delinquency was again under the spotlight as an example of what could happen when these

values were neglected. Ike promised to rid America of juvenile delinquents if reelected.

As election day approached, two international conflicts aided Eisenhower—the Suez crisis and the Soviet invasion of Hungary. Eisenhower ensured that America stayed out of both. This tense world situation only served to undermine two of the Democrats' key pledges—the suspension of nuclear weapons tests and the end of the military draft.

The Republican slogan "Peace, Prosperity, and Progress" seemed more appropriate to voters than the Democrats' "New America,"

with a feeling that because of the current peace and prosperity, there was no need for a new America. Eisenhower won hands down, with a huge lead in the popular vote and the electoral votes taking 41 of the 48 states.

I Like Elvis

Like a seasoned politician, Elvis Presley's manager, Colonel Tom Parker, was never one to miss a hot public relations opportunity. During the presidential election he launched an "Elvis for President" stunt, complete with button badges that read, "I Like Elvis," instead of Ike.

OPPOSITE: Girls wearing "I Like Elvis" badges lined up all night in New York for the opening of *Love Me Tender* at the Paramount Theater in November 1956.

ABOVE: Eisenhower hits the campaign trail again shadowed by Richard Nixon.

nixa
HIGH FIDELITY LONG-PLAYING MICROGROOVE RECORD 33⅓ rpm

L
O
N
N
I
E

"AND GOD CREATED WOMAN ...
BUT THE DEVIL INVENTED
BRIGITTE BARDOT"

And God Created Woman catapulted 23-year-old Brigitte Bardot onto the international movie scene in 1956. Director Roger Vadim's film displayed Bardot's natural sexuality in a way that left little to the imagination.

Criticized on its home ground in France, the movie caused a sensation—though often in a censored version—in the rest of the world. In America, *Time* magazine described Bardot's controversial appearance as "stretched end to end of the CinemaScope screen, bottoms up and bare as a censor's eyeball."

Shot on location in the southern French resort of St. Tropez, the film made the town an ultra-fashionable playground for the rich and famous, and Bardot's appearance at the Cannes Film Festival clad only in a bikini further confirmed her status as the world's new number-1 sex symbol. Nicknamed the "sex kitten" by a breathless media, Bardot brought a refreshingly uncontrived sensuality to the cinema screen, in contrast to the "manufactured" image of the Hollywood goddesses of the era.

The frank approach to sex in the movie was way ahead of its time, a forerunner of more liberal attitudes that would prevail in the sixties. Bardot's sensual, half-girl, half-woman mystique inspired a "casual" look with women worldwide, apparent in the image adopted by subsequent film icons such as Catherine Deneuve, Jane Fonda, and Julie Christie.

OPPOSITE: Bardot caused a sensation in her first major movie role.

BELOW: The poster that launched the new screen goddess to stardom.

1957

WHY DO FOOLS FALL IN LOVE?

Despite its domination of the pop charts, rock hadn't lost its ability to shock. The Everly Brothers' hit "Wake Up Little Susie" was banned from Boston airwaves on account of its lyrics and Jerry Lee Lewis prompted thousands of complaints when he kicked over his piano stool in a manic appearance on TV's Steve Allen Show. In the normally mainstream world of the stage musical, West Side Story, based on the violent confrontations between New York teenage gangs, caused a sensation when it opened on Broadway.

One of rock 'n' roll's earliest pioneers Johnny Otis scored his first (and only) big hit single with "Willie and the Hand Jive" in April. Elvis, meanwhile, paid just over $100,000 for his Memphis mansion, Graceland.

Elsewhere, as always, the year had its share of craziness. The Wham-O Company produced the first Frisbee, initially naming it the Pluto Platter; a stripper called Tempest Storm signed a $100,000 contract to tour the burlesque circuit; and the Gaither Report to the U.S. Congress called for more nuclear missiles and fallout shelters as Russian Sputniks—the world's first artificial satellites—circled the Earth.

Following hot on the heels of Allen Ginsberg's epic poem *Howl*, Jack Kerouac's novel *On the Road* caused a sensation when it was finally published by Viking on September 5, 1957. It received a rave review in the *New York Times*, and soon climbed to number 7 in the best-seller list.

Rejected by a number of publishers, Kerouac boasted that he'd written the book in a frantic three-week burst, prompting Truman Capote to comment, "That isn't writing, it's typing." The stream-of-consciousness style certainly suggested a highly spontaneous creative process. Kerouac claimed his method was influenced by the improvisation of jazz musicians.

Based on his own experiences when he'd motored, hitchhiked, and bused across America at the end of the forties, the novel extolled the virtues of individuality, hedonism, and sexual freedom which were central to Beat philosophy.

Described as "the bible of the Beat generation," *On the Road* was essential reading for young people looking for personal liberation from the straightjacketed society of the fifties. With Kerouac's espousal of sex, drugs, and music as keys to that liberation, his work was later regarded as a catalyst for the sixties counterculture—though he rejected the hippie movement not long before his death in 1969.

The White Negro

In his essay *The White Negro*, Norman Mailer described the phenomenon of the hipster, the new bohemian who embraced existentialism, drugs, and jazz. Instead of political rebellion, the hipster propounded a lifestyle revolution, rejecting middle-class values in favor of "cool," stereotypically African-American, attitudes. The hipster was what Mailer called "a psychic outlaw," who looked to Harlem for social role models, finding inspiration in the art of Charlie Parker rather than William Shakespeare.

Mailer, who had achieved fame with his World War II novel *The Naked and the Dead* in 1948, was known by the midfifties as an anti-establishment essayist, and was one of the founders of the highly influential *Village Voice* newspaper in 1955. *The White Negro*, published as a paperback book by City Lights in late 1957, first appeared in the summer of 1957 under its full title *The White Negro: Superficial Reflections on the Hipster* in the magazine *Dissent*. The "underground press" became a major platform for Beat writers in the fifties.

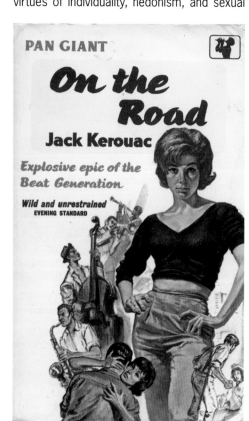

PAN GIANT

On the Road
Jack Kerouac

Explosive epic of the Beat Generation

Wild and unrestrained
EVENING STANDARD

LEFT: Jack Kerouac's *On the Road* was rejected by all of the publishers who first saw it.

RIGHT: Norman Mailer with his wife, Adele, by his side even though he had just been charged with stabbing her at a party.

MEN EVER COME TO CHILDBEARING."

NORMAN MAILER

HOLLY
CRICKET
BRUNSWICK RECORD STA
O-MINUTE
AGE SHOW
P.M.
DANC
8:30 P.M
ETIC
PARK
E SALE)
ROTHSCHIL
PAVILION
$1.50
(ADVANCE SALE)
ULY 13

ROCK 'N' ROLL TAKES OVER

Rock 'n' roll, it seemed, could produce one superstar after another. A product of the Sun Records' school of rockabilly, piano-pumping shouter Jerry Lee Lewis made his chart debut in July 1957 with "Whole Lot of Shakin' Going On." This was down-home boogie with a hillbilly beat, and Jerry Lee's wild stage act sent audiences crazy wherever he played—he was even known to set fire to the piano if things were going really well. And his records sold by the million. "Whole Lot of Shakin'" was followed at the end of the year with his biggest, "Great Balls of Fire," which hit number 2 in the Billboard chart and number 1 in the United Kingdom.

Then, out of Lubbock, Texas, via a studio in Clovis, New Mexico, came Buddy Holly and his group, the Crickets. Holly's strident brand of guitar-driven rock shot to number 1 on both sides of the Atlantic with his chart debut "That'll Be the Day" in September 1957, swiftly followed into the Top Ten by "Peggy Sue" and "Oh, Boy!" His bespectacled image endeared him to teenage rock fans everywhere, demonstrating that you didn't have to have Elvis's sultry sex appeal to be a rock 'n' roll star.

Little Richard Retires

The 1957 charts were dominated by records aimed at the teenage market. Elvis alone had four number 1s—"Too Much," "All Shook Up," "Teddy Bear," and the iconic "Jailhouse Rock." The Everly Brothers made number 2 with "Bye Bye Love" then topped the chart with "Wake Up Little Susie"; Chuck Berry scored with his teen anthems "School Day" and "Rock 'n' Roll

Music"; the Coasters had their first two hits; Fats Domino had four singles in the Top Ten; and Little Richard charted three times—then announced he was giving up rock for religion.

Non-rock teen-appeal records included two chart-topping versions of the schmaltzy "Young Love," first by Sonny James and then Tab Hunter, three massive hits by squeaky-clean Pat Boone ("Don't Forbid Me," "Love Letters in the Sand," and "April Love"), and Debbie Reynolds's cloyingly sentimental "Tammy." Paul Anka zoomed to the top of the charts in the summer of 1957 with "Diana," selling over nine million copies worldwide.

Other rock 'n' roll-influenced number 1s included "Party Doll" by Buddy Knox, Charlie Gracie's "Butterfly," and the rockabilly-tinged "Honeycomb" from Jimmie Rodgers. Plus, at the end of the year, sweet-voiced soulman Sam Cooke had his first time at the top with "You Send Me."

Rock 'n' roll was now a world phenomenon, not just in terms of record sales around the globe, but with live tours featuring the major U.S. stars. As well as Little Richard, Australian fans got to see a sensational tour headlined by Jerry Lee Lewis and Buddy Holly, and Bill Haley and his Comets made their first trip to Europe in the spring when they toured the United Kingdom—the first appearance on the continent by any American rock act. When he arrived in London, Haley was mobbed by thousands of fans at Waterloo Station in a near-riot dubbed the "Second Battle of Waterloo" by the media.

Buddy Holly and the Crickets' poster advertising one of their 1957 gigs.

"WE DON'T WRITE SONGS, WE WRITE RECORDS."

When the Coasters made their chart debut with their double-sided hit "Searchin' " and "Young Blood" in May 1957, it was the first of a string of classics written by the greatest rock 'n' roll songwriting team of the fifties, Jerry Leiber and Mike Stoller.

Sharing an enthusiasm for rhythm and blues, the two met in Los Angeles as teenagers in 1950, and by 1952 had their first national R&B hit, "Hard Times" by Charles Brown. The same year (and still in their teens) they had even more success with "Hound Dog" by Big Mama Thornton—which was a far bigger smash in 1956 when it was covered by Elvis Presley. They formed the Spark label in 1953, their first signing being a doo-wop group called the Robins, whom they picked to perform their "playlets," humorous songs that told little stories. The Robins' performance of "Riot in Cell Block No. 9" led to Atlantic Records' buying the Spark label. The group then became the Coasters, moving to New York with their songwriting mentors.

Leiber and Stoller were contracted to Atlantic as independent producers and created a series of minidramas for the Coasters, with the members of the group playing different parts, which included such classics as "Smokey Joe's Café," "Yakety Yak," "Charlie Brown," and "Along Came Jones," most of them Top 10 hits.

Leiber and Stoller's place as the most successful songwriting team in rock 'n' roll was confirmed with hits for Elvis—including "Love Me," "Jailhouse Rock," and, of course, "Hound Dog"—but it was their continuing association with the Atlantic label that marked their importance in rock history. Throughout the fifties they had been providing Atlantic with hits in addition to those achieved by the Coasters' records, for LaVern Baker, Ruth Brown, Joe Turner, and others, but it was with the Drifters that they made their most indelible mark.

They'd written several hot R&B sides for the vocal group in the midfifties, but it was right at the end of the decade that they set the seal on a new R&B sound when they first introduced strings to a Drifters record, "There Goes My Baby," in 1959. Their highly crafted approach as producers (with up to 60 takes on some sides) was hugely influential to the other pop music writers who collaborated with Leiber and Stoller on Drifters' hits that included "Save the Last Dance for Me" in 1960, "Up on the Roof" in 1962, and "On Broadway" in 1963.

Throughout the fifties Atlantic's R&B and rock 'n' roll catalog was second to none, including (as well as the above-mentioned Coasters, LaVern Baker, Ruth Brown, and Joe Turner) the Clovers, Clyde McPhatter, Chuck Willis, Ivory Joe Hunter, R&B sax supremo King Curtis, Bobby Darin, and its greatest star, soul pioneer Ray Charles—whose "What'd I Say" was one of the label's biggest hits of the decade.

MONO HA-K 2318   THE DRIFTERS' GREATEST HITS   LONDON ATLANTIC

FULL *dynamics-frequency* SPECTRUM   ATLANTIC

THE DRIFTERS' GREATEST HITS

LEFT: Leiber and Stoller composed many of the Drifters' best-known songs.

RIGHT: Ray Charles was Atlantic's biggest star but he left the label in 1959.

ROCK 'N' ROLL TELEVISION

TV variety shows like *The Milton Berle Show* and Ed Sullivan's *Toast of the Town* had brought rock 'n' roll into family living rooms across America, most famously with Elvis Presley's groundbreaking appearances. Those were, however, guest spots on all-round family entertainment programs, not performances on shows made for rock 'n' roll fans.

The first specific rock 'n' roll show to be broadcast nationally on U.S. television was *American Bandstand*, hosted by Dick Clark and first aired on August 5, 1957. Like Alan Freed, the enterprising Clark had been in the forefront of rock 'n' roll radio, and had hosted his own show on Philadelphia's WFIL. The station also had an affiliated television outlet, on which he often co-presented a pop show, *Bob Horn's Bandstand*, taking over as the full-time host in July 1956. The show was picked up by the ABC network in 1957 and renamed *American Bandstand*. From the outset it was a huge success and rock 'n' roll television was born.

In that first edition of *American Bandstand*, the very first record played was Jerry Lee Lewis's "Whole Lotta Shakin' Going On," which had entered the national charts a couple of weeks before. Guests on the debut broadcast were Billy Williams and vocal group the Chordettes, but a big feature of the show proved to be the studio audience of teenagers dancing to the music as they would in a club. Kids across America started copying their dance moves and clothes. The formula caught on, becoming a template for rock TV shows worldwide. *Bandstand* was broadcast out of its Philadelphia studios every weekday afternoon for six years, then weekly from 1963 to 1987.

Rockin' the BBC

Even before *American Bandstand* hit the airwaves, in London the BBC had launched *Six-Five Special* on February 16, 1957. Like *Bandstand*, it was broadcast live with a youthful studio audience, while the weekly Saturday show helped boost the careers of innumerable British rock and pop names including Tommy Steele, "Skiffle King" Lonnie Donegan, and Marty Wilde. The opening announcement on the first show from host Pete Murray set the frantic tone: "Welcome aboard the *Six-Five Special*. We've got almost 100 cats jumping here, some real cool characters to give us the gas, so just get on with it and have a ball." Murray's co-host, Josephine Douglas, then "translated" the intro into "square" language for all the adults watching!

The guiding hand behind *Six-Five Special* was producer Jack Good, a key innovator in rock 'n' roll TV. He and the BBC didn't always see eye-to-eye, and by June 1958 he'd left to launch a new show on the rival ITV network, *Oh Boy!* On this show, the pace was even more electric, with an audience of (mainly female) fans encouraged to scream at their idols like they would at a live concert. As well as a regular roster of British rock 'n' rollers, *Oh Boy!* introduced, for the first time on live British TV, American rock legends Eddie Cochran and Gene Vincent. From that point on both stars were more popular in the U.K. than in their home country. Jack Good went on to produce rock shows *Boy Meets Girl* and *Wham!* for U.K. television before moving to the United States and playing a part in launching the hugely popular *Shindig* in the sixties.

Dick Clark and his *American Bandstand* audience admire a spinning toy on the studio floor.

I WAS A TEENAGE MOVIEGOER

Low-budget rock 'n' roll movies were proving to be such a commercial success that it became clear that there was a substantial teenage audience to be tapped and 1957 saw a boom in teen exploitation films. Less than a dozen pictures geared primarily to a youth audience had appeared in 1956, while the total in 1957 was almost 40.

AIP (American International Pictures), which had jumped on the rock bandwagon with *Shake, Rattle, and Rock* in 1956, rushed out its first all-teen double bill at the end of the year, *Girls in Prison* and *Hot Rod Girl*. It was so successful that others quickly followed. The films were certainly "budget," each only costing between $50,000 and $100,000, and although they weren't box-office blockbusters, they made enough money to justify making more of the same. In 1957 alone, AIP's output included teen epics such as *Dragstrip Girl*, *Reform School Girl*, *Confessions of a Sorority Girl*, and the cult hit *I Was a Teenage Werewolf*. *Werewolf* was one of the biggest success stories, costing around $100,000 and grossing over $2 million within a year. Originally billed with *Invasion of the Saucer Men*, it was followed at the end of 1957 with *I Was a Teenage Frankenstein*.

As is evident from AIP's releases, the "bad girl" theme was incredibly popular. Other 1957 releases along the same lines included *The Careless Years* and *Teenage Doll* from United Artists, Republic's *Eighteen and Anxious*, and *Untamed Youth* from Warner Brothers. *Untamed Youth* starred blond bombshell Mamie Van Doren, the undisputed queen of the teen exploiter pic. Her portfolio included 1955's *Runnin' Wild*, and *High School Confidential* in 1958, now regarded as a classic of the genre and featuring an appearance by Jerry Lee Lewis singing the title song. Among Van Doren's later contributions were *Girls Town* (1959), *College Confidential* (1960), the marvelously titled *Sex Kittens Go to College*, also in 1960, and *The Beat Generation*.

The *Beat Generation* (1959) was typical of the way the exploitation moviemakers jumped on a trend, usually getting it wrong in the process.

Its publicity ran copy such as: "The wild, weird world of the Beatniks!…Sullen rebels, defiant chicks…searching for a life of their own! The pads…the jazz…the dives…those frantic 'way-out' parties…beyond belief!" Needless to say, little in the film had anything to do with Beat culture, any more than did *The Beatniks*

(1959), *The Rebel Set* (1959), and the U.K.-produced *Beat Girl* (1960).

Just as the record industry responded to the new teenage affluence of the fifties, the movie studios did exactly the same thing. This was an audience that simply hadn't existed as a separate "market identity" before. The very word "teenage" in a movie's title would draw the kids in, or so the producers thought, and they were usually right. Hence *Teenage Crime Wave* (1955) and *Teenage Rebel* (1956), the U.K.'s *Teenage Bad Girl* and the German-made *Teenage Wolfpack*, both in 1957. Not to mention the flights of fantasy represented by 1957's *Teenage Monster*, *Teenage Caveman* in 1958, *Teenagers from Outer Space* (1959), and *Teenage Zombies* in 1960.

RIGHT: The movie poster for one of the biggest teenage exploitation films.

BELOW: Mamie Van Doren singing and dancing in *Untamed Youth*.

"I'D LIKE TO CONGRATULATE THE RUSSIAN SCIENTISTS BUT I DON'T SPEAK GERMAN."

BOB HOPE

With its insistent "beep" signal beaming down to Earth as it circled the globe every 98 minutes, the 183-pound Russian *Sputnik* (meaning "fellow traveler"), launched on October 4, 1957, represented a huge embarrassment for America. The world's first artificial satellite was only about the size of a basketball but had been launched into orbit by America's Cold War enemy, apparently with the aid of U.S. secrets stolen by Soviet spies. It was followed on November 3, by *Sputnik II*, carrying the first living passenger, a dog named Laika.

"Red scare" paranoia was about to enter a new phase and the space race was underway. America's first attempt at launching a satellite in 1958 would go badly, resulting in newspaper headlines that read simply, "Kaputnik." And the sudden focus on real-life space exploration gave a new boost to the popularity of space-travel science-fiction novels and movies.

ANTI-U.S. RIOTS SWEEP TAIWAN

KEEP 'EM FLYING!

U.S. AIR FORCE

Some of the most violent anti-U.S. riots yet seen in the Far East erupted on the island of Taiwan—formerly known as Formosa—during the summer of 1957. The riots were sparked by America's decision to send missiles to the offshore state, which Eisenhower saw as one of the "dominoes" the United States had to defend to help prevent the spread of communism in the region.

Initially called the Republic of China, Taiwan was established in 1949 after the nationalist troops led by Chang Kai-shek withdrew from the Chinese mainland, having been defeated by Mao Tse-tung's Communist army. As a small anti-Communist bastion on the doorstep of the giant People's Republic of China, it was a natural friend for the United States to adopt in its foreign policy of "containment" of Communist regimes and their allies.

Unlike many anti-U.S. outbreaks in the Far East and elsewhere during the fifties, the riots, mainly concentrated in the capital Taipei, were not the carefully organized demonstrations usually witnessed, but spontaneous uprisings demonstrating genuine popular concern. Many Americans were shocked by what they saw as an "ungrateful" response by the people of Taiwan to Uncle Sam's gesture of military support. To the average Taiwanese, however, the presence of U.S. missiles on their soil made them feel more of a target for their Communist neighbors than they already were.

Student Riots in Boston

Riots of a rather different kind rocked the normally sedate campus of the Massachusetts Institute of Technology (MIT) in March 1957, when students protested against a rise in the dormitory rent and the unsatisfactory food served in the college dining facility.

Waving homemade posters declaring, "We protest" and "Lower rent," students gathered outside the college dean's home, exploding firecrackers and tossing snowballs. Then, as hi-fi sets blasted music from open windows, the rioters began to block traffic, setting fire to piles of garbage in the road. Three fire trucks and four police cars arrived, and then the tension rose as a police wagon rolled up and several students were arrested. More wagons were soon on the scene and the students started chanting, "Let's go to jail!" with the police more than happy to oblige them. By this time—it was an hour or more past midnight—the electricity had been turned off, adding to the general chaos.

Eventually, over 100 students gathered outside the dining room of Baker House, the focus of the food protest, and many were arrested when the police rushed them with searchlights sweeping the area. Everyone arrested was bailed out the next morning. They subsequently appeared in court on various charges including disrupting the peace, inciting riot, breaking glass, refusing to follow police instructions, and resisting arrest.

When the riots hit the nation's headlines, many Americans were stunned that this latest example of youthful rebellion was not perpetrated by rock 'n' roll movie fans or juvenile delinquents, but by normally "respectable" college kids, the presumed cream of the nation's youth.

OPPOSITE: Violence flared at the U.S. Tachikawa Air Base in Tokyo as 1,500 protesters attacked 2,500 armed Japanese police.

ABOVE: Despite the apparent rebelliousness of the nation's youth, the military continued to recruit them into service.

LITTLE ROCK ROCKED BY RACE RIOTS

The struggle for African-American civil rights hit the world's headlines in early September 1957 when the State National Guard was called in to prevent nine African-American students from entering a high school in Little Rock, Arkansas.

The United States Supreme Court ruled in 1954 that segregated schools were inherently unequal and therefore unconstitutional, but several states in the Deep South refused to accept the judgment, including Arkansas. Its governor, Orval Faubus, was adamant that segregation would stay, and when the nine African-American students enrolled at Central High in Little Rock, he ordered units of the Arkansas National Guard physically to prevent them from entering the school.

The images of the children, six girls and three boys, blocked from going to school by state troops—and crowds of baying white supremacists—were circulated around the world. After three weeks, a federal judge ordered the guard's withdrawal. But when a white mob took their place in the streets of Little Rock, ineffectually monitored by the local police, the mayor appealed to the president to help control the escalating crisis.

On September 24, 1957, President Eisenhower appeared on nationwide television and told the American people that the situation was intolerable, in terms of the Constitution, the civil rights of American citizens, and the country's image abroad. The next day, on his orders, 1,000 paratroopers of the 101st Airborne Division moved into Little Rock in full battle gear with rifles and fixed bayonets, to ensure that the nine African-American children could attend school. Governor Faubus was furious, calling the federal troops an army of occupation,

and the "Little Rock Nine" suffered physical violence and constant racial abuse as they entered Central High School over the following days. Despite the pressure to leave the school, they were determined to stay, and in doing so struck another blow in the long struggle of the Civil Rights Movement that would continue into the sixties.

Civil Rights Act

Another step to racial equality was the 1957 Civil Rights Act. It came as a result of the Civil Rights Bill in Congress, which ensured that all African Americans could exercise their right to vote, and that any abuses would be monitored by the Justice Department.

President Eisenhower, reeling from the events in Little Rock, publicly supported the legislation. It was, however, eventually much watered down due to the lack of support from Democrats. The Senate leader, future President Lyndon Baines Johnson (a Democrat), knew that his party would never agree on many key points, with the southern right wing contesting the liberal West Coast senators' views. And so they agreed to less stringent measures in the bill.

The subsequent Civil Rights Act reflected the spirit of the bill —to increase the number of registered African-American voters. Although anyone found guilty of obstructing someone's right to register faced scant punishment, since only whites could be jury members in the South. Nevertheless, the act was seen as another step in the right direction, and became historically symbolic as the first civil rights legislation to be passed by the U.S. government in 82 years.

A woman and a child protest school integration in front of the Arkansas capital building.

1958

THE INTERNATIONAL TEENAGER

The world was changing, and fast. Vice President Richard Nixon was shoved, stoned, booed, and spat upon on a "good-will" tour of Peru and Venezuela, while nine people died in anti-U.S. riots in Panama. And over 9,000 scientists from 43 nations worldwide petitioned the United Nations for a nuclear test ban.

Nearly 40,000 people were killed on America's roads that year, compared to 125 in the air, but that didn't stop the rise in the number of automobiles on the roads. As the Japanese companies Toyota and Datsun introduced "small" cars into the United States, stereophonic records appeared for the first time, the first-ever "greatest hits" album was produced (Johnny Mathis's Johnny's Greatest Hits), and the Grammy Awards were launched by the U.S. music industry.

The cult of youth gripped Eastern bloc Poland with the appearance of screen idol Zbigniew Cybulski, dubbed "the Polish James Dean." In San Francisco, newspaper columnist Herb Caen coined the term Beatnik to describe the Beat Generation writers and their followers.

The hula hoop arrived, and it was promptly banned in Japan (where they thought it would incite improprieties, much like Elvis's hips) and likewise in Russia, where it was denounced as an example of "the emptiness of American culture."

"THE ARMY CAN DO ANYTHING IT

When Elvis received his notice from the Memphis Draft Board just before Christmas 1957 informing him that he was to be conscripted for military service, it could have marked the end of his career. Two years out of the spotlight was the last thing you needed in the here-today-gone-tomorrow world of rock 'n' roll. On the other hand, if he found a way out of serving Uncle Sam the inevitable bad press would have put a huge dent in his image.

So manager Colonel Tom Parker decided Elvis should "do the right thing" like a good all-American kid, and made sure that he and the army would play it for all the publicity it was worth. Appealing for time to finish his next movie in the new year, Elvis managed to persuade the board to defer his entry into the army until March 24, 1958, when he was to report to the induction center in Memphis. From there on Parker's publicity machine was in full swing. Over 50 journalists and photographers followed Elvis's progress that day, from his swearing-in with 13 other rookies, to his physical at a nearby hospital, to the base at Fort Chafee where he would receive the most publicized haircut in U.S. Army history.

Throughout Elvis's service, Tom Parker took advantage of whatever photo opportunities the army would allow, and when the rock 'n' roll idol was posted to Germany, he made sure that there was blanket media coverage of the star's departure by troop ship from New York. There was even an EP released of interviews conducted with Elvis just before he left, entitled *Elvis Sails*, which, amazingly, went to number 2 in the *Billboard* chart.

His time in Germany also received massive coverage—Elvis on tank maneuvers, Elvis on weekend leave in Paris, and Elvis buying a BMW sports car were all turned into media events. When it was revealed he'd started dating a new girlfriend, Priscilla Beaulieu, stepdaughter of an Air Force captain, every newspaper and magazine featured the story of his romance. Elvis's relationship with the 14-year-old Priscilla began just a few weeks before his departure from Germany at the end of his two-year Army service in March 1960, so there was even more press interest when they picked up on the story of "the girl he left behind" as he returned to America and civilian life.

The ballyhoo on his homecoming was enormous, with a press conference at which reporters asked about his new love, and whether he felt the absence from the music business had harmed his career—but no one needed to worry. Between the time of his induction in March 1958 and his release from the army two years later, Elvis had a dozen singles in the *Billboard* Top 20, including three number 1s, five entries in the album chart, and another hit movie—*King Creole*—released in July 1958.

Jerry Lee's "Child Bride"

When Jerry Lee Lewis decided to take his 13-year-old bride with him on a tour of the United Kingdom, he didn't imagine the furor it would cause, leading to the cancellation of his tour and blighting his rock 'n' roll career for years to come.

Jerry Lee was first married at the age of 16, and before he was 19 he'd already married a second time—23 days before his divorce from his first wife was final. Then, in December 1957, Lewis (now 22) married for a third time, although he neglected to divorce wife number 2. His bride this time, Myra Gale Brown, was only 13, and his second cousin.

In Jerry Lee's rural South, marrying at 13 and wedding a second cousin wasn't that unusual, so when he landed in London for a U.K. tour in May 1958, and told reporters that the girl with him was his wife (though giving her age as 15), he didn't think too much about it.

The British press—and their counterparts in the United States—soon found out Myra's real age, the fact that the couple were related, and that Jerry Lee hadn't divorced his second wife. The headline writers had a field day, labeling the rock 'n' roller a "cradle robber" and "baby snatcher" and calling for a boycott of his concerts. After only three performances on the 37-date tour, with many dates already canceled, Jerry Lee and Myra left England for New York. There things did not improve; his records were banned by U.S. radio and TV, and his concert fee dropped from $10,000 a night to $250. He tried to apologize, but his career as one of the great originals of rock 'n' roll was severely damaged.

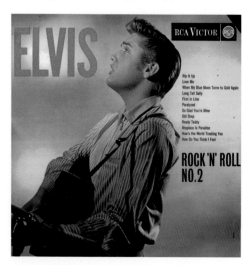

LEFT: Fears that Elvis's time in the army might harm record sales proved unfounded as the fans continued to clamor for every new release.

RIGHT: Every aspect of Elvis's army service was photographed, documented, and used by the army and Colonel Tom Parker for publicity.

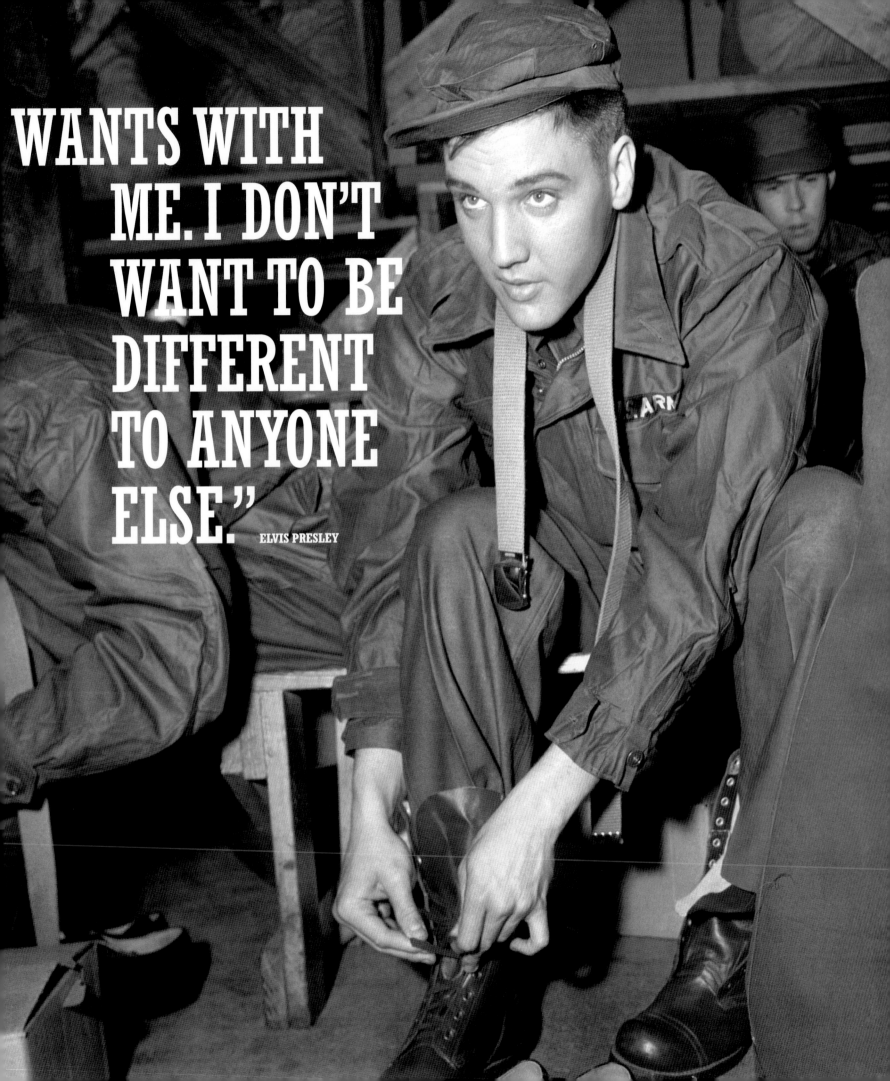

WANTS WITH ME. I DON'T WANT TO BE DIFFERENT TO ANYONE ELSE."

ELVIS PRESLEY

SEX, DRUGS, AND ROCK 'N' ROLL

PHOTOPLAY

MAY 1958

THE WORLD'S TOP FILM MAGAZINE

1'3

INSIDE
Sex and Violence on the screen — where will it end?

KATHY GABRIEL

High School Confidential was one of the first movies to explore the campus dope-ring scare that swept the American media in the late fifties. And, for rock fans, it had the added attraction of a guest appearance by Jerry Lee Lewis, singing on a parked wagon outside the school gates. Elvis Presley's fourth movie, King Creole, was also pitched as a serious drama, based on the Harold Robbins novel A Stone for Danny Fisher. Even so, Elvis managed to get through 11 songs during the course of the action!

The widespread outrage over the way that movies aimed at teenagers portrayed the passion of youth and juvenile delinquency could no longer be ignored by film magazines. Photoplay (left) managed to voice its "concern" while still exploiting the sex angle.

JUVENILE RIOTS ROCK CITIES AROUND THE WORLD

Race riots broke out in London's Notting Hill area at the end of August 1958. Spurred on by Oswald Mosley's neo-fascist Union Movement, groups of white thugs ran riot through the area armed with knives, leather belts, and iron bars, attacking West Indian residents wherever they found them.

The area had been settled by a large number of Caribbean immigrants during the post-war years, and tensions rooted in bad housing and job discrimination came to the surface when the 300-strong "Keep Britain White" mobs went on a rampage. The trouble subsided after five nights of running battles, but the police at the time earned the distrust of the local Caribbean community by playing down the racial aspects of the riots, saying they were caused merely by hooligans on both sides. But the police and other eyewitnesses did agree on the strong presence of "Teddy" boys among the white rioters.

"Teds" had been a teenage subculture in Britain since the early fifties, and had long been associated with juvenile delinquency in the press. With their long, draped jackets, narrow "drainpipe" trousers, and decorative waistcoats based on early twentieth-century Edwardian fashion (hence the name "Ted"), they'd first appeared four or five years before the advent of rock 'n' roll. But, as soon as rock arrived, they adopted it as their music.

Similar to events surrounding motorcycle gangs in America, notorious incidents involving some of the Teddy boys—when reported by a hysterical media—made them all delinquents in the public mind. Most of them, however, along with their Teddy-girl partners, were just part of the teenage revolution that was sweeping the Western world with rock 'n' roll as its theme music. Like their (albeit more affluent) counterparts in the United States, they had money to spare as a social group for the first time, and there were clothing retailers, record companies, and film distributors all too ready to help them spend it.

Rock 'n' roll had come to represent an international culture of youth, evidenced by the teenage "riots" that often accompanied rock movies or appearances by American rock acts in countries as varied as Germany, Australia, Italy, and Japan.

Even behind the "iron curtain" that divided communist Eastern Europe and Russia from the West, rock 'n' roll made its presence known. Bill Haley's "Rock Around the Clock" took the East by storm, prompting the state authorities to do what they had earlier tried unsuccessfully to do with jazz—ban it. Seeing rock as an example of Western decadence that would threaten the moral and political fiber of Soviet youth, the Russian government stamped down hard on the music. The Communists tried to break up local rock bands, clandestine concerts were raided by the police, and Western records were outlawed.

But rock 'n' roll's appeal continued. African-American markets in musical instruments, recordings of Western and domestic rock bands, and "secret" rock concerts flourished, and the authorities were gradually forced to allow homegrown forms of rock to be played and recorded.

"Teddy Boys," named after the Edwardian-style clothes they preferred, were vilified by the press as mindless hooligans bent on violence.

ALL I HAVE TO DO IS DREAM

Country-inspired rock was appearing on the 1958 charts, particularly in hits by Texan singer Ricky Nelson and the Kentucky-born brothers Don and Phil Everly.

Ricky Nelson had six singles enter the Top 20 during 1957, and followed through in 1958 with another five, including his first number 1 "Poor Little Fool" (and the first record to top *Billboard's* new "Hot 100" chart). Although only 18, he was a seasoned performer, having joined the cast of his parents' radio sitcom *The Adventures of Ozzie and Harriet* at the age of nine. The show moved to television in 1952, and by the time he began making records in 1957, his clean-cut good looks had already assured him a substantial fan base.

His records had good credentials, too, many of his rockabilly-flavored songs having been written by Dorsey and Johnny Burnette. Lead guitarists on his discs also included jazz virtuoso Barney Kessel, top session man Joe Maphis, and a regular member of his backing group, the great James Burton.

Nelson continued with best sellers through to the end of the decade, including another chart-topper "Travelin' Man" in 1961, after which he moved more toward straightforward country music, changing his name to Rick Nelson. His pop-rock hits of the late fifties can be seen as the first manifestation of late sixties' country rock.

Brotherly Love Songs

Like Ricky Nelson, the Everly Brothers started their professional career on their parents' radio show while still children. In 1958 they were at their chart-busting peak, with four Top 10 entries including "Problems" at number 2 and two number 1s. "All I Have to Do Is Dream" and "Bird Dog." Their records ranged from the romantic love song typified by "Dream" to the hard-edged "Bye Bye Love," "Wake Up Little Susie"—both hits in 1957—and "Bird Dog." Many of their most successful songs were written by the country songwriting team of Felice and Boudleaux Bryant. They were witty or achingly romantic expressions of teenage angst perfectly crafted with the forceful delivery of the Everlys.

With their first three years' of hits produced for the independent Cadence label—which they would leave after a royalty dispute in 1960—the Everly Brothers' presence on both the country and pop charts gave the country capital of Nashville a new lease on life at the height of the rock 'n' roll boom. It also established Don and Phil as superstars and, ultimately, rock music legends.

Along with other styles that graced the best-seller lists in the late fifties, the country harmony singing of the Everlys would influence a generation of musicians in the sixties, from the Beatles and the Byrds to Gram Parsons, Simon and Garfunkel, and Crosby, Stills, and Nash. And in 1958, the two good-looking rockers were on a par with Elvis in the popularity stakes, their records now fondly remembered anthems of the era.

OPPOSITE: The Everly Brothers started their entertainment careers on their parents' radio show.

ABOVE: Ricky Nelson was a child actor before rock 'n' roll provided a springboard for his adult career.

Life in Hollywood
by Ricky Nelson

I AM just eighteen. For seventeen years and three months I've lived in Hollywood, on the same street, in the same house. Frankly, I never thought much about it until lately.

But just last week I received a letter from a girl in the Midwest. She told me that her biggest dream is to come to California and that she's saving her allowance so she can afford to move her family out West.

She ended by saying, "I envy you being able to live in Hollywood all your life."

This letter started me to thinking about it, really for the first time. And the funny thing is, nothing that happened to me was planned. It just happened.

I was born in Teaneck, New Jersey, but by the time I was nine months old my folks had quit travelling around the country with Pop's band. They bought a house in Hollywood and we moved West permanently.

Hollywood never seemed out of the ordinary to me.

To a lot of people, Hollywood sounds like one big glamorous movie set.

But I've just grown up here, played with the same kids, climbed trees, and gone to school a few blocks from home and none of this seemed very glamorous.

I did have one "exotic" experience though. One day my grandmother set my cot in the backyard and then went into the house. A few minutes later, my brother Dave and some friends came into the yard. They were playing cowboys and Indians.

One look at me just sitting there in the cot gave them an idea. They thought I'd make a perfect papoose. Only one trouble : I was a little pale for a paleface. Dave found a can of paint and a brush in the garage and he and his friends painted me from head to toe.

When I was little, a lot of interesting people used to come to the house.

I remember one nice man, mainly because he had bright red hair and he used to bring me toys.

His name was Red Skelton and, at the time, Mom and Pop were on his radio show. But at the age of three I was impressed by the toys and his hair.

I didn't know he was famous. I guess a lot of well-known people were at our house during the years I was growing up, but honestly I don't remember much about it ; I suppose I was more interested in my roller skates than in sitting in the living room listening to people talk.

I can't even remember when I first discovered that Mom and Pop were "celebrities."

We Got The Job

I was four years old when Mom and Pop left Red Skelton's show. Skelton went into the Army and at that time Pop thought up the idea of doing a family radio show, called "The Adventures of Ozzie and Harriet."

For the first five years, two professional child actors played Dave and me.

In 1949, when they'd outgrown the parts, Pop decided to audition some other kids to replace them. Dave and I seemed like the type to play ourselves, so we got the job !

Even when I started working on radio my childhood routine didn't in any way differ from the kids on my block. We did the show one evening a week, no rehearsal time at all. I continued going to school. The only difference was that one night a week I'd go to a studio, sit down at a table—I was too short to stand up and reach the microphone—and I'd just talk into it.

I never thought too much about what I was doing. I never considered myself an actor ; neither did Dave. We were just being ourselves. It wasn't really hard work ; it was more like fun.

Sometimes Dave and I would fool around with the scripts and occasionally we'd lose our place. I couldn't (Continued on page 50)

DOO-WAH DOO-WAH, DOO-WAH DOO-WAH

Doo-wop was still making its presence known as vocal groups continued to loom large in the pop charts through 1958. This trend started at the beginning of the year when Danny and the Juniors had a seven-week run in the number 1 spot with the anthemic "At the Hop"—which they followed into the Top 20 with "Rock and Roll Is Here to Stay" in March.

Formed at high school in Philadelphia, Danny & the Juniors were typical of white and mixed-race doo-wop outfits whose style was based on the same a cappella renditions of teen ballads and upbeat rock 'n' roll songs as the African-American "bird" groups—like the Penguins, Ravens, and Crows—who had flourished earlier in the fifties.

The first of these singers to make a mark were the Crests, who got together in Brooklyn in 1955 and were spotted singing on the Lexington Avenue subway by a talent scout for Coed Records. They had their first hit, "16 Candles," toward the end of 1958, which made the Top 10 in both the R&B and pop charts. The Crests were actually a mixed-race group, but their leader, Johnny Mastrangelo, typified the Italian sweet voice and good looks of the white doo-woppers.

Far more significant over the long term were Dion & the Belmonts. Named after Belmont Avenue, a major Bronx thoroughfare in New York, they consisted of Carlo Mastrangelo singing baritone, Angelo D'Aleo and Fred Milano first and second tenors, and their lead tenor voice Dion DiMucci. The teenage DiMucci, after making one single, "The Chosen Few," with the Timberlanes, put the Belmonts together in 1958 and signed to Laurie Records. Their debut on the label, "I Wonder Why," was an instant success, a street-jargon chant, as was the teen-angst follow-up "No One Knows," in 1958. Dion's natural phrasing and warm vocal texture marked them as the best—and ultimately most successful—of the white doo-wop groups, a

status confirmed with their biggest smash, the international hit "Teenager In Love" in 1959.

Imperial Status

Also from New York City, Little Anthony & the Imperials were an African-American group formed by Anthony Gourdine in 1957. At age 15, Gourdine had joined a doo-wop group called the Duponts, and when it folded a short time later he then founded his own group with Clarence Collins, Ernest Wright Jr., Glouster "Nat" Rogers, and Tracy Lourd, calling themselves the Chesters. They made one record, performed at Harlem's most prestigious venue, the Apollo, and (on signing with End Records) changed the name of the group to the Imperials. The new name was suggested by DJ Alan Freed, who also dubbed Gourdine "Little Anthony" on account of his size.

With his high-pitched falsetto voice up front, Little Anthony and the group had an immediate Top 5 hit with "Tears on My Pillow" in August 1958, followed by "A Prayer and a Jukebox" in 1959, and "Shimmy, Shimmy, Ko-Ko-Bop" in 1960. Gourdine then left to go solo, but when he rejoined in 1964, they continued with hits in the sixties soul vein right through the decade.

Other doo-wop hits in 1958 included a chart-topping smash for the Philadelphia group the Silhouettes with "Get a Job," its hard-luck-to-teenager theme similar to that of the Coasters's "Yakety Yak," also a number 1 that year. The Elegants, an Italian-American quintet from New York's Staten Island, peaked in July 1958 with "Little Star." And vocal group veterans the Platters, who'd been appearing in the charts since 1955, had two number 1s, "Twilight Time" in April and the evocative "Smoke Gets in Your Eyes" released at the end of the year.

First appearing in October, "To Know Him Is to Love Him," the debut disc for Los Angeles teen trio the Teddy Bears, was a huge international hit, climbing to the top of the

charts by December. The group was formed by 17-year old Phil Spector when he was still at Fairfax High School, with schoolmates Annette Kleinbard and Marshall Leib. The teen ballad was written by Spector, its title taken from the inscription on his father's grave.

The enterprising youngster produced the record himself after raising the $40 dollars needed for studio time; his mother contributed $10, as did Kleinbard, Leib, and Harvey Goldstein, bass singer on the demo who didn't appear on the final record when it was recorded for the Dore label. Spector would go on to mastermind many more hits as the architect of a new wave of rock 'n' roll vocal groups, the sixties successors to the doo-wop sound of the fifties.

Dion DiMucci (center) with Belmonts Fred Milano and Angelo D'Aleo.

STAR WARS PART I

After the Russian's *Sputnik* triumphs a few months earlier, the space race went into orbit—literally—as America launched its first satellite, *Explorer I* (right), on January 31, 1958. It was quickly followed by *Explorer II* and *III*, both launched in March.

In London, 10,000 people marched 52 miles to the atomic weapons establishment at Aldermaston over the Easter weekend, in protest of Britain's first hydrogen bomb tests. The protest marked the launch of the Campaign for Nuclear Disarmament (CND), which developed a very strong following among young people in Britain over the next few years. Some of the marchers, seen at left in London's Hyde Park, chose distinctive headgear to put their point across.

NORTH OF THE BORDER

Canada's first rock 'n' roll star to make it really big was Paul Anka, who as a baby-faced 16-year-old topped the charts around the world in 1957 with the self-penned "Diana." As a result, Anka, who was said to have written the smash for a babysitter five years his senior, was an established superstar by 1958 when he went on to score in the charts with another five hits—a track record that continued into the early sixties, by which time "Diana" had sold over 9 million copies.

Also in 1958, southern rockabilly singer Ronnie Hawkins made a historic move north of the border when he recruited a bunch of aspiring Canadians for his band, the Hawks. Arkansas-born Hawkins already had a band of that name when he was playing around the South through 1956–57, auditioning unsuccessfully for the Sun label in Memphis before cutting a version of "Bo Diddley" for the small label Quality. Then in 1958 he relocated to Toronto, Canada, taking with him fellow Arkansan, the Hawks' drummer Levon Helm. Among the local musical fraternity he soon found guitarist Robbie Robertson and bass player Rick Danko, forming the nucleus of the new Hawks, which would go on to include Canadian multi-instrumentalist Garth Hudson and keyboardist Richard Manuel.

Despite only having limited chart success, "Mary Lou" hit the U.S. Top 30 in 1959, and the Hawks' reputation as a live act with dynamic backing for Hawkins' wild vocals became the stuff of legend. And even more so when, minus their lead singer, they became the Band in the midsixties—famously backing Bob Dylan as well as establishing themselves as pioneers of country rock in their own right.

Teenage singer-songwriter Paul Anka achieved superstar status within a year of his first smash hit "Diana."

NATURAL BORN KILLERS

The most notorious incident of teenage crime in the fifties occurred early in 1958 when a 19-year-old youth and his 14-year-old girlfriend launched a killing spree. They left 10 people dead and sent shock waves throughout America.

At school in Lincoln, Nebraska, Charlie Starkweather had been something of a loner. Most kids avoided him because of a violently mean streak. By his late teens, he had become fascinated with the James Dean "rebel" image, which he cultivated as best he could while holding down a job as a garbage man. He felt angry and isolated, until he started dating Caril Ann Fugate, five years his junior and besotted by his rebel persona. Basking in her attention, Starkweather felt that he could be somebody.

In November 1957, he robbed a gas station of about $100 in cash, then took the attendant out at gunpoint and shot him. The crime hit the headlines, and Starkweather told his girlfriend that he'd committed the robbery but not the murder. She didn't believe him, and the shared knowledge bound them together even closer. Starkweather was on a high—he had money, a pretty girl who adored him, and now he felt he was above the law.

On January 28, 1958, Starkweather visited the home of Fugate and her parents, who were seriously opposed to his relationship with their daughter. During an argument, Starkweather shot and killed his girlfriend's mother and stepfather, then strangled her two-year-old sister. The two lovers hid the bodies at the back of the house, and stayed there for several days, taping a note to the door telling folks to stay away because everyone was down with the flu. Eventually, Fugate's grandmother became suspicious and alerted the police, but by the time they arrived the two had taken off—Starkweather and Fugate were on the run.

First they appeared at the home of a 72-year-old family friend to seek shelter, rewarding the old man by shooting him in the head. Then,

when their car got stuck in mud, they fled on foot, hitching a lift from two teenagers. The teenagers were also shot dead, and the couple stole their car. Driving to the wealthy district of Lincoln, they entered a home where they murdered the lady of the house and her maid, also killing her husband when he returned home in the evening.

By this time a manhunt was underway, and the pair left for Wyoming where they planned to change vehicles. Spotting a Buick parked with the driver asleep inside, they had found their tenth victim. Struggling to start the car (and with its owner's body on the passenger seat), they drew the attention of a passing deputy sheriff. When he stopped, Fugate rushed to him, claiming that Starkweather had kidnapped her.

Her boyfriend fled in the Buick, giving himself up after a 100-mph chase and a shootout with the police. Both Starkweather and Fugate were found guilty of murder, though it was never clear how much Fugate was involved in the actual killings. Charles Starkweather was executed in the electric chair on June 25, 1959, and Caril

Ann Fugate—on account of her age—was sentenced to life, eventually being paroled after 17 years. The case, later forming the basis for the 1994 film *Natural Born Killers*, shocked all of America, and prompted more questions by "moral guardians" about the state of the nation in the rock 'n' roll age.

Dr. King Stabbed

While signing copies of his book about the Montgomery bus boycott, in which he had been a leading figure, Dr. Martin Luther King Jr. was stabbed in a Harlem department store on September 20, 1958. He was autographing the book *The Stride Towards Freedom* when an African-American woman asked if he was Martin Luther King. When he said yes, she pulled a letter opener from her purse and stabbed him in the chest. The near-fatal injury required King to undergo three hours of surgery in a Harlem hospital. The woman, Izola Ware Curry, was mentally deranged and King made a personal plea for her not to be jailed but to be hospitalized instead.

The John Birch Society

In the wake of incidents like the King assault and spectacular homicides on the scale of the Starkweather-Fugate rampage, it was inevitable there would be a moral backlash. It came in the form of an upsurge in conservative attitudes, typified by the formation of the John Birch Society. Virulently right-wing, the society (named after an American intelligence officer who was killed in 1945 by Chinese Communists) even opposed the Civil Rights Movement, claiming it was backed by the American Communist Party.

OPPOSITE: Teenage sweethearts Caril Ann Fugate and Charlie Starkweather embarked on a murderous crime spree that led him to the electric chair and her to prison.

ABOVE: Dr. Martin Luther King Jr. is comforted by his wife and family in the hospital after being stabbed in a Harlem bookstore.

GUITAR MAGIC

The electric guitar was the instrument that came to symbolize rock 'n' roll, and Gibson and Fender were the leading manufacturers. The Fender Stratocaster, in particular, became an icon as the solid-bodied electric guitar.

It was not, however, one of the new breed of rockers who pioneered the development of the electric guitar. Instead, Les Paul, a gentle jazz musician who recorded easy listening music with his wife, Mary Ford, was the great guitar innovator. Paul had played in bands for many years and began experimenting with building electric guitars in the thirties. He developed his ideas and designs to such an extent that the Gibson company signed a deal with him to produce guitars bearing his name—the Gibson Les Paul. His experiments with recording techniques, echo, multitracking, and effects were developed for use in the record, radio, and television industries and he certainly had a huge influence on rock 'n' roll music.

Link Wray's atmospheric "Rumble" was released early in 1958. Pioneering the use of distortion and feedback in rock 'n' roll, it was the first rock guitar instrumental to make the charts. But the king of the guitar instrumental was Duane Eddy, who twanged his way through a string of echo-laden chart hits after his July 1958 debut "Rebel Rouser." Many more rock artists over the coming decades would have cause to thank Les Paul for channeling his talent and ingenuity into the development of the electric guitar.

**Mary Ford and Les Paul at home
experimenting in the recording studio.**

"IT IS NOT ABOUT SEX. IT IS ABOUT LOVE.

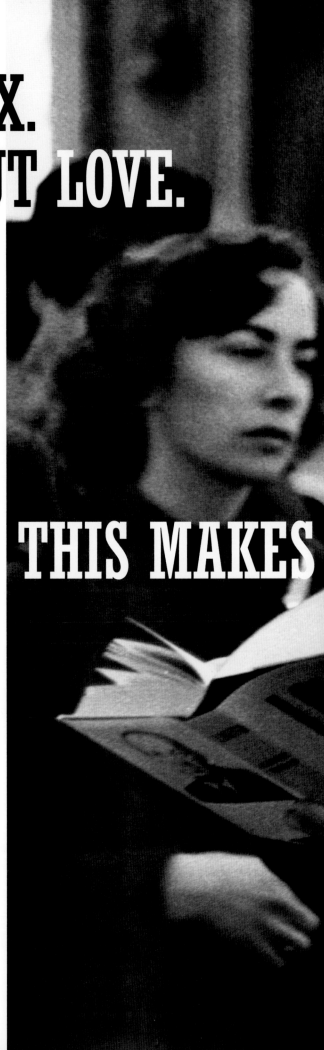

THIS MAKES

First published by the Paris-based Olympia Press in 1955, Vladimir Nabokov's novel *Lolita* finally appeared in the United States on August 18, 1958. The novel was applauded for its innovative style, but received most attention because of its taboo-breaking subject matter.

The first-person narration by a middle-aged man, Humbert Humbert, who becomes sexually attracted to a young pubescent girl, made it difficult for Nabokov to find a publisher, hence his choice of the French "erotica" specialists Olympia. But some favorable critical reviews, particularly one by the English author Graham Greene, led to its U.S. publication by G. P. Putnam's Sons.

The book was successfully adapted for the cinema by Stanley Kubrick in 1962, with Nabokov involved in the screenwriting, Humbert being played by James Mason, and the girl by Sue Lyon. It was made for the screen again in 1997 by director Adrian Lyne. As far as Nabokov was concerned, the downside to the book's eventual acceptance was the adoption of the name "Lolita" in everyday slang to mean a sexually attractive (or sexually precocious) young girl.

In 1958 it represented the breaking down of another barrier in terms of subjects considered "fit" for publication, and another step toward the freedom of the individual to choose what he or she should read rather than choices dictated by official or semiofficial moral guardians who purported to know better.

In the same year another groundbreaking novel that dealt with modern morality was published. "I would not have changed two words in *Breakfast at Tiffany's*, which will become a small classic," wrote Norman Mailer on the publication of Truman Capote's short novel. Although it received mixed reviews when it first appeared, the story of good-time girl Holly Golightly struck a chord with the mood of personal liberation at the time. The character was a seemingly freewheeling spirit who nevertheless has her own personal demons that she ultimately can't ignore.

Although Capote had a deal with Random House to publish the book in the fall of 1958, he also signed up with the magazine *Harper's Bazaar* to publish in the summer before the book came out. The Hearst Corporation, however, which owned *Harper's*, wanted Capote to cut the four-letter words and avoid mention of how Holly made her living, which the author refused to do. A Hearst executive went ahead and made the cuts.

Three years later, the book became a celebrated movie starring Audrey Hepburn, although Capote had wanted Marilyn Monroe to play the part. But he was even more upset by the film's changed ending, which had Golightly staying in New York with the narrator (played by George Peppard) rather than continually searching for the place where she feels she belongs, as in the novel.

A highly influential best seller of a different kind came in *The Affluent Society*, John Kenneth Galbraith's critique of American economics, in which he called for greater government spending on education and health care, and the expansion of the "new class" of citizens able to pursue work they find inherently enjoyable— both notions anathema to the conservative thinking of the time.

Customers in a London bookshop browse through copies of Nabokov's *Lolita* on the day of its release.

IT UNIQUE IN MY EXPERIENCE
OF CONTEMPORARY NOVELS."

LIONEL TRILLING, LITERARY CRITIC

SOME LIKE IT HOT

1959

As the fifties came to a close, the U.S. space agency, NASA, announced the names of seven astronauts it planned to rocket into orbit, while the U.S. Air Force appointed its first African-American major general.

Soul-music pioneer Ray Charles had a huge hit with "What'd I Say," despite the overtly sexual connotations of his delivery, which got the record banned on radio stations across America. Bobby Darin's chart-topping hit "Mack the Knife" was also banned from WCBS Radio in New York, in light of a spate of teenage stabbings in the city.

In the movies, Italy gave us a taste of La Dolce Vita (The Sweet Life), starring the statuesque Swedish film diva Anita Ekberg, while Marilyn Monroe famously sashayed down a railroad platform in Some Like It Hot. And a new blond bombshell called Barbie made her debut at the New York Toy Fair.

All across the United States, college kids were seeing how many could cram themselves into telephone booths. Elsewhere, references to glue-sniffing among young people first appeared in print and the media-hyped stereotype of the goatee-bearded, bongo-playing beatnik became an international craze in cartoons, B movies, and magazine articles.

"JAZZ IS STRICTLY FOR STAY-AT-HOMES."

BUDDY HOLLY

The biggest tragedy yet to hit rock 'n' roll occurred on February 3, 1959, when Buddy Holly (inset) was killed in a fatal plane crash that also claimed the lives of chart stars Richie Valens and the Big Bopper along with pilot Roger Peterson.

The three performers had been playing a concert in Clear Lake, Iowa, and were on their way to their next date in Moorefield, Minnesota, when bad weather brought the aircraft down just 8 miles (13 km) from where they'd taken off in Mason City, the nearest airport to Clear Lake.

THE HIT FACTORY

When singer and composer Neil Sedaka had his first big hit in 1959 with "Oh! Carol," it signaled the start of an avalanche of successes to come out of New York's Brill Building, the celebrated rock 'n' roll "song factory" of the late fifties and early sixties.

The main thrust of the music from the Brill Building, located at 1619 Broadway, just north of Times Square, was provided by Aldon Music, a music publisher situated across the street from the Brill. The company was formed by Al Nevins and Don Kirshner in 1958. Nevins was a guitarist with a group called the Three Suns, and Kirshner was already part of the songwriting and publishing world. Their idea was to bridge the gap between the new culture of rock 'n' roll, with its huge pool of local talent and already proven market potential, and the songwriting and publishing traditions of Tin Pan Alley. This was before the days when rock artists wrote strong material of their own, so the kids who were pouring into recording studios off the

streets of New York were, more often than not, making do either with covers of old standards or with mediocre self-penned songs.

Nevins and Kirshner brought together some of the city's brightest new songwriters, including three teams that initiated most of Aldon's hits—Gerry Goffin and Carole King, Barry Mann and Cynthia Weill, and Neil Sedaka and Howard Greenfield. Other teams also emerged as part of the Brill Building sound. They were actually located on the premises, though not part of the Aldon empire, and included Jeff Barry and Ellie Greenwich, Doc Pomus and Mort Shuman, Burt Bacharach and Hal David, and Gerry Leiber and Mike Stoller.

As well as penning hits for stars such as LaVern Baker and Connie Francis, many of the Sedaka-Greenfield numbers were sung by Sedaka himself, such as "Calendar Girl," "Breaking up Is Hard to Do" (a U.S. chart-topper in 1962), and the aforementioned "Oh! Carol," which was written for Carole King.

With Gerry Goffin, King was responsible for some classic teen ballads, including the Drifters' "Up on the Roof," "It Might as Well Rain Until September" (which she recorded herself), and "Will You Love Me Tomorrow," a 1961 chart-topper for the Shirelles. The team also famously put their babysitter, Little Eva, on the pop-music map with the 1962 smash "The Locomotion."

The husband-and-wife team of Barry Mann and Cynthia Weill had their first hit with the Diamonds' "She Say (Oom Dooby Doom)" in 1959 but they also produced hits for, among others, the Crystals and Jay & the Americans.

Of the non-Aldon writers based at the Brill, Jeff Barry and Ellie Greenwich were among the most prolific, with hits for the Phil Spector stable that included the Crystals' "Da Doo Ron Ron" and "Then He Kissed Me," as well as the Ronettes with "Be My Baby" and "Baby I Love You." Veteran songsmiths Doc Pomus and Mort Shuman's first Brill hit was 1959's "Teenager in Love" for Dion & the Belmonts. Meanwhile, Burt Bacharach and Hal David, in their celebrated association with Dionne Warwick on numbers like "Anyone Who Had a Heart" and "Walk On By," helped define pop songwriting into the midsixties.

ABOVE: Burt Bacharach shares a joke with Hal David.

RIGHT: Neil Sedaka's 1959 hit "Oh! Carol" was written with Carole King in mind.

MAD ABOUT THE BOYS

A profusion of magazines exploded onto the newsstands as the new rock 'n' roll idols started to achieve superstar status. Naturally, most were aimed at teenage girls, with plenty of photographs of their idols scattered throughout the pages.

Elvis Presley, of course, was rarely far from the front page of any publication aimed at the youth market, even though he was thousands of miles away in Germany. His house in Germany generally had a cluster of fans gathered outside but when he was on the military base, there were no fans. The media was rigidly controlled, and he could at least escape from the spotlight for a while. Others, like Frankie Valli, began to feel the pressure of their newfound celebrity and revealed their sensitive nature in interviews. Now not only were the fans expected to adore their idols, buy the records and the magazines, and go crazy at the concerts, they were obliged to feel sorry for them, too!

PHOTOPLAY
THE WORLD'S TOP FILM MAGAZINE
NOVEMBER 1959
1'3
ELVIS PRESLEY

Sure, my name's in lights and people make a fuss over me, but sometimes .. even in the middle of a crowd . . .

I feel
sort (
shy
and
alon

The giddy
name across
York does no
It's my fa
tened of g
meeting pe
When I w
I hid from
of my own
I thoug
change (
same.
friends.
with no
I do
what
man.

52

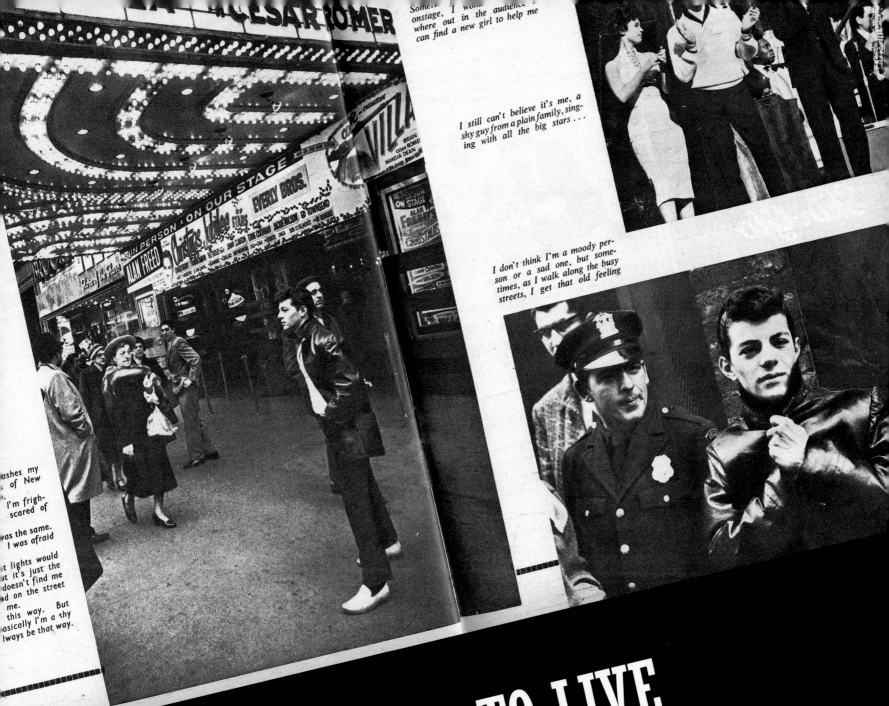

I still can't believe it's me, a shy guy from a plain family, singing with all the big stars . . .

Some... onstage, I wo... where out in the audience... can find a new girl to help me

I don't think I'm a moody person or a sad one, but sometimes, as I walk along the busy streets, I get that old feeling

...ashes my ...of New

...I'm frigh-...scared of

...was the same. ...I was afraid

...lights would ...t it's just the ...doesn't find me ...d on the street ...me. ...this way. But ...asically I'm a shy ...ways be that way.

"IT'S VERY HARD TO LIVE UP TO AN IMAGE." ELVIS PRESLEY

THE NEW R&B

Entering the best-sellers list on January 5, one of the earliest chart toppers of 1959 was "Stagger Lee" by Lloyd Price, a no-holds-barred rocker based on the traditional folk song "Stagolee." It represented a new wave in R&B that was crossing over into pop territory and it heralded big changes to come.

Price, who'd hit early in the decade with his self-penned debut disc "Lawdy Miss Clawdy," made further inroads into the Top 10 in 1959 with the raucously pop "Personality" and "I'm Gonna Get Married," both topping the R&B charts. His musical background was solidly based in New Orleans, a city that also produced some of the other new cutting-edge names in rhythm and blues.

Among them was Frankie Ford, whose "Sea Cruise," which hit the charts in March 1959, became a firm favorite with R&B bands for decades to come, even though its isolated success made Ford a one-hit wonder. Backing Ford's vocals on the record were Huey "Piano" Smith & the Clowns, who'd made the pop charts the previous year with the million-selling "Don't You Just Know It," but they are better remembered for 1957's "Rocking Pneumonia and the Boogie Woogie Flu."

Jimmy Clanton also hailed from the Crescent City and surrounded himself with the best New Orleans session players, including Huey Smith and sax man Lee Allen. He'd had a Top 5 hit in 1958 with "Just a Dream," and an appearance in a rock 'n' roll movie produced by Alan Freed, *Go, Johnny, Go!* set the seal on his mainstream success in 1959, when a spin-off single "Go, Jimmy, Go" hit the number 5 spot.

OPPOSITE: The Flamingos let it rip in the movie *Go, Johnny, Go!*

BELOW: Jackie Wilson drifted seamlessly from R&B into the pop charts.

Another R&B number made it to the pop charts in April 1959, when "Kansas City" topped the list for Wilbert Harrison, becoming a popular rock 'n' roll standard in the process. Harrison, also a product of the New Orleans scene, would make the best-seller list again over a decade later with the 1970's "Let's Work Together," covered the same year by the blues band Canned Heat.

Although he was from the Deep South, Barrett Strong made his mark in the northern city of Detroit. After he left the R&B vocal group the Diablos to go solo, he was one of the first artists to be signed by Motown founder Berry Gordy in 1959. Along with his sisters, Gwen and Anna, Gordy had formed the Anna label. Distributed by Chicago's Chess Records, they had a hit with Strong's recording of "Money (That's What I Want)," at the end of 1959. The hit—just missing the pop Top 20 but reaching number 2 on the R&B charts— provided vital capital for Gordy to expand his operation, creating the Tamla, then Tamla-Motown, labels. The song went on to be a rock standard after it was covered by the Beatles in 1963.

It was Barrett Strong's only hit as a vocalist, but as a composer, he was a pivotal figure in Motown's formative years and in the midsixties he became a Motown staff lyricist, teaming with the producer Norman Whitfield. Together they wrote some of the greatest songs ever recorded by Motown artists, including "Papa Was a Rollin' Stone" by the Temptations, "War" by Edwin Starr, and the all-time classic "I Heard It Through the Grapevine," a hit for both Gladys Knight & the Pips and Marvin Gaye.

Singing with Soul

One of the greatest R&B singers of the period to cross over into the world of pop with ease was Detroit-born Jackie Wilson, whose early career was also entwined with Berry Gordy.

After replacing Clyde McPhatter in the seminal R&B vocal group Billy Ward & the Dominoes in 1953, Wilson went solo in 1957 with the release of "Reet Petite," a raunchy slice of big band backed R&B written by the then unknown Gordy.

Wilson had his first Top 30 entry in 1958 with "To Be Loved," followed at the end of the year by his first big success "Lonely Teardrops," which climbed to the number 7 spot on the pop charts by early 1959. The song, which was also written by Berry Gordy, became Jackie

Wilson's signature tune, and his performance of it on Ed Sullivan's TV Show is considered a classic in the annals of rock 'n' roll television.

The hits continued through 1959 and the early years of the sixties, and Jackie Wilson, with his amazing vocal range and dynamic delivery, became the first of a new breed of African-American pop idols—a seminal inspiration for the soul singers who followed. Jackie Wilson suffered a heart attack while performing onstage; and after eight years in a coma died in 1984.

"THE LAW CANNOT MAKE A MAN LOVE ME, BUT IT CAN KEEP HIM FROM LYNCHING ME."

DR. MARTIN LUTHER KING JR.

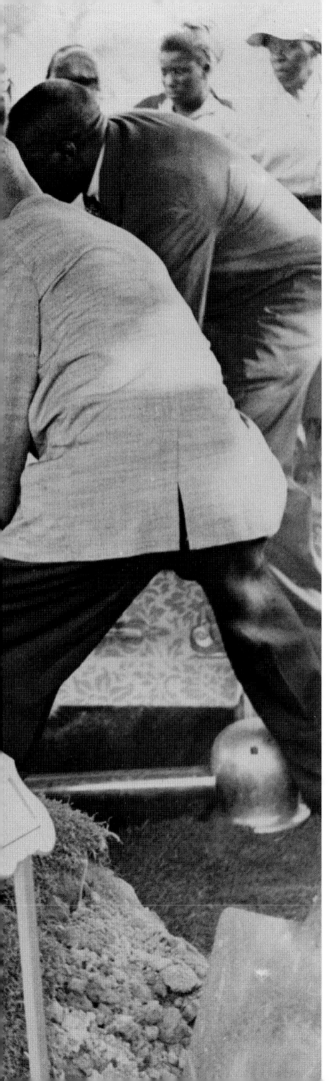

THE HATE THAT HATE PRODUCED

As the American Civil Rights Movement gained momentum by the day, issues of racial discrimination continued to dominate the American domestic scene, with "Jim Crow" bigotry still showing its ugly face in the southern states. Sometimes it seemed as if progress had not been made at all, such as on April 25, when Mack Charles Parker, an African American accused of raping a white woman, was taken from the jail where he was being detained in Poplarville, Mississippi, and lynched by a mob.

After Virginia's school-closing law (a device to avoid integration) was ruled unconstitutional in January 1959, the state general assembly repealed the compulsory school-attendance law and made the operation of public schools a local option for the state's counties and cities. As a result, several schools that had been closed reopened because citizens preferred integrated schools to none at all, but that was not the case in Prince Edward County. Ordered to integrate its schools, the county instead closed its entire public-school system.

The experience of African Americans in the face of prejudice was highlighted by a series of accounts in *Sepia* magazine from the pen of a white writer, John Howard Griffin, who underwent medical treatments in order to darken his skin. Passing himself as black in the South gave him some small idea of the everyday experiences of African Americans, from casual insults to institutionalized (though increasingly outlawed) racism. His essays in the series were later collected together in the best-selling book *Black Like Me*, published in 1961.

When Lorraine Hansberry's *A Raisin in the Sun* appeared on Broadway on March 11, 1959,

the 29-year-old writer became the youngest American playwright, the fifth woman, and the only African American to date to win the New York Drama Critics Circle Award for Best Play of the Year. Telling the story of a family's living and struggling on Chicago's South Side in the fifties, the play was a landmark work in its authentic depiction of African-American life. Acclaimed by the *Washington Post* as "one of a handful of great American plays," the production made it impossible for the American stage to ignore African-American creativity and subject matter from then on. In 1961, a film version won a special award at the Cannes Film Festival, and the screenplay—written by Hansberry— was nominated for a Writer's Guild Award. Hansberry died of cancer in 1965 at the age of 35, after finishing *To Be Young, Gifted, and Black*, an autobiographical portrait that was posthumously produced in 1968 and won the record for longest run of an off-Broadway drama.

July 1959 saw the airing of a television documentary called *The Hate That Hate Produced*, an account of the African-American Muslim group the Nation of Islam, which brought to the general public's attention for the first time the fiery passion of a young man who called himself Malcolm X. It was the first of many public appearances of the man that racist white America would come to hate. A former drug dealer and burglar, he discovered the Muslim faith and became a member of the Nation of Islam on release from prison in 1952. In 1953 the FBI opened its first file on him supposedly because someone named Malcolm X was a Communist. He wasn't.

Mack Charles Parker's flag-draped coffin is lowered into his grave in Lumberton, Mississippi, in May 1959.

"IN LOVE, WOMEN ARE PROFESSIONALS. MEN ARE AMATEURS."

FRANCOIS TRUFFAUT

When François Truffaut's movie *400 Blows* burst onto cinema screens in 1959 (Truffaut is at right, at the Cannes Film Festival with his star Jean-Pierre Léaud), followed by Jean-Luc Godard's *Breathless*, released in 1960, the films caused a sensation worldwide. They were part of the French "New Wave" (*la Nouvelle Vague*), a radical group of directors who rejected cinematic convention and produced young, dynamic works infused with extreme editing, a naturalistic visual style, and concern for social and political issues of the day.

Regarding directors as the "authors" of their movies, they also made a case for Hollywood names such as Alfred Hitchcock and John Ford to be judged more seriously than they were at the time.

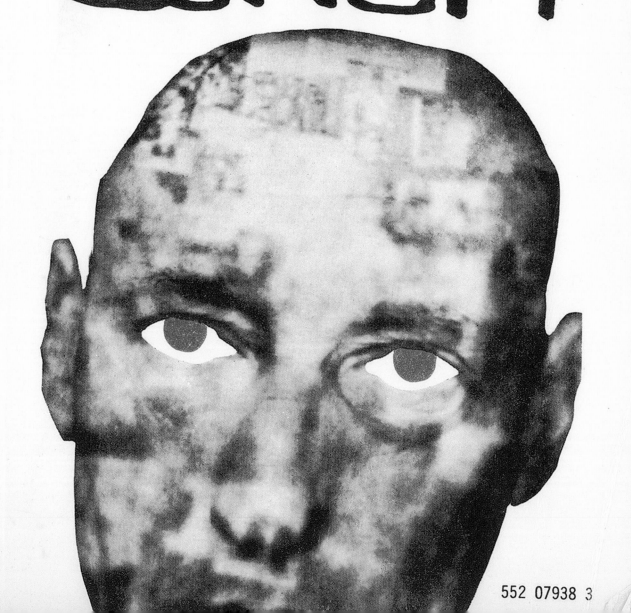

WILLIAM BURROUGHS
THE NAKED LUNCH

552 07938 3

NAKED LUNCH AND MAGIC CHRISTIANS

Literary taboos were still being challenged as the sixties approached, especially in William Burroughs's third novel, *Naked Lunch* (also called *The Naked Lunch* in some editions). Now considered to be the Beat generation author's seminal work, when it first appeared in 1959 it was controversial both in its extreme language and its shocking themes.

Touching graphically on highly sensitive subjects, including gay sex, sadomasochism, and pedophilia, the book broke new ground with its scattershot use of language (much of it still considered obscene in the late fifties) and heralded Burroughs's "cut-up" technique of writing, in which he would cut up a body of text, rearranging it so that a "new" piece emerged.

The book found an immediate publisher in France, and later in the year, the first English-language edition was published by Grove Press in New York. There were immediate legal challenges to its sale, and the book was actually banned by Boston courts in 1962 on grounds of obscenity. The decision was subsequently reversed in a historic ruling by the Massachusetts Supreme Court in 1966, the last major case of literary censorship to be fought in an American courtroom.

The Magic Christian

A satire on capitalism and the greed it seemingly encourages, Terry Southern's comic novel *The Magic Christian* was a sensation when published in 1959. The narrative consisted of a series of episodes concerning an eccentric multimillionaire given to practical jokes, who doesn't care how much money his stunts cost him as long he gets a laugh out of it. Although much of its comedy would seem labored and tame by today's standards, at the time it was seen as a breakthrough in humorous writing.

A film made 10 years later based on the book was even more heavy-handed in its "wacky" approach, despite a formidable cast that included Peter Sellers, Ringo Starr, Richard Attenborough, Yul Brynner, and Raquel Welch.

Absolute Beginners

Set in London in 1958, *Absolute Beginners*, by Colin MacInnes, was regarded by many as a milestone British novel when it appeared in 1959 because it dealt with a subject hitherto ignored—the modern teenager.

Through the eyes of an 18-year-old freelance photographer, it describes a London of jazz clubs, casual sex, fashion wannabes, and racial tension, a backdrop to an emerging youth culture that few writers at the time had identified in this way. With its keen feel for the atmosphere of the times, it captured the contrast between the gray postwar society of their elders and the neon-lit aspirations of the young. It was published along with a wave of British "kitchen sink" novels that included *Saturday Night and Sunday Morning*, by Alan Sillitoe, and Keith Waterhouse's *Billy Liar*, all signaling the fast-approaching demise of the old, established order in society.

OPPOSITE: William Burroughs's novel *The Naked Lunch* became the focus of a landmark court case in the United States when the decision to ban it was overturned.

LEFT: *Absolute Beginners* and *Billy Liar* were part of a new wave of writing from British novelists.

"OURS ARE BETTER THAN YOURS."

NIKITA KHRUSHCHEV, ON RUSSIAN ROCKETS

Two new states became part of the United States in 1959, and two more stars were added to the national flag.

Alaska was the first to join, after years of campaigning on the part of many Alaskans. The vast territory, which is larger than Texas, California, and Montana combined, was purchased by the United States from Russia in 1867 for just over $7 million. With President Eisenhower's signing of the Alaska Statehood Act on July 7, 1958, Alaska formally became a state of the union on January 3, 1959. The new American flag, for just a matter of months, featured seven rows of seven stars each.

In August, Hawaii's statehood was finally granted. The islands had enjoyed "territory" status since 1900, which allowed them a degree of self-governance, but most Hawaiians wanted true statehood. Resistance to the idea came mostly from the plantation owners, who imported cheap foreign labor on a scale prohibited in many other states of the union.

After continuous agitation from workers' groups in Hawaii (many of them descendants of the original immigrant laborers), both houses of the U.S. Congress passed the Admission Act in March 1959, and the president signed it into law. On June 27, a referendum was held asking the residents of Hawaii to vote on accepting the statehood bill. The vote was 17 to 1 in favor of acceptance, and on August 21, Hawaii was proclaimed the 50th state of the union. The flag was configured once again, with the now-familiar alternating rows of six and five stars across.

The Kitchen Debate

While on an official visit to Moscow in July 1959, Vice President Richard Nixon was engaged in a lively and much-publicized exchange of angry words with the Soviet leader Nikita Khrushchev, which became instantly known as the "kitchen debate." The confrontation took place at a model kitchen exhibit at the U.S. Trade and Cultural Fair held in Moscow's Sokolniki Park. The two men were touring the exhibition ahead of its opening that evening, July 24, when they stopped in front of an American mock-up displaying the latest gadgets such as washing machines, toasters, and juicers.

"I want to show you this kitchen. It is like those of our houses in California," Nixon began, pointing to a dishwasher. "We have such things," came the Soviet reply, continuing, "You Americans expect that the Soviet people will be amazed. It is not so. We have all these things in our new flats."

From there on, the "debate" developed into a verbal sparring match that soon escalated from talk of household gadgets to nuclear missiles. Reporters, government officials, and workmen putting the finishing touches to the stands looked on amazed and then began to applaud their respective leaders.

Pointing out that Russia had rockets that would answer any threat, Khrushchev declared, "Ours are better than yours." Finally, Nixon apologized for being a poor host, and the two men agreed to thank the exhibit hostess for letting them argue in her kitchen.

Nixon and Khrushchev swap Cold War words in the kitchen exhibit at the U.S. Trade and Cultural Fair in Moscow.

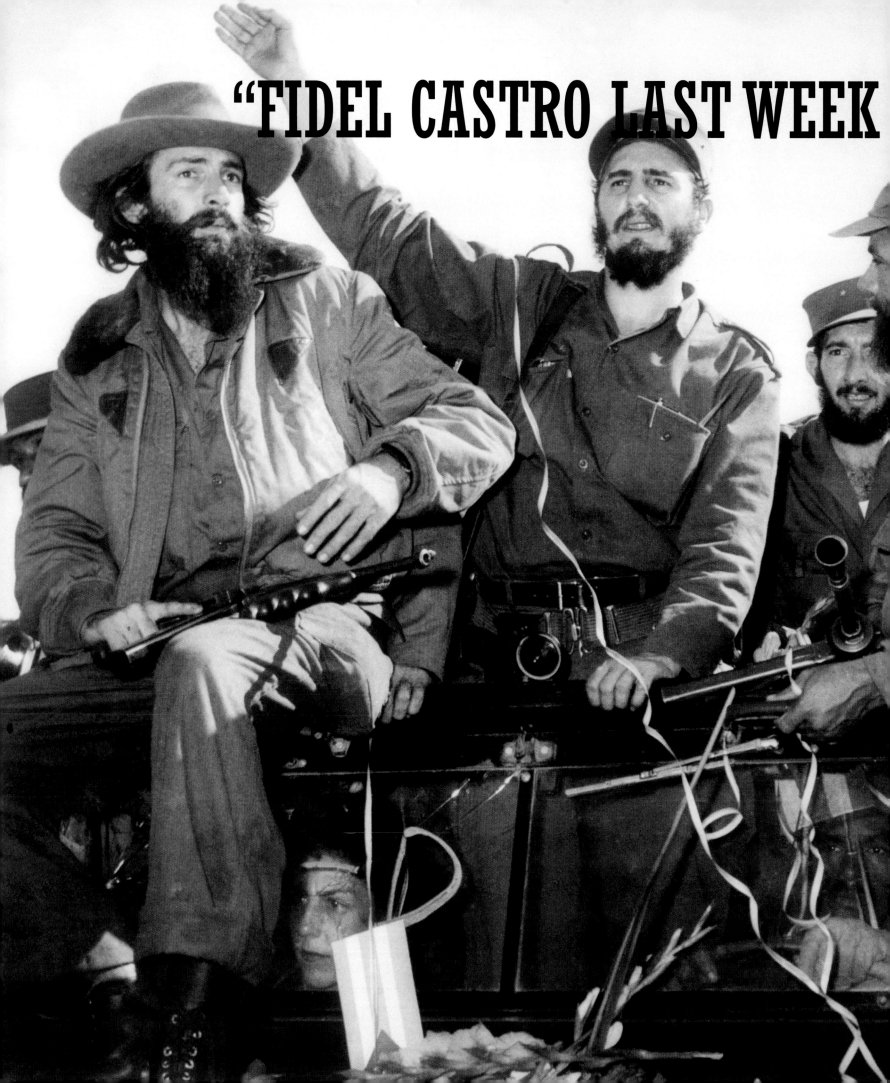

"FIDEL CASTRO LAST WEEK

MARCHED IN TUMULTUOUS TRIUMPH THROUGH THE TOWNS AND VILLAGES OF POST-BATISTA CUBA. THEY SCREAMED 'VIVA!,' AND FLUNG FLOWERS WHEN CASTRO APPEARED."

LIFE MAGAZINE, JANUARY 19, 1959

VIVA LA REVOLUCIÓN!

When Fidel Castro, Che Guevara, and the core of their ragtag band of revolutionary fighters led a victory parade through the Cuban capital, Havana, on January 8, 1959, it captured the imagination of the world. Not only had the tiny guerrilla army overthrown the hated regime of the right-wing dictator Fulgencio Batista in the face of thousands of U.S.-equipped troops, but these rebels looked cool.

After two years fighting in the jungle, their hair was long and their beards looked unkempt. On cinema and television newsreels across the world, the cigar-smoking revolutionaries appeared decidedly "Beat" as their triumphant cavalcade by jeep wound its way through the adoring crowds.

And their victory was genuinely welcomed by the vast majority of the downtrodden populace. At the time of the revolution, the largely rural population of Cuba had an average annual income per person of $91.25, an eighth of that of the poorest state in the United States, Mississippi. Only 11 percent of Cubans drank milk, 4 percent ate meat, and 3 percent had access to running water. Less than 10 percent had electricity, and 43 percent were illiterate, while Batista ruled with an iron fist an economy dependent on the vast estates of U.S. fruit growers and the mafia-driven gamblers' paradise of Havana.

Granma Sets Sail

The revolution was known as the July 26 Movement, named after a failed assault by poorly armed guerrillas on the Batista army's Moncada Barracks on that date in 1953.

The revolution began in November 1956, when Castro and 81 comrades set sail from Mexico in the tiny yacht Granma. Castro and his brother Raúl had been jailed after the Moncada incident, and then exiled to Mexico when Batista, under pressure from civil leaders, freed political prisoners.

While in Mexico, the Castro brothers recruited more exiled Cubans to launch a revolution to overthrow Batista, during which they met the Argentine doctor Ernesto "Che" Guevara, who joined their forces. They left Mexico on November 25, 1956, intending to make their landing in eastern Cuba coincide with planned uprisings in the cities and a general strike, when they would launch an armed offensive to topple the Batista regime.

Things didn't go as planned, however; the would-be insurgents were immediately attacked as they landed by hundreds of government troops and warplanes. As they regrouped, they were betrayed by a guide and forced into the jungle, their numbers decimated. Eventually, just 12 survived to launch a long-fought guerrilla war in the mountains of the Sierra Maestra, from where, in August 1958, Castro ordered Guevara and his fellow comandante Camilo Cienfuegos to lead two columns westward toward Havana.

Batista Flees

Eventually, as the cities of Santa Clara and Santiago de Cuba fell to the rebels, Batista fled the country in the small hours of New Year's Day 1959, leaving a military junta in command. As Cienfuegos and Guevara continued to lead their guerrilla columns into Havana, workers and peasants all over Cuba responded to Castro's call for a general strike—the revolution had triumphed.

The immediate reforms enacted by the revolutionary government were spectacular, earning them popular support not just in Latin America but the world over. In January, it was also announced that 50 to 60 percent of casino profits would be directed to welfare programs, and the first of a series of land reforms was enacted by May. Large estates were expropriated and turned into state farms, and the massive U.S.-owned United Fruit Company was dispossessed without compensation. Land was turned over to small farmers, and sugarcane farms were made into cooperatives.

The Havana Hilton Hotel was famously turned into a hospital—and the celebrated Coppelia ice cream park, where previously only the white middle classes could sample its 200-plus flavors, was thrown open to ordinary Cubans of all races. And, as many well-off Cubans (and Americans) fled to Miami with what they could carry, they left behind hundreds of fifties-vintage American cars that are still seen on the streets of Havana today.

The strategic fallout of the Cuban Revolution was traumatic as far as America was concerned. As the United States tightened an economic embargo on the new Socialist regime, Castro's reliance on the Soviet Union for trade and aid became inevitable. As the Cubans would soon realize, there were strings attached to the Russian benevolence. Suddenly, Uncle Sam had a new recruit to the Communist bloc in his own backyard. The Cold War was about to enter a new, dangerous phase, which would bring the world to the brink of nuclear Armageddon less than four years later.

Driving commandeered cars, Cuban rebels arrive in the capital, parading victoriously up Havana's 23rd Street.

1960

With a new decade, 1960 promised changes, one of the most important being the introduction of the first oral contraceptive. In May the U.S. Food and Drug Administration approved "the pill"—Enovid—as safe for birth-control use.

The first wave of "war babies," children born in the early forties, were reaching college age as economies in the West continued to boom; Pepsi-Cola adopted the slogan "For those who think young." In the United States, there was expansion in civic building of art galleries and museums, while bidding levels in art auctions rose steadily—always a sign of prosperity. And 90 percent of American homes now had television.

The first two-way telephone conversation by satellite took place. And, in California, smog-control devices were made compulsory on cars—the first such law in the country.

Among the intelligentsia, the writer and social commentator Gore Vidal published his satirical fantasy Visit to a Small Planet, and sociologist C. Wright Mills introduced the term "the New Left" to describe contemporary radical thought.

At the other end of the cultural spectrum, The Flintstones premiered as the first animated show on U.S. prime time television, Brian Hyland topped the Billboard pop charts with the memorably titled "Itsy Bitsy Teenie Weenie Yellow Polka Dot Bikini," and Chubby Checker first did the twist.

ELVIS IS BACK!

Although his records had been released regularly in his absence, when Elvis Presley arrived back in the United States on March 3, 1960, Colonel Tom Parker made sure the whole world knew about it. A press conference was arranged at Fort Dix when he arrived from Germany and another at his home, Graceland.

He was then off to a recording studio in Nashville to lay down a new single for RCA Records, which was frantic for new material. Joined by his old partners, Scotty Moore and D. J. Fontana, plus the Jordanaires and various session musicians, he cut "Stuck on You" with "Fame and Fortune" for the flip side. The labels were printed before the session, RCA pressing 1.4 million advance orders and billing them as "Elvis's First New Recording for His 50,000,000 Fans All Over the World." The publicity for the disc hinted at a far less threatening Elvis than before, calling it "a clever, catchy rhythm piece with exactly the kind of mild rock beat that today's kids like."

They were right about the kids. RCA's first stereo single shot to number 1 on the day it was released.

The new, mainstream-friendly Elvis next appeared on *The Frank Sinatra-Timex Show*, recorded on March 26, an ABC-TV special billed as "Frank Sinatra's Welcome Home Party for Elvis Presley." Elvis received a then-record $125,000 for a TV-guest spot and appeared in a formal black suit. However, the biggest irony was that, only two years before, the host had castigated rock 'n' roll as being "sung, played, and written for the most part by cretinous goons." Broadcast in May, the show captured nearly 70 percent of the total audience share. Elvis was back, and all of America knew it.

Elvis at the Movies

At the April recording session in Nashville, Elvis also recorded two numbers that would be another indication of the musical direction his career was taking. "It's Now or Never" was a

kitsch adaptation of a Neapolitan-style Italian ballad "*O Sole Mio*" projecting Elvis into Mom and Dad's (or even Grandma's) territory. The instinct behind the choice seems to have been Tom Parker's as much as Elvis's, and it was an actual request by Parker that nominated "Are You Lonesome Tonight," another song heavy on the dramatics—including the famous "all the world's a stage" soliloquy in the middle—as a potential single release. Both songs topped the charts when they were released in July and November.

Another, some would say blatant, exercise in post-army marketing came with the movie *GI Blues*, set in a U.S. Army unit based in Germany. The songs in the film were lightweight stuff; in fact, one scene in which Elvis sings "Doin' the Best I Can" in a club is only notable because someone is playing "Blue Suede Shoes" on the jukebox in the background.

Nevertheless, the film became one of the top 15 box office hits of 1960 and the album topped the long-playing charts. Less typical (unfortunately) of the way Elvis's movie career would develop was the film *Flaming Star*, in which he had a "serious" nonsinging role as a Native American. It was a part originally planned for Marlon Brando and reflected Elvis's personal ambition for dramatic acting roles. Instead, the frothy musical outings that dominated his movie career throughout the sixties would see Elvis Presley become less and less relevant to the rock 'n' roll he helped create.

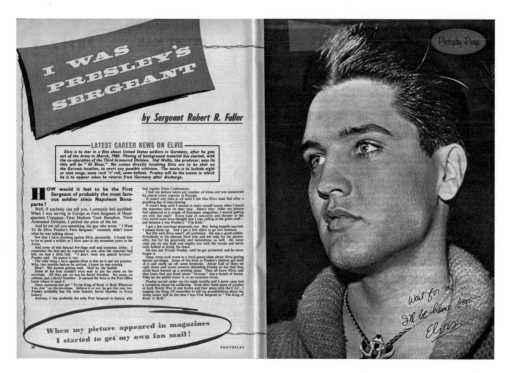

LEFT: Some of Elvis's army buddies were quick to exploit their acquaintance.

RIGHT: An enthusiastic journalist grabs a photo opportunity at Elvis's homecoming press conference at Fort Dix.

BUT BOBBY ROCKS!

While Elvis had been in the army, basic rock 'n' roll was looking like a thing of the past. Buddy Holly was dead, and Jerry Lee Lewis's career was in shambles after the 1958 child bride scandal. At the beginning of 1960, Chuck Berry was awaiting trial, accused of "transporting a woman across state lines for immoral purposes" after employing a 14-year-old Arizona girl as a hatcheck attendant in his St. Louis nightclub. He would eventually be jailed for three years and paroled in 1963.

Meanwhile, what Jerry Lee Lewis dismissed as "Bobby rock" was making itself known; a trend for clean-cut, safe-sounding teen idols who were about as threatening to the status quo as a high school prom. And they all seemed to be called Bobby!

There was Bobby Vee, directly inspired by Buddy Holly. Vee and his backup band, the Shadows, played as part of Holly's tour the night after the fateful plane crash, and he had two Top 10 hits in 1960, "Devil or Angel" and "Rubber Ball," the first of a string of hits over the next couple of years.

Then there was Bobby Darin. Darin had been a hit maker since 1958, when he'd debuted with some fine up-tempo songs including "Splish Splash" and "Queen of the Hop," followed by "Dream Lover" and his dynamic chart topper "Mack the Knife" in 1959. The year 1960 saw the finger-clicking Darin moving toward a nightclub style with the ballad "Beyond the Sea" and two "swingin'" covers of previously corny oldies, "Clementine" and "Won't You Come Home, Bill Bailey."

Bobby Rydell hit the charts no less than six times in 1960, his successes including the smoother-than-smooth "Volare" and "Sway," a song that still resonates with folks today. Bobby Vinton topped the pop chart in 1962 with the schmaltzy "Roses Are Red (My Love)," the first of 28 Top 40 entries over the next 10 years.

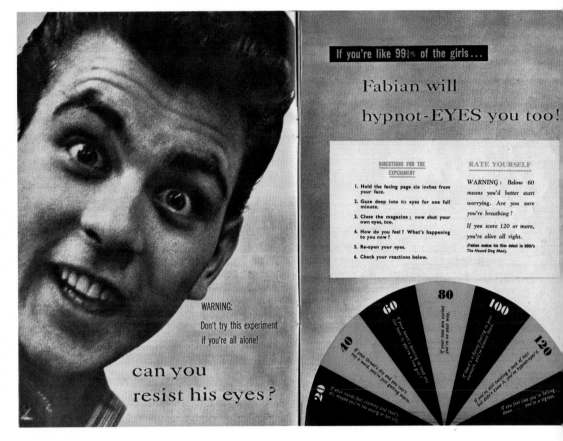

WARNING:
Don't try this experiment if you're all alone!

can you resist his eyes?

If you're like 99¾% of the girls...

Fabian will hypnot-EYES you too!

DIRECTIONS FOR THE EXPERIMENT

1. Hold the facing page six inches from your face.
2. Gaze deep into his eyes for one full minute.
3. Close the magazine; now shut your own eyes, too.
4. How do you feel? What's happening to you now?
5. Re-open your eyes.
6. Check your reactions below.

RATE YOURSELF

WARNING: Below 60 means you'd better start worrying. Are you sure you're breathing?

If you score 120 or more, you're alive all right.

(Fabian makes his film debut in 20th's The Hound Dog Man).

Bikini Hits

Also part of this good-looking genus, Fabian was pinup number 1 for millions of females through 1959 and 1960, as was Frankie Avalon—the latter having two chart toppers in 1959 and four hits in 1960. Avalon went on to be the costar of innumerable "beach movies" with bikini-clad Annette Funicello (who also had three hit records in 1960) through the early sixties.

A novelty smash, "Itsy Bitsy Teenie Weenie Yellow Polka Dot Bikini," took Brian Hyland to the top of the charts in 1960. He followed with several more hits that included two memorable teen tearjerkers, "Ginny Come Lately" and "Sealed with a Kiss," both in 1962—the same year that Tommy Roe hit the front pages of girls' magazines and set the record-store cash registers ringing with his number 1 "Sheila."

Britain also had its quota of postrock photogenic heartthrobs, including John Leyton, Adam Faith, Ricky Valance, and Eden Kane. Canada also had a Bobby of its own—Bobby Curtola, who first hit the charts with "Hand in Hand with You" in 1960 and went to the top spot in 1962 with "Fortune Teller."

OPPOSITE: Bobby Darin veered away from rock toward the middle-of-the-road in 1960.

ABOVE: There was no escaping Fabian's hypnotic personality.

"IS IT A BOOK YOU WOULD WISH

In London, the trial under the 1959 Obscene Publications Act over Penguin Books's publication of D. H. Lawrence's *Lady Chatterley's Lover* ruled in favor of Penguin, marking another anticensorship breakthrough in publishing. The book had been published in Italy in 1928 and in France a year later but had been banned in Britain up until now. Penguin wanted to issue an uncensored edition of the steamy story of Lady Chatterley's affair with her gamekeeper to complete a set of Lawrence's works commemorating the 30th anniversary of his death.

The trial, during which the prosecution counsel astounded the jury with his "wife and servants" question (apparently assuming that, like Lady Chatterley, they all lived in country mansions), was the best publicity Penguin could hope for. The book sold 200,000 copies on the first day of publication and 2 million within a year.

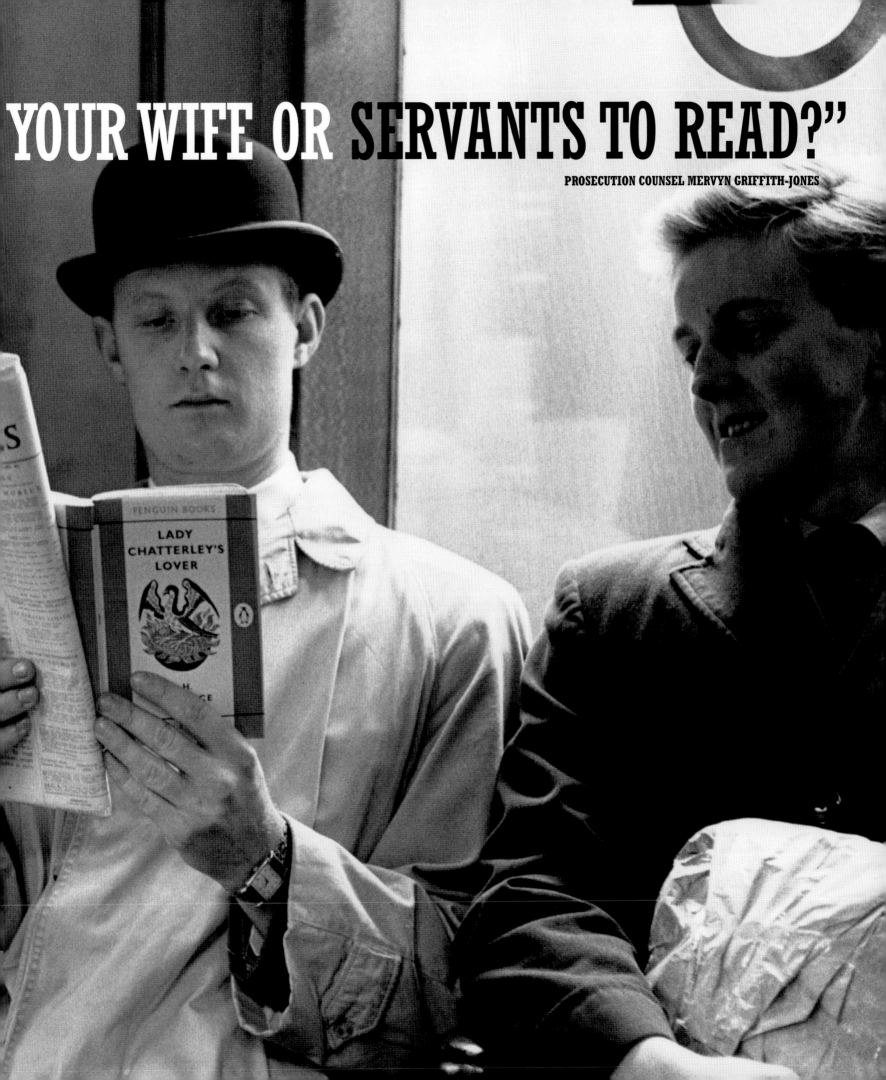

YOUR WIFE OR SERVANTS TO READ?"

PROSECUTION COUNSEL MERVYN GRIFFITH-JONES

"I WAS A PILOT FLYING THAT WHERE I WAS MADE WHAT I WAS DOING SPYING."

HAPPENED FLYING DOING

FRANCIS GARY POWERS, U-2 PILOT

A major diplomatic incident was triggered in May 1960, when an American U-2 spy plane was shot down by a Russian missile while photographing military installations in Soviet territory. The pilot, Captain Francis Gary Powers, was convicted of espionage against the Soviet Union and sentenced to three years' imprisonment and seven years of hard labor. He was released after 21 months (along with an American student also accused of espionage) in a celebrated "spy swap" during which the United States handed over a Soviet KGB colonel. Powers is seen, right, with a model of the U-2, testifying before a Senate Armed Services Committee following his release by the Soviets.

AN AIRPLANE AND IT JUST SO

"I THINK I MUST HAVE ONE OF THOSE FACES YOU CAN'T HELP BELIEVING."

NORMAN BATES, PSYCHO

The movies' master of suspense, Alfred Hitchcock, outdid himself in *Psycho*, in which Anthony Perkins as Norman Bates brought a new kind of villain to the screen. The famous shower scene, in which Janet Leigh's beautiful Marion Crane meets her bloody end (left), is still one of the most memorable sequences in cinema history.

Also that year Stanley Kubrick made *Spartacus*, in which Kirk Douglas played a different kind of hero (trade ad poster, below right). The world's favorite film magazine *Photoplay*, meanwhile, was getting along fine with the new wave of cinema-friendly, clean-cut American boy singers while still using cheesecake shots for its cover (right). It also ran suggestive stories about "troubled" Hollywood stars, such as Montgomery Clift, who starred in *Wild River* in 1960.

Despite all of the social changes taking place, Rock Hudson continued to play the doting husband of the doting, sexually submissive Doris Day. *Pillow Talk*, one of the pair's biggest hit movies, opened this year.

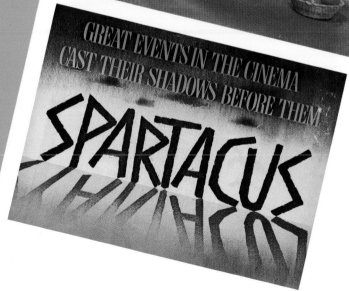

EVERY MAN IS EQUAL—EXCEPT AT THE LUNCH COUNTER

The civil rights struggle was fought in many arenas across the American South and elsewhere in America in the 1950s and 1960s.

On February 1, 1960, four African-American college students from the North Carolina Agricultural and Technical College in Greensboro staged a sit-in at the segregated lunch-counter of an F. W. Woolworth store. They were not served but refused to leave, and stayed there until closing time. The next morning, they came with 25 more students. Their sit-in captured media attention across the nation and led to similar demonstrations throughout the South.

Two weeks later, the demonstrations had spread to other cities, and by the end of the month 31 lunch-counter sit-ins had been staged in North Carolina, Maryland, Virginia, South Carolina, Georgia, Florida, Tennessee, Louisiana, and Texas, resulting in hundreds of arrests. Within a year, peaceful sit-in demonstrations of this kind took place in over a hundred cities in the North as well as the South. The students' bravery in the face of verbal and physical abuse during their sit-ins led to integration in many stores, even before the passage of the Civil Rights Act of 1964.

It was an indication that these students were at the forefront of the Civil Rights Movement, and at a conference held in Raleigh, North Carolina, in April 1960, the Student Nonviolent Coordinating Committee (SNCC) was founded. The group pledged to work for reform through peaceful confrontation. They would soon be usurped in America as the predominant student activist body by the Students for a Democratic Society.

New Civil Rights Act

On April 21, a civil rights act was passed by Congress, which introduced criminal penalties against anybody who obstructed someone's attempt to register to vote or someone's attempt actually to vote. Following two previous civil rights acts (in 1957 and 1958) under President Eisenhower, only an extra 3 percent of African-American voters were added to the electoral roll for the 1960 elections. What they had achieved, however, was to push the whole issue of civil rights into the White House, involving the lawmaking process in doing so. Now there was some legislation with teeth.

Signed by the president on May 6, the introduction of the act was accompanied by the establishment of a Civil Rights Commission, which would investigate complaints of citizens deprived the right to vote on grounds of "race, color, religion, sex, age, disability, or national origin." It monitored any attempts to deny equal recourse to the law and was a crucial move in paving the way for further civil rights legislation that followed in the sixties.

In his presidential election campaign, however, Democratic candidate John F. Kennedy argued that a new civil rights act was necessary. In the election on November 8, he narrowly defeated Republican Richard Nixon, with crucial support from African-American voters in the key states of Illinois and Texas.

After the election, it was discovered that over 70 percent of the African-American vote went to Kennedy. However, during the first two years of his presidency, Kennedy failed to enact his promised legislation. The battle for civil rights was still a long way from being over.

Men wait at a Woolworth's lunch counter, which only served white patrons.

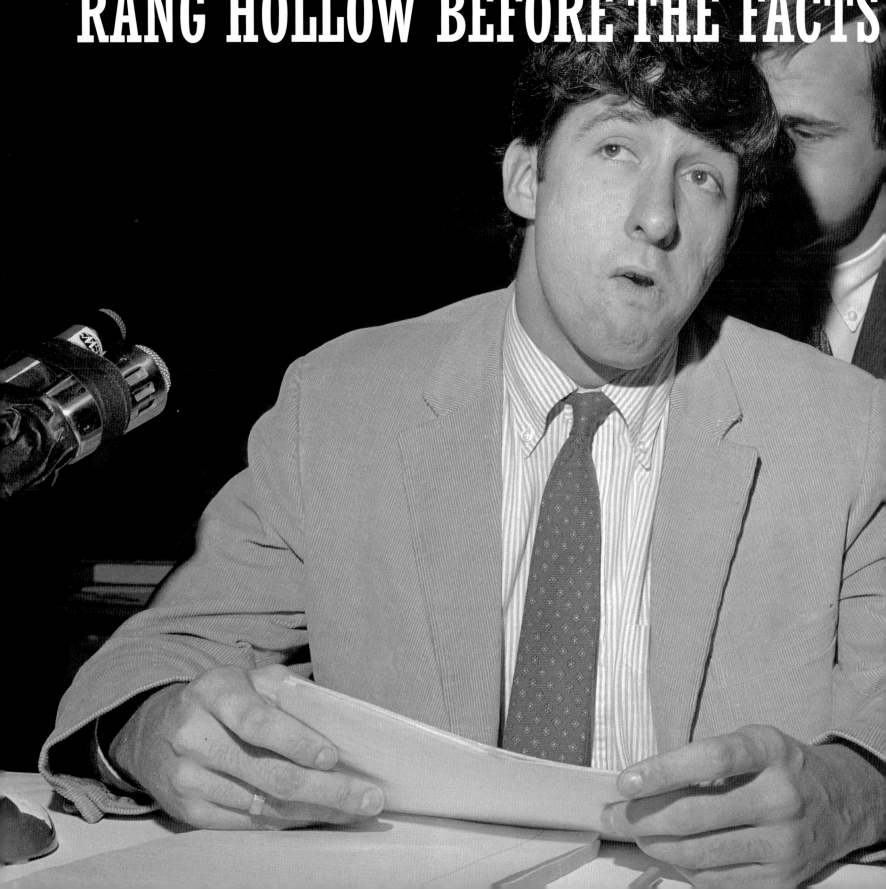

"THE DECLARATION RANG HOLLOW BEFORE THE FACTS

ALL MEN ARE CREATED EQUAL' OF NEGRO LIFE IN THE SOUTH."

SDS PORT HURON STATEMENT

Ann Arbor, Michigan, was the site of the first mass meeting of the Students for a Democratic Society (SDS)—the core of the student activist movement that would be at the center of radical protest throughout the sixties.

Founded the year before, the organization's roots went far back into American left-wing politics, where it had evolved from the youth branch of a Socialist educational group, the League for Industrial Democracy (LID), which in turn descended from the Intercollegiate Socialist Society, started in 1905. At the Ann Arbor inaugural meeting, Robert Alan Haber was elected president, and two years later, its political manifesto was adopted by the 60 or so founding SDS members at their first convention. Known as the Port Huron Statement, the manifesto—largely written by activist Tom Hayden—was a seminal text in the "New Left" movement that would galvanize American society.

Titled "Agenda for a Generation," the document criticized the American political system for failing to achieve international peace or to address effectively a myriad social ills, including racism, materialism, militarism, poverty, and exploitation. In sometimes naive language, it called for a nonviolent youth movement that would transform U.S. society into a model political system in which the people, rather than just the social elite, would control social policy.

"We would replace power rooted in possession, privilege, or circumstances with power rooted in love, reflectiveness, reason, and creativity," it declared, deriding "the permeating and victimizing fact of human degradation, symbolized by the southern struggle against racial bigotry … [and] the enclosing fact of the Cold War, symbolized by the presence of the Bomb." It called on the younger generation "to take responsibility for encounter and resolution" in campaigns of civil disobedience and what it called "participatory democracy." The seeds were sown for a culture clash based not on differences of race or class, but on generation.

Burning Draft Cards

Initially, the main focus of SDS activity was to aid and support the Civil Rights Movement and to improve conditions in the urban ghettos. But by the midsixties it was best known for its role in the youth-led opposition to the war in Vietnam.

"Make Love—Not War!" was the most familiar slogan of the SDS and it became the motto for the entire antiwar movement. The organization was responsible for the first highly publicized draft-card burnings, and in 1969, a massive SDS-orchestrated demonstration in New York's Central Park, the "Spring Mobilization to End the War in Vietnam," drew half a million protesters. Chanting "Burn cards, not people" and "Hell, no, we won't go!" hundreds of young men threw their draft cards into a large bonfire.

The most notorious confrontations between the powers of authority and the radical students would be at the Democratic Convention in Chicago in 1968, when Mayor Richard Daley's police attacked 5,000 antiwar demonstrators in what investigators would later term a "police riot." There would be an even greater trauma in May 1970, when Ohio National Guardsmen shot and killed four students at Kent State University.

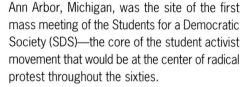

SDS founder Tom Hayden was a key figure in the drafting of the famous Port Huron Statement.

TWISTIN' THE NIGHT AWAY

When Chubby Checker shot to the top of the *Billboard* charts with "The Twist" in the summer of 1960, it was the start of a worldwide dance craze—and a craze for dance crazes—in the early sixties.

Checker (whose real name was Ernest Evans) was a native of Philadelphia and he launched the twist craze on the Philly-based Dick Clark TV show *American Bandstand*. The original twist record, simply titled "The Twist," was released by Hank Ballard and the Midnighters in 1959. But when Ballard didn't turn up for a *Bandstand* broadcast, Checker took his place and quickly recorded the number with the TV studio band. The resulting version was a smash in 1960 and again the following year (when it once more reached number 1), after which the dance took off worldwide as a genuine craze.

The catalyst for the fad—a dance that could be done by folks who couldn't dance and was described as "someone stubbing a cigarette with one foot while swinging their hips, arms rocking side to side as if toweling their back after a shower"—was the Peppermint Lounge, a club on West 45th Street in New York. The house band was the Starlighters, fronted by Italian-American Joey Dee, who had a follow-up hit to Checker's 1960 "Twist" chart entry with "Peppermint Twist." The club was an instant magnet for socialites, becoming the place to see and be seen with the good and the glam flocking to the venue where "the twist was born."

Checker also scored in 1961 with "Let's Twist Again," and in 1962 saw the great Sam Cooke with one of the most evocative twist records of all, "Twistin' the Night Away." A twist movie was inevitable, of course, and Checker obliged with the originally titled *Twist Around the Clock* in 1961. Not to be outdone, Joey Dee and the Starlighters defended the Peppermint Lounge's honor by fighting back with an appearance in *Hey, Let's Twist* the same year. Checker retaliated with *Don't Knock the Twist* in 1962.

Plain Craze Crazy

Meanwhile, the record companies launched other dance crazes, though none were anywhere nearly as popular as the twist, many emanating from Checker's Philadelphia-based label Cameo-Parkway. They included the "mashed potato" launched by Dee Dee Sharp, the "hucklebuck" (another Chubby Checker chart entry in 1960), the "wah watusi" (a hit for the Orlons), and the "hully gully"—"Hully Gully Baby" being a minor 1962 hit for the Dovells. There was also the "frug," the "pony" (Chubby again), the "funky chicken," and the "turkey trot"!

Even the Brill Building writers got in on the act when husband-and-wife songwriters Gerry Goffin and Carole King recruited their babysitter, Eva Boyd (hereafter known as Little Eva), for "The Locomotion," which became a much-remembered smash hit single and much copied dance step. And the indefatigable Chubby Checker carried on with more dance discs through the early sixties, including "The Fly" in 1961, "Limbo Rock" in 1962, "Hooka Tooka," in 1964, and "Let's Do the Freddie" in 1965.

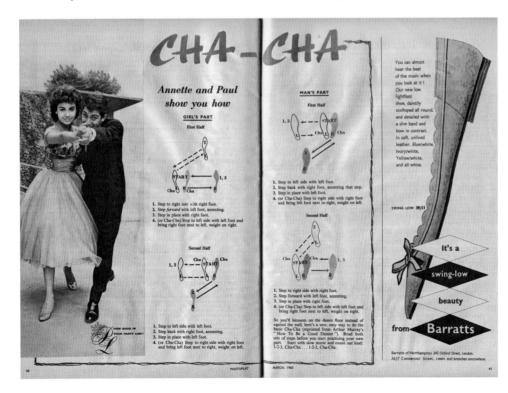

OPPOSITE: Chubby Checker shows the moves that made him famous.

LEFT: Magazines continued to demonstrate more conventional moves for the dance floor.

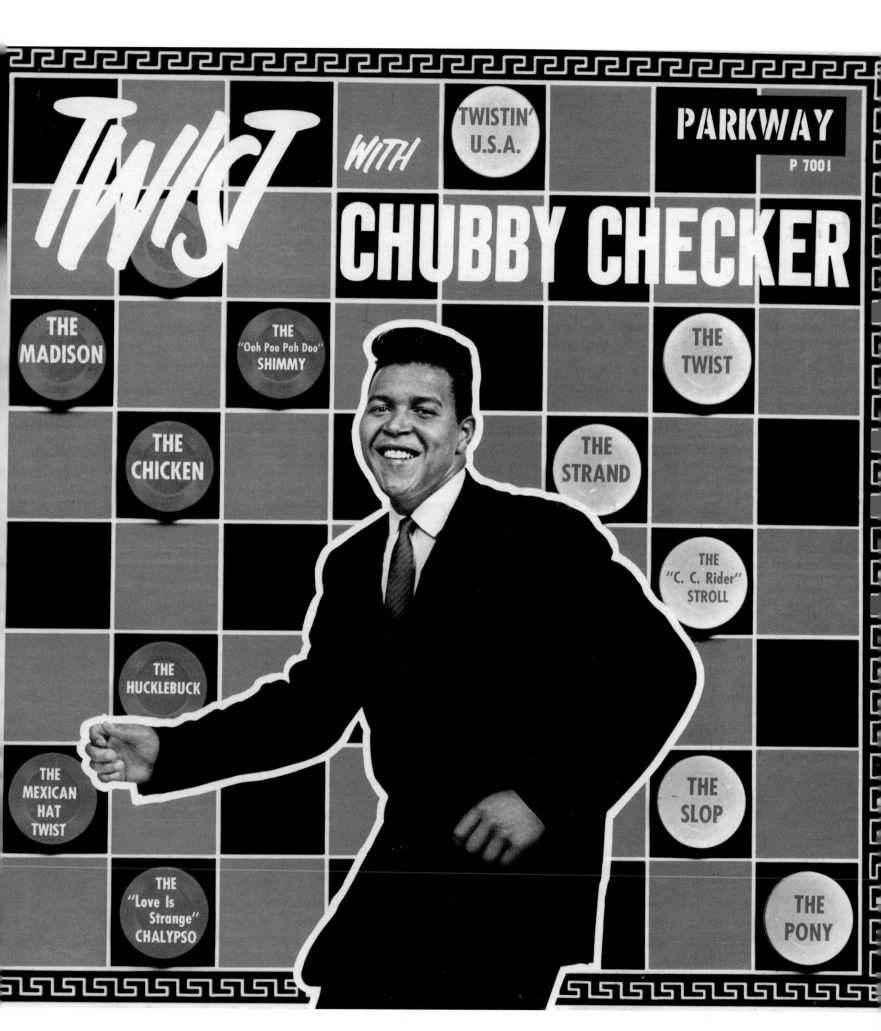

"WE WERE AS CLOSE AS TWO GUYS CAN GET WITHOUT BEING QUEER."

GENE VINCENT TALKING ABOUT EDDIE COCHRAN

The dynamic rock 'n' roller Eddie Cochran died on April 17 following a car crash that also involved Gene Vincent, while the two were on tour in England. Other 1960 hit makers who, like Cochran and Vincent, had roots in rockabilly included Johnny Burnette (who scored with "You're Sixteen"), and former Sun artist Roy Orbison, whose "Only the Lonely" was the first of many dramatic ballads to chart on both sides of the Atlantic. Cochran is pictured shopping for records in a Los Angeles store with his fiancée, songwriter Sharon Sheeley.

J.F.K. VS. NIXON: THE TV DECIDES

When John F. Kennedy won the 1960 presidential election by a narrow margin against Republican candidate Richard M. Nixon, it was greeted as the dawning of a new era. The 43-year-old senator from Massachusetts, a Harvard graduate and war hero, was the first Roman Catholic and the youngest elected president in U.S. history.

The election campaign itself was certainly historic in that it was the first time that the candidates took part in a head-to-head, televised debate. On September 26, 1960, 70 million U.S. viewers tuned in to watch the first of four televised "Great Debates," still a record number for a presidential election. The major theme was the threat of global communism, with only the first meeting of the two opponents concentrating on domestic issues. It was this first debate, however, that stuck in people's minds the most.

Kennedy was extremely photogenic, easily winning the image battle over Nixon, who (recovering from the flu) appeared pale and refused to wear studio makeup.

The voting was so tight that it was well into the early hours of the morning before Richard Nixon hinted from Republican headquarters in Los Angeles that he might be defeated. As his supporters chanted "We want Nixon!" he told the nation to back their new leader: "I want Senator Kennedy to know—I want you all to know—that if this trend continues and he does become president, he will have my wholehearted support." He did not officially concede victory until six hours later in a congratulatory telegram to the president-elect.

A Family Affair

When Kennedy delivered his victory speech the next day from Hyannis, Massachusetts, his family was present. Next to him was his father, Joseph Kennedy, a former U.S. ambassador to London and head of the Kennedy political dynasty, and his brother and campaign manager, Robert Kennedy. On his other side was his wife, Jacqueline, nine months pregnant with their second child. In his speech, he said they would now prepare for "a new administration and a new baby."

Urging all Americans to help him "move this country safely through the 1960s," he added, "I can assure you that every degree of mind and spirit that I possess will be devoted to the long-range interests of the United States and to the cause of freedom around the world."

It was a theme he reiterated in his inauguration speech in January 1961, when he pledged, "One form of colonial control shall not have passed away merely to be replaced by a far more iron tyranny." It was clearly a reference to continuing Eisenhower's policy of U.S. support for the government of South Vietnam.

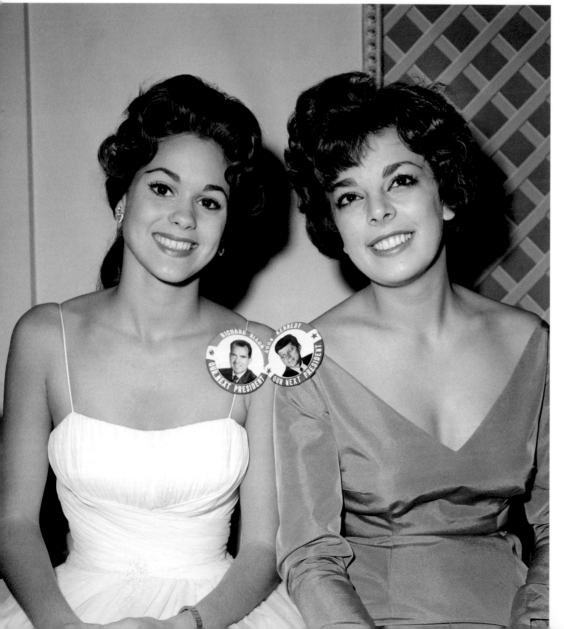

BELOW LEFT: Models sporting politically influenced hairstyles, "The Dick Dip" and "The Jack Flip."

BELOW: Kennedy and Nixon go head-to-head as the nation watches on TV.

HAIRCUTS, HIJACKERS, AND H-BOMBS

1961

As the Russian ballet star Rudolf Nureyev (left) made a "leap to freedom" and defected to the West, work began on the Berlin Wall to prevent similar departures by Germans in the Eastern half of the city.

Newly elected President Kennedy had plenty to worry about in his first year in office, especially the Soviet Union's testing of a 58-megaton hydrogen bomb, which broke a three-year nuclear test moratorium and caused the largest explosion ever recorded. In October, the U.S. president advised any Americans who had not already done so to build fallout shelters to protect themselves in the event of a nuclear exchange with the Communist bloc.

A U.S. commercial plane was hijacked to Cuba, beginning something of a trend—and resulting in Kennedy signing a law against hijacking that called for the death penalty for anyone convicted. The president also established the Peace Corps, with the first volunteers sent to Ghana.

In California, surfers began a new craze, skateboarding; the Mattel toy company introduced the Ken doll, marketing it as Barbie's boyfriend; and in Denmark, a strike of barber's assistants ended after 33 years, just as the fashion of longer hair for men began.

THE BIRTH OF THE MOTOWN SOUND

When "Shop Around" by Smokey Robinson and the Miracles hit the number 2 spot in the U.S. pop charts in 1961, it marked the hit-making debut of Tamla Motown, founded in 1959 by Berry Gordy.

Born in Detroit in 1929, Gordy's first involvement in the music business was as a songwriter for various local acts such as Jackie Wilson and the Matadors. He wrote a minor hit for Wilson, "Reet Petite" in 1957, followed by the singer's first big one, "Lonely Teardrops" in 1958. Encouraged by that success, in 1959 he started his own publishing company, Jobete Music, and later the same year launched Tamla Records with a loan of $800. He also started Motown, named after the nickname for Detroit—"Motor Town"—the center of the U.S. automobile industry.

Tamla was named after the Debbie Reynolds film *Tammy* and its first release was "Come to Me" by Marv Johnson. As the record started to sell, Gordy found he couldn't keep up with the demands of national production and distribution, so he leased the master to United Artists. Later in his first year of operation, he cowrote and produced "Money (That's What I Want)," which was recorded by Barrett Strong. But with Tamla not yet equipped to break a national hit, "Money" was released on Anna Records, owned by Gordy's sisters Gwen and Anna, and Gwen's husband, Harvey Fuqua. The record reached number 2 on the R&B chart and just missed the Top 20 pop chart.

Miracles Happen

In November 1959, Gordy recorded "Bad Girl" by a young singer, William "Smokey" Robinson and his group, the Miracles—for whom Gordy had written songs when they were called the Matadors. The record sold well but still only with the help of a national distribution deal, this time with Chess Records. Robinson convinced Gordy that Motown should distribute its own records,

so in 1960, Gordy cowrote and distributed "Shop Around" on Tamla. It was the beginning of a revolution in African-American pop music.

Gordy's ambition was to create African-American music that was acceptable to mainstream America, and to do it through a company owned and run by African Americans. As he signed more talent, mainly groups of streetwise kids from the Detroit area, he saw his dream beginning to come true.

Mary Wells was another early signing for Gordy. In 1959, when she was still only 16, she approached Gordy with a song she had written for Jackie Wilson. Unable to write music, Wells sang the song to Gordy, who immediately signed her and released her version of "Bye, Bye, Baby," which made the Top 10 on the R&B charts in 1960. In August 1961, she made a minor impression in the pop chart with "I Don't Want to Take a Chance" on Motown, and she would hit the pop Top 10 the following year with "The One Who Really Loves You."

In October 1961, Motown—via the Tamla label—had its first number 1 with "Please, Mr Postman" by the Marvelettes. Formed earlier that year at the high school in Inkster, a tiny suburb 30 miles outside Detroit, the all-girl quintet called themselves the Marvels. A teacher introduced them to Gordy, who signed them to Tamla and renamed them the Marvelettes. On the Marvelettes' first visit to the recording studio, which produced "Postman," the drummer was Marvin Gaye—a future Motown superstar

(and husband of Gordy's siter, Anna) who also released the first record under his own name on Tamla in 1961.

The Girl Groups

The "Motown sound" introduced some of the sixties' soul music's greatest names, including Stevie Wonder, the Temptations, and the Four Tops. There were also the archetypal "girl groups" who, along with the Marvelettes, included Motown's Martha & the Vandellas, and the Supremes.

The "girl group" phenomenon was not, however, confined to music coming out of Detroit. The Shirelles, believed to be the first of the "girl groups," hailed from New Jersey and had a minor hit with "Tonight's the Night" in 1960, before topping the charts early the following year with "Will You Still Love Me Tomorrow," penned by the Brill Building's Gerry Goffin and Carole King. There were also Phil Spector's protégées, the Crystals, who first charted in 1961 with "There's No Other (Like My Baby)," before scoring a string of huge hits through 1962 and 1963.

OPPOSITE: Mary Wells sang her way onto the Motown label at age 16.

ABOVE: Marvin Gaye's career began as drummer for the Marvelettes.

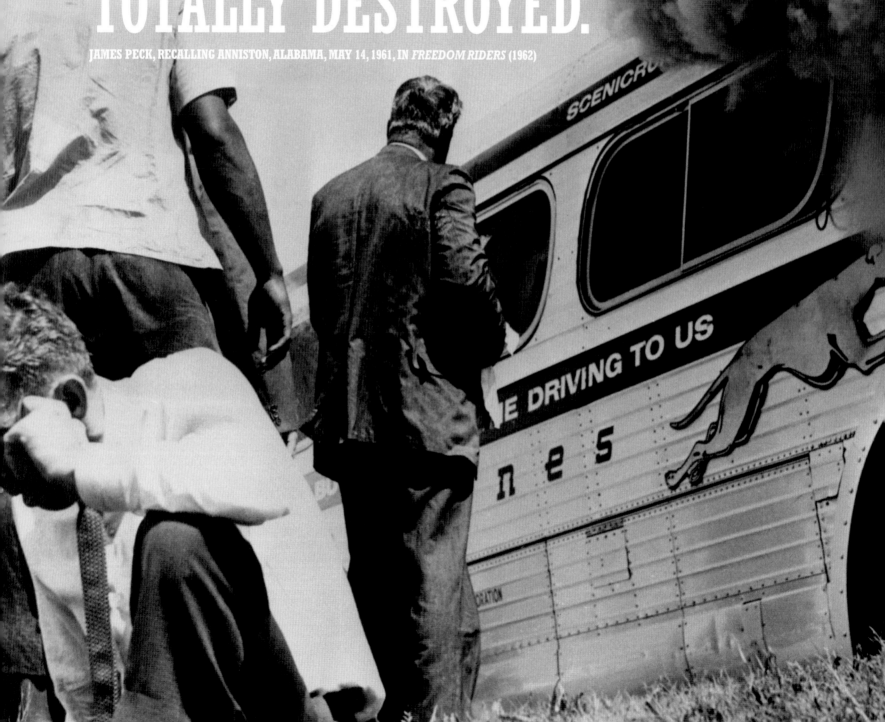

"A BOMB WAS HURLED INSIDE . . . TO ESCAPE BEFORE THE BUS BURST INTO FLAMES AND WAS TOTALLY DESTROYED."

JAMES PECK, RECALLING ANNISTON, ALABAMA, MAY 14, 1961, IN *FREEDOM RIDERS* (1962)

ALL THE PASSENGERS MANAGED

Despite the success of campaigns like the Montgomery bus boycotts of 1956, segregation continued in many parts of the Deep South. In 1961, the civil rights group CORE (Congress on Racial Equality) began to organize what it called Freedom Rides.

The idea was for teams of African-American and white volunteers to test the desegregation of buses, and bus, rail, and air terminals, by sitting next to each other as they traveled through the South. After three days of training in nonviolent protest techniques, CORE's national director, James Farmer, and 13 volunteers left Washington on May 4, 1961, for Georgia, Alabama, and Mississippi. The Attorney General, Robert Kennedy, sent his own representative, John Seigenthaler, to accompany the Freedom Riders.

As soon as the protesters reached the southern states, the violence began. In Anniston, Alabama, one bus was destroyed, and riders on another were attacked by men armed with clubs, bricks, iron pipes, and knives, while in Birmingham the passengers were greeted by members of the Ku Klux Klan. Some of the Freedom Riders were badly beaten. In the Alabama state capital, Montgomery, a white mob attacked the riders with chains and axe handles, and John Seigenthaler was knocked unconscious when he went to the aid of one of the passengers. When the Freedom Riders arrived in Jackson, Mississippi, on May 24, many were arrested.

Freedom Riders Ride On

The Ku Klux Klan and their local supporters hoped that the violent treatment meted out to the Freedom Riders would deter other people from taking part in the protests. Over the next six months, however, more than 1,000 people participated in the Freedom Rides. When it became clear that the local authorities were unwilling to protect the bus demonstrators from orchestrated violence, President Kennedy sent 500 federal marshals from the North to do the job.

During that long, hot summer of 1961, the Freedom Riders also campaigned against other forms of racial discrimination. They continued the sit-in campaigns of the previous year, sitting together in segregated restaurants, at lunch counters, and in hotels. This was especially effective when it involved large companies, which, fearing boycotts in the North, began to desegregate their businesses.

Robert Kennedy petitioned the Interstate Commerce Commission (ICC), urging it to draft regulations to end racial segregation in bus terminals. At first the ICC was reluctant, but in September 1961, it issued the necessary orders, which went into effect at the beginning of November.

As with the Montgomery bus boycotts, the conflict at Little Rock, and the lunch-counter sit-ins, the worldwide publicity about the Freedom Riders did much to accelerate change in the battle for civil rights.

Prior to being set on fire in Anniston, the Freedom Riders' Greyhound bus was attacked with iron bars and its tires were slashed with knives.

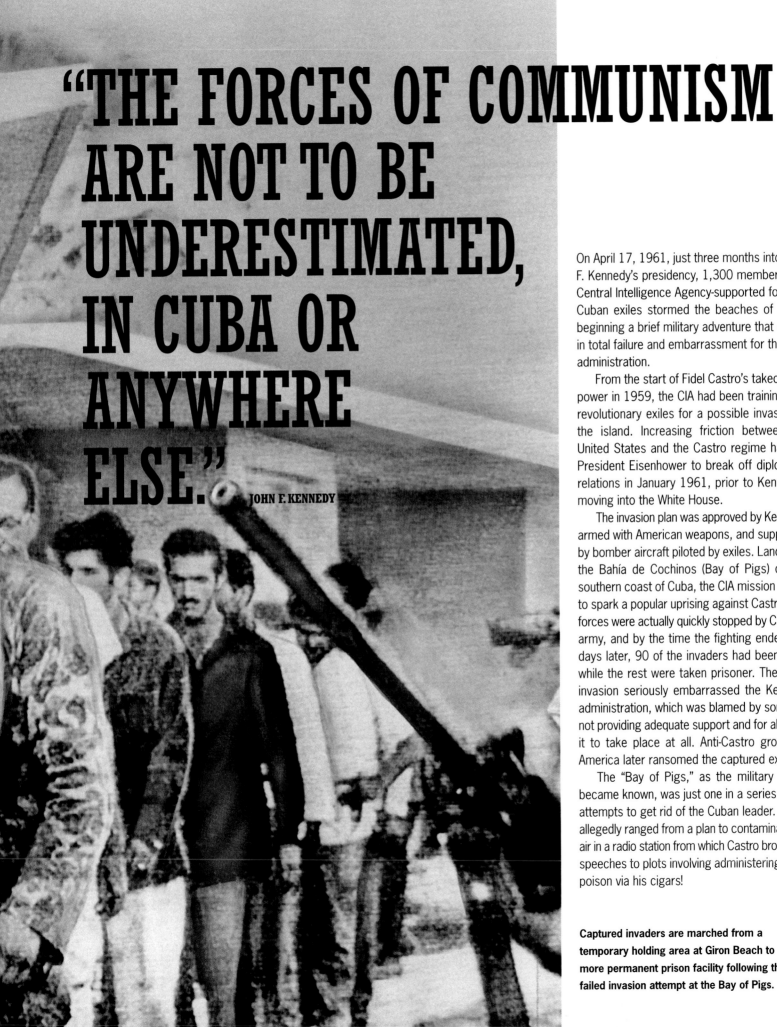

"THE FORCES OF COMMUNISM ARE NOT TO BE UNDERESTIMATED, IN CUBA OR ANYWHERE ELSE."
JOHN F. KENNEDY

On April 17, 1961, just three months into John F. Kennedy's presidency, 1,300 members of a Central Intelligence Agency-supported force of Cuban exiles stormed the beaches of Cuba, beginning a brief military adventure that ended in total failure and embarrassment for the U.S. administration.

From the start of Fidel Castro's takeover of power in 1959, the CIA had been training anti-revolutionary exiles for a possible invasion of the island. Increasing friction between the United States and the Castro regime had led President Eisenhower to break off diplomatic relations in January 1961, prior to Kennedy's moving into the White House.

The invasion plan was approved by Kennedy, armed with American weapons, and supported by bomber aircraft piloted by exiles. Landing at the Bahía de Cochinos (Bay of Pigs) on the southern coast of Cuba, the CIA mission aimed to spark a popular uprising against Castro. The forces were actually quickly stopped by Castro's army, and by the time the fighting ended two days later, 90 of the invaders had been killed while the rest were taken prisoner. The failed invasion seriously embarrassed the Kennedy administration, which was blamed by some for not providing adequate support and for allowing it to take place at all. Anti-Castro groups in America later ransomed the captured exiles.

The "Bay of Pigs," as the military fiasco became known, was just one in a series of CIA attempts to get rid of the Cuban leader. These allegedly ranged from a plan to contaminate the air in a radio station from which Castro broadcast speeches to plots involving administering lethal poison via his cigars!

Captured invaders are marched from a temporary holding area at Giron Beach to a more permanent prison facility following the failed invasion attempt at the Bay of Pigs.

THE FIRST MAN IN SPACE IS RUSSIAN

The space race took on a whole new human complexion on April 12, 1961, when the Russian cosmonaut Yuri Gagarin became the first human to travel into space, circling Earth in the *Vostok 1* spacecraft. The *Vostok 1* circled at 16,988 miles per hour (27,400 kilometers), the flight lasting 108 minutes. Following reentry into Earth's atmosphere, Gagarin ejected from the spacecraft and landed by parachute.

He was greeted as a hero in the Soviet Union and became a celebrity worldwide, even in the United States, which wasn't far behind in what was becoming—as opposed to the arms race, to which the space program was closely linked—a "peaceful" superpower rivalry.

On May 5, 1961, Alan Shepard became the first American in space when he took a 15-minute suborbital flight over the Pacific Ocean in the *Freedom 7* spacecraft. Shepard was launched by a Redstone rocket on a flight that carried him to an altitude of 116 miles (187 kilometers).

Just 20 days later, on May 25, 1961, President Kennedy made his famous speech to Congress, in which he called for a commitment that by the end of the decade the United States would land a man on the moon.

LEFT: A postcard illustration commemorating the *Vostok* Project with Yuri Gagarin and a branch with important dates for the Soviet space program written on its leaves.

RIGHT: The original seven Project Mercury astronauts: front row, left to right, Walter M. Schirra Jr., Donald "Deke" Slayton, John Glenn Jr., and M. Scott Carpenter. Back row, left to right, Alan Shepard Jr., Virgil "Gus" Grissom, and Gordon Cooper.

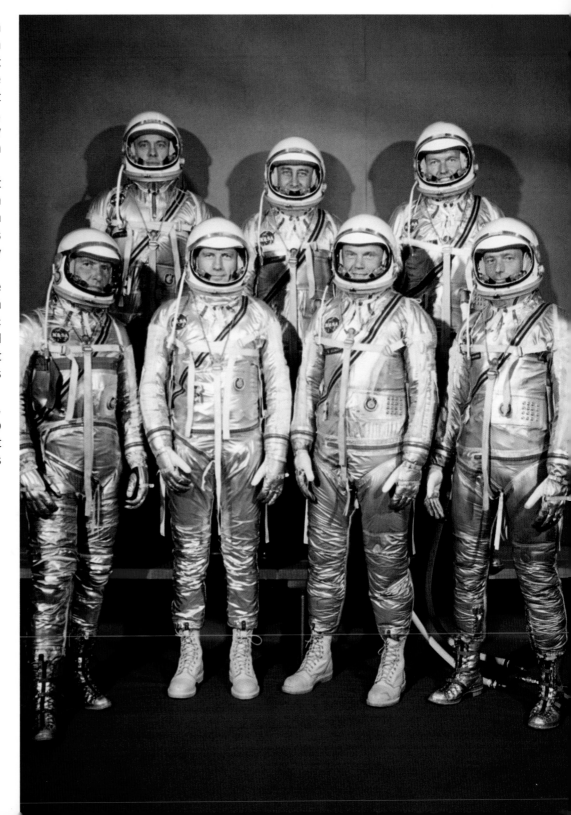

WHEN BOOKS BECOME MOVIES

Two seminal works of fiction appeared in 1961, one introducing a new phrase into the English language, the other extending the boundaries of what might be permitted in a modern popular novel.

Joseph Heller's novel *Catch-22* was set in a U.S. Army Air Force bomber squadron in World War II, based on an island off the coast of Italy. Seen mainly through the eyes of Captain John Yossarian, its frantic style and sardonic humor presented a highly effective critique of the absurdity of military—and most bureaucratic—"logic."

Central to the theme of the book is the concept of "catch-22," whereby the only excuse for a pilot's not having to fly a mission is if he's mentally unfit. Bizarrely, when someone claims he can't fly because he is going crazy, the authorities conclude that he'd be crazy if he *wanted* to fly; therefore, his objection means he's sane and he has to fly. There's no way he can get out of it.

The phrase "catch-22" has since come into common use in reference to any similar double-bind, particularly the kind of self-contradictory logic often applied by bureaucrats and those in positions of power. Because of this, the novel—made into a movie in 1970—helped feed the general skepticism of any kind of authority that characterized the sixties, especially in the context of the escalating war in Vietnam.

Obscenity Laws Relaxed

The Carpetbaggers, by Harold Robbins, one of many harbingers of the sexual revolution when it was published in 1961, demonstrated without being challenged in the courts what it was now permissible to print.

Less than two years earlier, the U.S. postmaster general had banned D. H. Lawrence's *Lady Chatterley's Lover* from the mail system because it was deemed obscene, although the American publisher, Grove Press, saw the ban overturned in a case taken to the Supreme Court. At the time, booksellers across America were still being sued for selling Henry Miller's sexually explicit *Tropic of Cancer*.

The phrase "carpetbagger" dates back to the end of the American Civil War, when would-be entrepreneurs from the North traveled south, hoping to profit from the misfortunes of the South and carrying their belongings in cheap luggage made from carpet remnants. It soon became a term applied to anyone hoping to find success in a new field. Thought to be based on the aircraft manufacturer and movie mogul Howard Hughes, the main character in *The Carpetbaggers*, Jonas Cord, moves from airplanes to Hollywood, in a narrative replete with sexual references that would have made it unpublishable just a few years earlier.

The Carpetbaggers was the most popular of Robbins's unprecedented string of best sellers that had begun with *Never Love a Stranger* in 1948. One of his earlier works, the 1952 novel *A Stone for Danny Fisher*, was adapted into the 1958 movie *King Creole*, starring Elvis Presley. A commercial writer who instinctively recognized the possibilities opened up by Grove Press's victory with *Lady Chatterley's Lover*, Robbins used a formula in *The Carpetbaggers* of page-turning action and glamorous settings spiced with plenty of sex and violence to sell more than eight million copies. He would become one of the world's best-selling authors, publishing over 20 books that were translated into 32 languages and selling over 50 million copies.

LEFT: The title of Joseph Heller's novel has now become a well-known phrase throughout the English-speaking world.

RIGHT: Elizabeth Ashley and George Peppard starred in the film version of Harold Robbins's novel *The Carpetbaggers*.

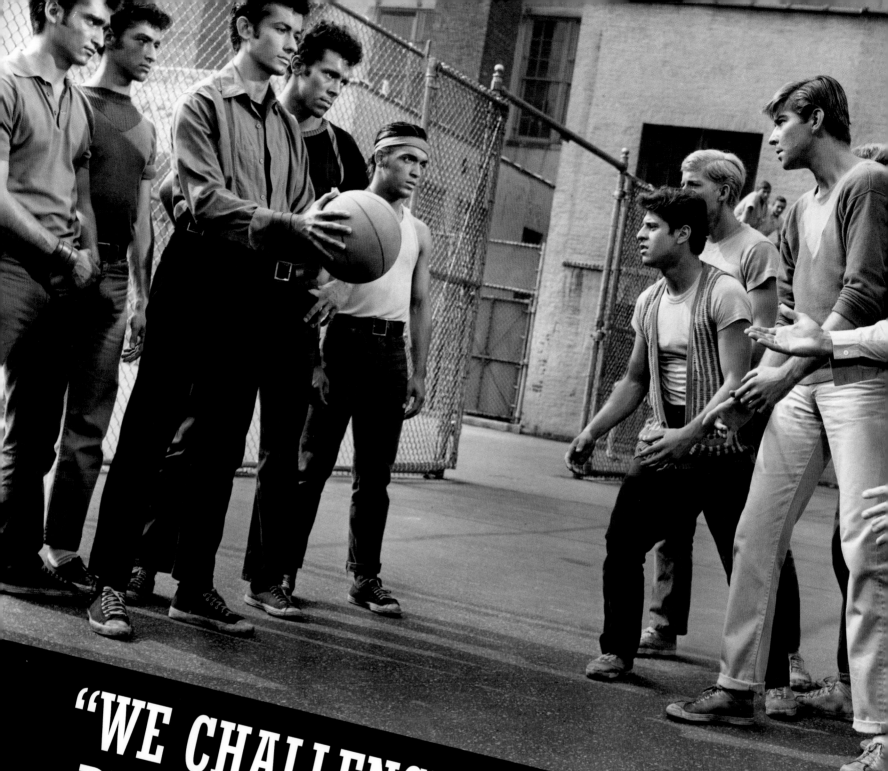

"WE CHALLENGE YOU TO A RUMBLE. ALL OUT, ONCE AND FOR ALL. ACCEPT?"

RIFF, WEST SIDE STORY

"WHEN YOU'RE A JET . . . "

The teen-gang musical *West Side Story* moved from stage to screen, winning 10 Oscars in the process, including Best Picture. Although it was a mainstream hit focused on the teen-related problems of sex and violence, and had a contemporary setting, it was actually based on Shakespeare's *Romeo and Juliet*. Shakespeare, of course, had based the story of his two lovers on earlier material including a narrative poem by Arthur Brooke called *The Tragicall Hostorye of Romeus and Juliet*.

The theme of social feuds or circumstances contriving to create a barrier between two lovers dates back even further to ancient writings on Troilus and Cressida or Tristan and Isolde, but Stephen Sondheim's lyrics set to Leonard Bernstein's music brought the story right up to date. Inspired by newspaper stories about rioting teenagers in Los Angeles, the setting was transferred to New York and the soundtrack albums from stage and screen versions (right) became huge hits.

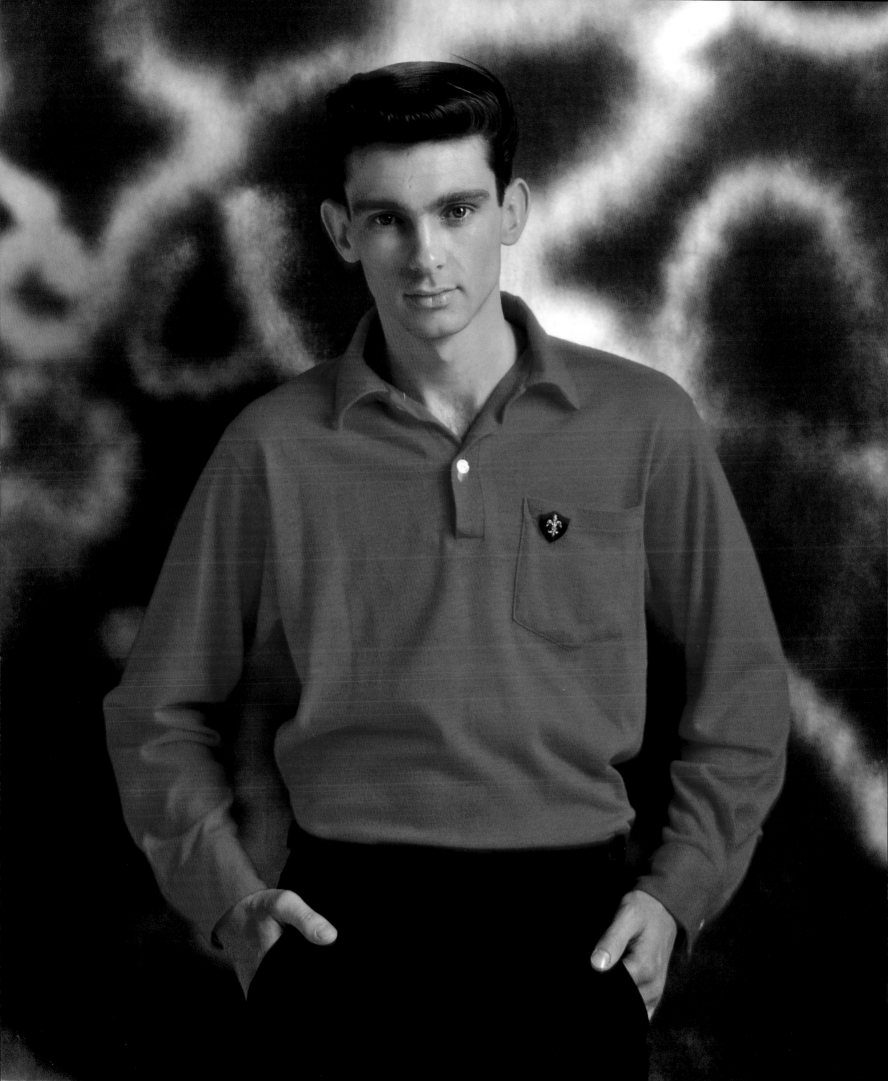

THE TOWN WITHOUT PITY

The world of rock 'n' roll was in something of a state of flux in 1961—a lot of new names hit the charts, although some never saw the best-seller lists again, while others went on to make their mark in the annals of pop music.

Elvis soundalike (and look-alike) Ral Donner made his Top 20 debut in May 1961 with a cover of Presley's "The Girl of My Best Friend," but went one better in July with "You Don't Know What You've Got (Until You Lose It)," which made number 4. New Orleans soul man Lee Dorsey had the first of a series of funky R&B charters with "Ya Ya." Other one-hit wonders of 1961 included the Mar-Keys, an instrumental group from Memphis who scored with "Last Night," and Ernie K-Doe, whose "Mother-in-Law" topped the charts in April.

Bobby Lewis also had a debut number 1 with "Tossin' and Turnin'," as did the Marcels with their off-the-wall doo-wop rendition of the old Rogers and Hart standard "Blue Moon." But the biggest debut record of 1961 came from Del Shannon, whose "Runaway" (with its memorable solo played on the musitron, an early form of synthesizer) was one of the top sellers of the year. It put the stridently voiced singer on course for a clutch of hits through the first half of the sixties. In the United Kingdom, the black-leather-clad Vince Taylor had little record success, but impressed both the Beatles and Elvis with his stage outfit.

Ex-Drifter Ben E. King had his first solo chart entry with the marvelous Leiber and Stoller song "Spanish Harlem" in January 1961, followed by "Stand by Me" in the middle of the year. And a long string of dramatically delivered hits for Gene Pitney began when "Town Without Pity" became a Top 20 debut for the singer and songwriter.

LEFT: Gene Pitney in a somber mood.

RIGHT: English rocker Vince Taylor.

HERE COME THE 1960S . . .

The era of sexual liberation really took off with the successful trial of the oral female contraceptive pill announced on November 3, 1961. "The pill" became widely available in most Western countries soon after. Overt references to sex became ever more commonplace in the open-minded sixties, and the sleek E-Type Jaguar (right) was described as "sex on wheels" when it first appeared at the Geneva Motor Show in 1961.

Fashion was becoming ever more daring and outrageous, too. Women's hemlines were creeping higher, showing ever longer legs, and the miniskirt was on its way. The profusion of magazines aimed at young women had become an avalanche by the early sixties, providing a dedicated conduit through which advertisers could reach their target market. The glamour explosion of the fifties mushroomed along with the consumer boom and young women especially were bombarded with information and offers on new products. Sexy high-heeled shoes helped to give newly revealed legs a well-defined shape, while the range of cosmetics now available was truly bewildering.

Man!
the slick chick
who wears
this slipper
must be strictly
on the moon

Airborne
Cool shoes with the far out feel of fashion

SMOOTH!

The only make-up that gives you
the LIVING COLOUR look
NEW GOYA BEAUTY PUFF

Only Goya can create a make-up that covers perfectly— and yet is fine as gossamer. Only Goya spins wonder-ingredient, titania, to unbelievable fineness, tinting each tiny particle to give you "living colour". Beauty Puff nourishes ... cherishes ... moisturises your skin, keeps it smooth, keeps you cool 'n' confident all day. Beauty Puff is perfumed by Goya!

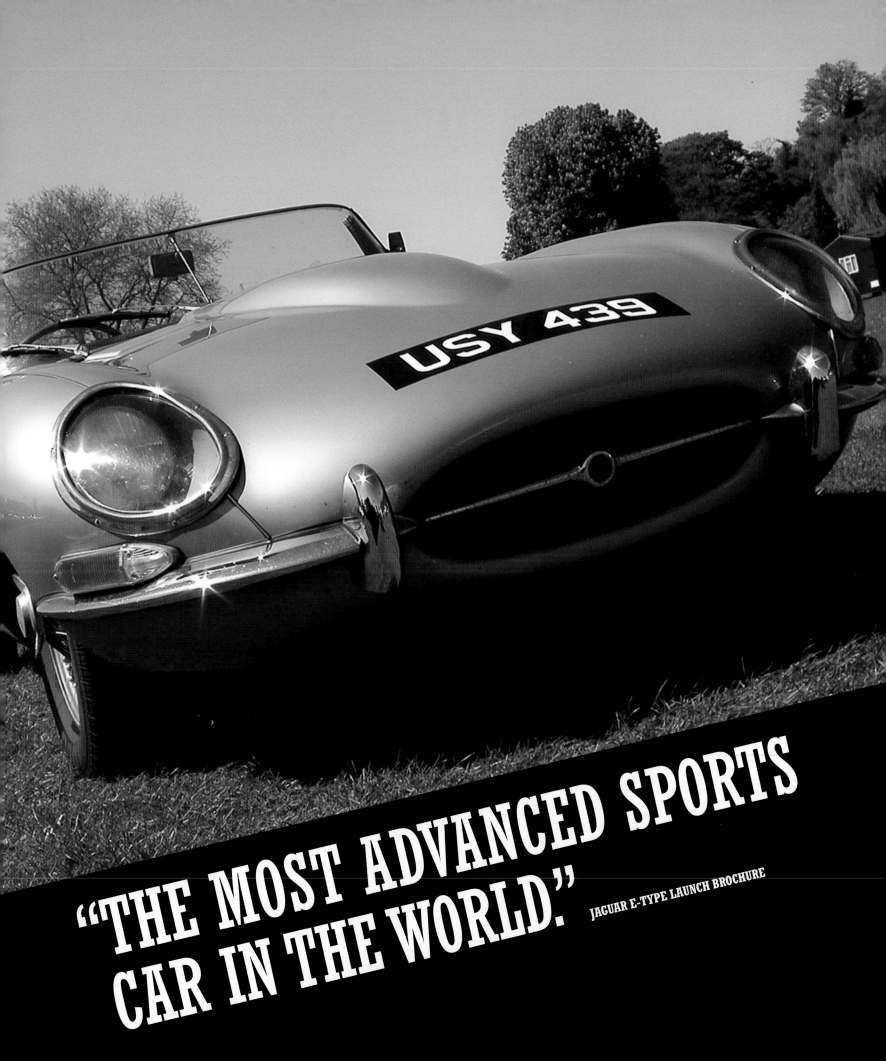

"THE MOST ADVANCED SPORTS CAR IN THE WORLD." JAGUAR E-TYPE LAUNCH BROCHURE

THE BIRTH OF BRITISH BEAT

After years of producing secondhand Hollys and poor-man's Presleys, something was stirring in Britain that was going to shake the rock 'n' roll scene to its foundations.

Yet to be discovered by the record companies, a new breed of British rockers was playing their first tentative gigs in local dance halls and jazz cellars across the country. As schoolkids in the skiffle era of the midfifties, they took their musical cues from vintage rock 'n' roll and African-American R&B and were in the process of creating a tough, guitar-driven Beat music that sounded as new as tomorrow.

One such group who had started out as a skiffle-inspired act named the Quarrymen were now a leather-clad five-piece band and had been playing in the German port of Hamburg for much of 1960 before returning to their native Liverpool. On February 9, 1961, they played their first gig (a lunchtime session) at the city's Cavern Jazz Club; they were billed as "The Beatles."

Consisting of John Lennon, Paul McCartney, and George Harrison on guitars, Stuart Sutcliffe on bass guitar, and Pete Best on drums, their months playing long hours in the nightclubs of Hamburg had paid off. With a raucous repertoire of rock 'n' roll classics by the likes of Little Richard, Carl Perkins, and Chuck Berry, they were starting to sound like a real group. It was not as if they had no competition in Liverpool; the Beatles were just one of hundreds of rock 'n' roll groups, many of whom had made the Hamburg trek before them.

On March 21, the Beatles made their first nighttime appearance at the Cavern, three days before leaving for another three-month stint in Hamburg. While in Germany, they made their first-ever studio recordings, seven tracks— some of which they played as a backup band for singer Tony Sheridan. Also, while in Hamburg, Stuart Sutcliffe left the group to enroll in the local art school and develop his talent as a painter—it was as an art student in Liverpool that he'd met John Lennon in 1957.

Beatles Go Home

The group returned to Liverpool in July (with Paul McCartney now playing bass guitar), where they found the rock scene buzzing as never before. Back in Germany, a single from their recording session was released: "My Bonnie" backed with "The Saints (When the Saints Go Marching In)," credited on the label to "Tony Sheridan and the Beat Brothers."

The Beatles were starting to build a strong following in Liverpool and, in October, the manager of a local record store ordered copies of the German single in response to persistent pestering from Beatles fans. Curious to see what all the fuss was about, he went to the

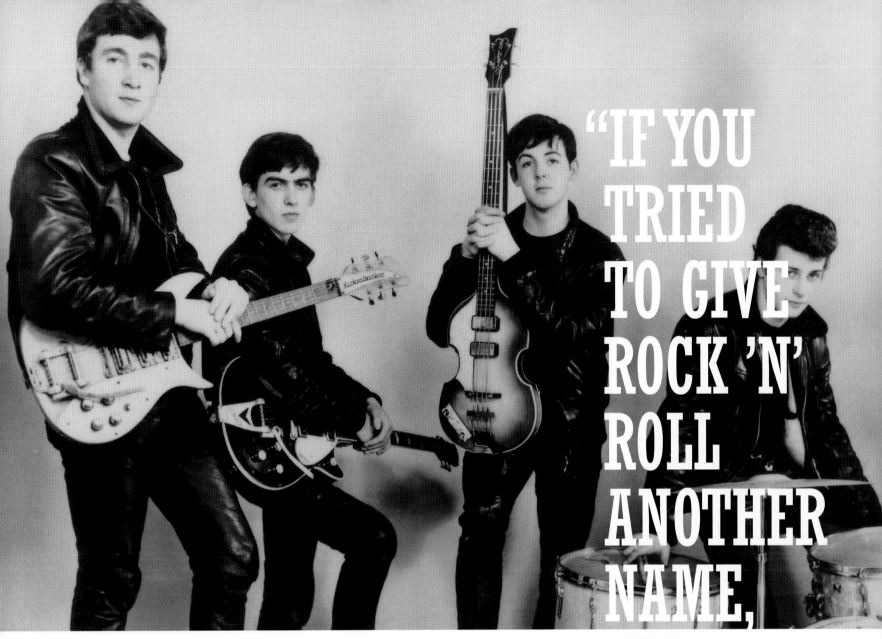

"IF YOU TRIED TO GIVE ROCK 'N' ROLL ANOTHER NAME, YOU MIGHT CALL IT 'CHUCK BERRY.'"

JOHN LENNON

Cavern to check out the band himself. His name was Brian Epstein, and on December 3, 1961, he offered to manage the Beatles. The four, eager for fame, signed right away.

Meanwhile, in the London suburb of Dartford, a chance meeting that July between economics student Mick Jagger and art student and former schoolmate Keith Richards led to their discovering a mutual interest in the music of Chuck Berry. By autumn, they were in a local group together, pounding out Chicago-style rhythm and blues and calling themselves Little Boy Blue and the Blue Boys. By the following summer, after meeting up with fellow blues fanatic Brian Jones, they had changed their name to the Rolling Stones.

Just as there was a burgeoning rock 'n' roll scene in Liverpool and its suburbs, hardly noticed in the rest of the country, the embryonic Stones were part of an "underground" rhythm-and-blues circuit based in and around the capital. The catalyst for the R&B interest in

London was a band called Blues Incorporated, led by guitarist Alexis Korner. When it secured a residency at the Ealing Jazz Club in 1962, its lineup included a young Jack Bruce on bass and Charlie Watts on drums; Mick Jagger would join them and sing guest vocals from time to time.

Although there were rock and R&B groups springing up in other parts of the United Kingdom around the same time, it was these two scenes—Liverpool rock 'n' roll and London rhythm and blues—that were the key triggers for the British "Beat boom" that would transform pop music in the early sixties.

OPPOSITE: Alexis Korner with fellow R&B artists Sonny Terry and Brownie Maghee.

ABOVE: The Beatles with Pete Best, rather than Ringo Starr, on drums.

VILLAGE VOICES

When 19-year-old Robert Zimmerman—now calling himself Bob Dylan—arrived in Manhattan from Minnesota in January 1961, the folk scene that had been based in Greenwich Village since the forties was thriving as never before.

Washington Square Park, close to the student population at New York University, had long been the focus of impromptu folk sessions. Now, along with venues in coffeehouses and bars like the Café Wha?, Hip Bagel, and Why Not?, the Folklore Center on MacDougal Street had become a focal point, featuring books, records, and instruments as well as a performance space.

But the most successful folk venue was Gerde's Folk City, a former jazz/poetry club. The key to its popularity was the Monday night "hootenanies," where amateur and professional singers would "jam" in front of the capacity crowd. A new, young breed of performers was emerging—singers and songwriters like Tom Paxton, Joan Baez, and Phil Ochs—singers more concerned with contemporary social issues than preserving "purist" folk traditions.

Like Dylan, a disciple of the legendary left-wing balladeer Woody Guthrie, Paxton had moved into the Village in 1960 and quickly established himself as one of the leading songwriting talents on the scene. His first album was issued by the Gaslight Club, where he performed, and the quality of his writing was recognized by the inclusion of many of his songs in the influential Village-based magazines *Broadside* and *Sing Out!*

With a background in the Harvard student folk scene in Boston, Joan Baez was a sensation at the Newport Folk Festival in 1959. This brought her to the attention of Columbia Records' John Hammond, who would also subsequently discover Dylan for the label. But Baez wasn't comfortable with the corporate giant as an artistic home and ended up on a modest classical label, Vanguard, based on West 14th Street in the Village.

Described by one music historian as "the finest topical folk singer of his generation," Phil Ochs (again like Dylan) was another middle-class kid drawn into folk singing largely through the influence of Guthrie. While at Ohio State University, he'd spent a brief period with a group called the Singing Socialists, and when he made the inevitable move to New York City in 1961, he became a central character on the Village music scene almost immediately.

Dylan quickly involved himself in the folk fraternity, playing anywhere he could perform. In September 1961, he received a glowing review in the *New York Times*; bringing him to the attention of John Hammond, who subsequently produced his first album, *Bob Dylan*, in November for release in March 1962.

OPPOSITE: Greenwich Village's Cafe Wha? sign lures passersby to a thriving music scene.

BELOW: Like Dylan, Phil Ochs was a disciple of balladeer Woody Guthrie.

BLOWIN' IN THE WIND

In March 1962, Marilyn Monroe sang "Happy Birthday" to President John F. Kennedy at Madison Square Garden, wearing a dress described as "skin and beads"—on August 5 she was found dead in her Los Angeles home.

Across the Atlantic, the Beatles' first single reached number 17 on the British charts, even though they were virtually unknown outside Liverpool. Meanwhile, in America, the Isley Brothers released "Twist and Shout," which the four U.K. "mop tops" would take into the U.S. charts less than two years later.

Meanwhile, in the folk clubs of Greenwich Village, Bob Dylan (left) was capturing hearts and minds alike with his unique brand of protest songs.

On the publishing front, Helen Gurley Brown authored the proto-feminist Sex and the Single Girl, while Marvel comics launched The Incredible Hulk and The Amazing Spider Man to an unsuspecting world.

Jackie Robinson became the first African-American player to be elected to the Baseball Hall of Fame; Nelson Mandela was arrested for incitement to strike and illegally leaving South Africa; and the United Nations announced that the Earth's human population had reached three billion.

The final days of October could have marked the final days for everybody, as America and the Soviet Union confronted each other eyeball-to-eyeball during the Cuban missile crisis, almost triggering the doomsday scenario that they said could never happen.

SURF'S UP!

Originating in the "sun and sand" youth culture of southern California, surf music celebrated not just surfing itself but the whole outdoor lifestyle of beach parties, bikini-clad girls, hot-rod cars, and dance music. The phenomenon had its roots at the beginning of the decade, when the Ventures had a huge instrumental hit with "Walk—Don't Run" in 1960, but otherwise it was still very much a local West Coast trend until 1962, when it made the transition to being a national craze.

There were two distinct strands of surf music, vocal and instrumental, and the earliest hint of it in the charts was in 1959, when the vocal duo Jan & Dean made the Top 10 with "Baby Talk." Los Angeles-based Jan Berry and Dean Torrence followed that with genre classics like "Surf City" and "Deadman's Curve," all featuring their trademark high-harmony vocals and bouncy Chuck Berry-inspired guitar riffs. Despite Jan & Dean's having no less than 24 entries in the U.S. Top 10 between 1959 and 1966, the group most closely associated with the surf vocal sound was the Beach Boys.

Formed in Hawthorne, California, in 1961 by the brothers Carl, Dennis, and Brian Wilson, plus their cousin Mike Love and Al Jardine, the Beach Boys played their debut gig on New Year's Eve 1961, and by September 1962 they had their first chart entry with "Surfin' Safari." They had the first surf record to make the Top 5 with "Surfin' USA" in April 1963 but were beaten to the top spot by Jan & Dean two months later with "Surf City"—though the latter was written by Beach Boy Brian Wilson. Between then and the midsixties, they had a dozen or so surf-style hits in the charts, including classics such as "Surfer Girl," "Fun, Fun, Fun," "I Get Around," and "California Girls," before launching into more ambitious territory with "God Only Knows" and "Good Vibrations."

Distinctive Sound

While the Ventures' "Walk—Don't Run" and "Perfidia," both hits in 1960, were the earliest surf-style instrumentals to make the charts, the origination of the classic surf instrumental sound is credited to Dick Dale and his group the Del-Tones. Born in Beirut, Dale—whose real name was Richard Monsour—grew up on the southern California coast and joined the hordes of young surfers who flocked there. A guitar enthusiast, he had released a few unremarkable singles on his own label in 1960. But, more important, he worked closely with Leo Fender, the manufacturer of the first mass-produced, solid-body electric guitar and the president of Fender Instruments. Together they developed the reverberation unit that would give surf music its distinctive "fuzzy" sound.

During the summer of 1961, Dale and his band unveiled their new surf sound during weekend dances at the Rendezvous Ballroom in Balboa, California, and went on to release records specifically aimed at the surf crowd. In September 1961, "Lets Go Trippin'" topped the California charts and edged toward the national Top 50, followed by "Surfbeat," "Surfing Drums," and "Shake 'n' Stomp." In

1962, they released what is considered the classic surf instrumental, "Miserlou," and in early 1963, Capitol Records signed Dale, dubbing him "King of the Surf Guitar." The same year, he appeared in a "surf-exploitation" movie *Beach Party*, and although never a household name, he had become a California celebrity.

Dick Dale's influence on surf music can't be overstated. He was a surfer himself and aimed to transfer the excitement and adrenaline of the sport through his guitar playing. His fast staccato playing and generous use of reverb were a highly influential and important part of the early surf sound. His unique left-handed guitar technique—playing it upside down instead of restringing the instrument—was also said to have later influenced Jimi Hendrix.

Other surf instrumentals that graced the early sixties' charts included "Bustin' Surfboards," a minor hit for the California group the Tornadoes in 1962. To avoid confusion with the U.K. chart-topping Tornados, they subsequently changed their name to the Hollywood Tornadoes. The Duals' "Stick Shift" charted the previous year.

Probably the best-known surf instrumental record of all, however, was "Wipe Out," by the Surfaris. Although only one-hit wonders (admittedly their hit did reenter the charts in 1966), the teenage five-piece from Glendora, California, captured the mood of surf music—and surf culture—perfectly, when "Wipe Out" climbed to number 2 in the charts during the summer of 1963.

OPPOSITE: Traditional rockers like Bo Diddley were swift to cash in on the beach craze.

ABOVE: The Beach Boys played their first gig on New Year's Eve 1961.

"HE'S A REBEL AND HE'LL NEVER EVER BE ANY GOOD."

GENE PITNEY, FOR THE CRYSTALS

When the Crystals, right, topped the charts in October 1962 with "He's a Rebel," it was the first of a series of smashes for producer Phil Spector's "wall of sound." This revolutionized rock recording through its use of echo, multitracking, and tape loops. He called his records, which also included hits by the Ronettes, Darlene Love, and Bob B. Soxx and the Blujeans, "three-minute symphonies." A millionaire by the age of 21, he was dubbed the Tycoon of Teen by an industry in which it seemed he could do no wrong.

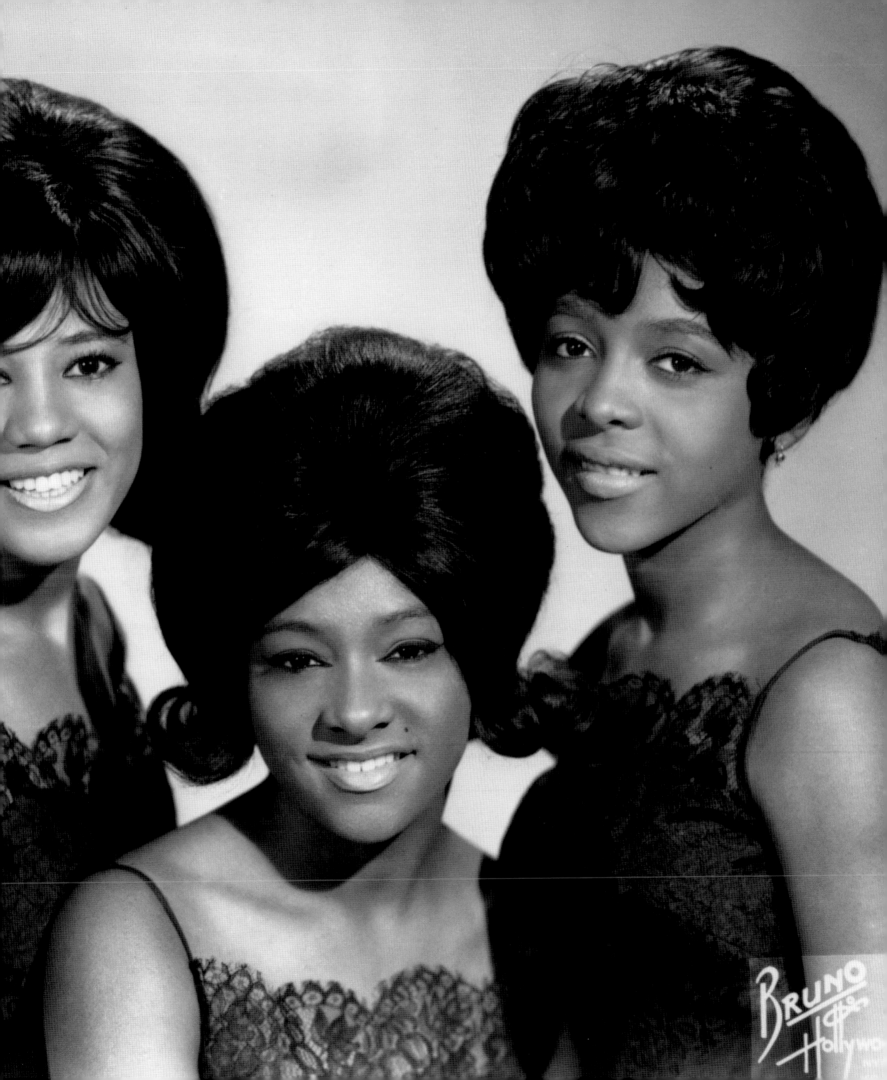

BRUNO
Hollyw

LAST OF THE DOO-WOPS

With the studio-oriented vocal groups of the Brill Building writers (Phil Spector in particular) and Berry Gordy's Motown protégés all ascending the charts, the old school of self-trained doo-wop groups was all but a thing of the past.

Dion

Following their 1959 hit "Teenager In Love," Dion and the Belmonts stayed together for another year or so, charting with a trio of covers of standards—"Where or When" (by Rogers and Hart), the old Disney favorite "When You Wish upon a Star" (by Harline and Washington),

and Cole Porter's "In the Still of the Night"—all in 1960. Then Dion decided to go solo.

After an inauspicious start with "Lonely Teenager" he released two smash hits in 1961, "Runaround Sue" (a chart topper) and "The Wanderer" (a number 2). He was into meatier material now, with an even sexier, more strident delivery. Moving from the Laurie label to Columbia at the end of 1962, he had sensational hits with covers of two earlier Drifters R&B hits "Ruby Baby" and "Drip Drop," plus the spirited "Donna the Prima Donna," all in 1963. He became *the* Italian-American doo-wop idol.

The 4 Seasons

The 4 Seasons had been together for six years when they finally charted in 1962. Formed in New Jersey in 1956, their founder and lead singer Frankie Valli (born Francis Castellucio) teamed up with the Varietones (vocalist Tommy DeVito and vocalist/guitarists Nick Massi and Nick DeVito). They renamed themselves the Four Lovers and Valli believed that they could hit the big time by reworking the doo-wop formula. DeVito was not convinced and left. He was replaced by Bob Gaudio on piano.

In 1960, Bob Crewe hired the group as demo singers for Philadelphia's Swan label, intending ultimately to record them in their own right. In 1962—by this time Crewe had renamed them after the 4 Seasons Cocktail Lounge where they occasionally played in a Newark bowling alley—they released the chart-topping "Sherry." It epitomized the 4 Seasons sound, taking full advantage of Valli's three-octave voice, and came out on the Chicago Vee-Jay label, which, prior to Motown, had been the largest African-American-owned record company.

More hits followed in the same vein, with "Big Girls Don't Cry," another number 1 later in 1962, and "Walk Like a Man" and "Rag Doll" also topping the charts in 1963 and 1964, respectively.

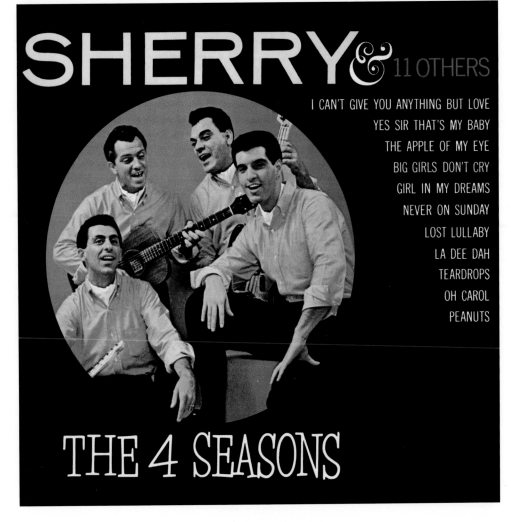

SHERRY & 11 OTHERS

I CAN'T GIVE YOU ANYTHING BUT LOVE
YES SIR THAT'S MY BABY
THE APPLE OF MY EYE
BIG GIRLS DON'T CRY
GIRL IN MY DREAMS
NEVER ON SUNDAY
LOST LULLABY
LA DEE DAH
TEARDROPS
OH CAROL
PEANUTS

THE 4 SEASONS

OPPOSITE: Dion had changed his sound and his image by 1962.

LEFT: Frankie Valli and the 4 Seasons reworked the doo-wop sound to find success.

IT'S A MAN'S, MAN'S, MAN'S WORLD

Taped at the legendary Apollo Theater in Harlem, New York, on October 24, 1962, James Brown's album *Live at the Apollo* broke new ground in live recording, capturing perfectly his dynamic stage act and confirming his reputation as the "hardest-working man in show business."

Born James Joseph Brown Jr. (Brown later changed his name to drop the "Jr.") in Barnwell, South Carolina, in 1933, Brown drifted into crime as a youngster, serving a prison sentence for armed robbery when he was just 16. On his release, Brown tried his hand as a boxer and a baseball pitcher before an injury put aside his sports career. Next, he teamed up with Bobby Byrd, who had a group called the Avons. Renaming themselves the Famous Flames, Brown and Byrd's band toured the South playing R&B, eventually catching the eye of Syd Nathan, who signed them for his Cincinnati label, King Records.

Their first single, "Please, Please, Please," was released in 1956, reaching number 5 in the R&B charts under the name James Brown with the Famous Flames, although Brown's dynamic stage presence, along with the fact that he wrote or cowrote almost all of the band's material, soon led to the group's billing themselves simply as James Brown, with the Famous Flames becoming his backing band. Subsequent releases were disappointing until "Try Me" hit the top of the R&B charts as well as becoming a Top 50 pop success in 1958.

The live recording in 1962 brought Brown national renown, paving the way for more albums and a string of hits throughout the sixties, seventies, and eighties.

SEE YOU IN COURT

The normally staid precincts of "Ole Miss," the University of Mississippi, in the quiet town of Oxford, witnessed scenes of violent confrontation on October 1, 1962, between federal troops and locals trying to prevent 29-year-old James Howard Meredith from enrolling as the first African-American student at the university. The clashes left two people dead, 300 injured—including 48 soldiers—and 30 U.S. marshals with gunshot wounds.

Meredith was born in Kosciusko, Mississippi, of Native American and African-American parents. He enlisted in the United States Air Force when he left high school, before attending the all- African-American Jackson State College for two years. While there, he applied for admission to the University of Mississippi on January 31, 1961. As swiftly as February 4, he received a telegram denying his admission. He then wrote to the Department of Justice requesting assistance and continued to write several letters to the university, requesting that his application be considered for the summer session.

Supreme Court Ruling

Eventually, with the aid of the NAACP, on May 31, he filed a complaint in the U.S. District Court that he was refused admission to the university solely on the grounds of his race. The District Court rejected the assertion, but after a series of legal battles and appeals, the United States Supreme Court handed down a decision on September 10, 1962, upholding Meredith's right to admission at the University of Mississippi.

Despite the Supreme Court's ruling, it was clear that enforcing it would not be easy. Mississippi Governor Ross Barnett publicly vowed to block Meredith's admission; Barnett was appointed registrar of the university and used his position to prohibit Meredith's attempts to register on September 20, and again on September 25. In another move to prevent Meredith's registration, the Mississippi legislature passed a law that prohibited any person who was convicted of a state crime from admission to a state school. The new law was clearly targeted at Meredith, who had been convicted of false voter registration.

Governor Barnett had, however, been in secret talks with U.S. Attorney General Robert Kennedy in an effort to end the confrontation, and on September 30, Meredith was escorted onto the university campus by Deputy Attorney General Nicholas Katzenbach and 400 federal marshals, after President Kennedy had federalized the Mississippi National Guard. Deputy federal marshals, U.S. border patrolmen, and federal prison guards were also stationed on and around the campus to protect the new student.

A mob of more than 2,000 people converged on the campus, assaulting the National Guard and marshals throughout the night with guns, bricks, Molotov cocktails, and bottles. Tear gas was used to try to control the crowd. The violence finally came to an end on October 1, when U.S. Army troops arrived from Memphis, forcing the mob to retreat.

That morning, October 1, 1962, Meredith registered at the University of Mississippi, the first African-American person to do so. He would go on to finish his education at the university and graduate in 1964. In 1966, his book *Three Years in Mississippi* was published, giving an account of his experiences at "Ole Miss."

Just like the confrontation over the admission of African-American children to the high school in Little Rock, Arkansas, in 1957, the Meredith incident was another example of the entrenched views of certain southern politicians standing in direct opposition to what was now federal policy—the complete racial integration of educational institutes.

The campaign for civil rights that had engaged people of all races, particularly over the previous decade, was coming to a head and would stage its most spectacular demonstration of intent in 1963, when Dr. Martin Luther King Jr. gave his famous "I Have a Dream" speech from the steps of the Lincoln Memorial in Washington, D.C., to a crowd of more than a quarter of a million people.

James Meredith, with his attorney, Mrs. Constance Baker Motley, fought a legal battle in the courts to gain admission to the University of Mississippi, yet he still needed the protection of the National Guard and federal marshals when he first walked on to the university campus.

"TELSTAR IS . . . CONSIDERED BY
USHERED IN
THE ERA OF
SATELLITE
COMMUNICATIONS."

LEONARD JAFFE, NASA SATELLITE COMMUNICATIONS CHIEF

MOST OBSERVERS TO HAVE

On September 12, 1962, President John F. Kennedy gave what became known as the "Moon Speech" at Rice University in Houston, pledging the commitment that he'd called for in Congress 18 months before—that the United States would land a man on the moon by the end of the decade.

There was a new air of confidence regarding America's place in space, especially since February, when John Glenn became the first American to orbit Earth.

At the age of 38, Glenn had been assigned to the National Aeronautics and Space Administration (NASA) as one of the original group of astronauts for the Mercury Project. On February 20, 1962, during the Mercury Atlas 6 mission, he piloted *Friendship 7*, the first American-manned spacecraft to achieve full orbit on a three-orbit circuit of Earth that lasted 4 hours, 55 minutes, and 23 seconds. When he returned safely, all of America greeted him as a national hero, with a traditional New York ticker-tape parade staged in his honor.

Telstar

On July 10, the practical use of space technology was demonstrated with the launch of Telstar, the world's first active communications satellite. Designed to transmit telephone, television, and high-speed data communications, it was the first private-owned satellite, belonging to the giant AT&T company. It had been developed jointly by AT&T, Bell Telephone Laboratories, NASA, the British General Post Office, and the French National PTT (Post & Telecom Office).

Launched by NASA aboard a Delta rocket from Cape Canaveral in Florida, the medium-altitude satellite orbited Earth once every 2 hours, 37 minutes. Telstar relayed its first television pictures the same day it was launched, the image of a flag outside its ground station in Andover, Maine. Then, a couple of weeks later, on July 23, the first-ever transatlantic television signals were bounced off the satellite, followed by the first telephone call to be transmitted via space and the first live TV transmissions. President Kennedy went on to give a live transatlantic press conference via Telstar.

"Telstar" was also the name given to a hit instrumental single by a British group, the Tornados. Producer Joe Meek conceived the idea of a "spacey-sounding" hit that would celebrate the much-publicized satellite's success, bringing in a group of studio session players to form the Tornados. Meek's approach to recording was ahead of its time in many ways, and he was adept at electronic special effects. For "Telstar," he created the sound of "radio signals" by recording a pen running round the rim of an ashtray and then playing the tape in reverse. The resulting record was as successful as its satellite namesake and it rocketed to the top of the charts on both sides of the Atlantic.

Telstar takes to the air aboard a Delta rocket at Cape Canaveral in Florida.

"WHICH LEAVES ME ONLY ONE NUCLEAR WEAPONS—WHICH

At the end of October 1962, the world came closer to nuclear catastrophe than at any time before or since. Triggered by America's discovery of Soviet missile bases in Cuba, U.S. armed forces were at their highest state of readiness, and Soviet field commanders in Cuba were prepared to use battlefield nuclear weapons to defend the island if it was invaded. The two superpowers—and the rest of the world—were on the brink of Armageddon.

The Soviet Union was falling behind the United States in the arms race. Its missiles were only powerful enough to be launched against Europe, but America's missiles were capable of striking the entire Soviet Union, with some U.S. bases in Turkey less than 200 miles from the Russian border. In late April, Soviet Premier Nikita Khrushchev came up with the idea of placing intermediate-range missiles in Cuba— a deployment that would double the Soviet

strategic arsenal, providing a deterrent to what it felt was the real threat of a U.S. attack.

Cuban leader Fidel Castro was also anxious to defend his island nation against a U.S. attack, which, since the aborted Bay of Pigs invasion in 1961, he felt was inevitable. He readily agreed to Khrushchev's plan to place missiles on the island, and in the summer of 1962, the Soviet Union began covertly building its missile installations in Cuba.

As far as America was concerned, the crisis began on October 15, when reconnaissance photographs revealed the Soviet missile bases under construction just 90 miles from the coast of Florida. Early the next day, President Kennedy was informed of the missile installations, and he immediately called together a group of his 12 most important advisers (known as EX-COMM) to handle the crisis. After a week of intense, top-secret debate within the upper echelons of government, Kennedy and his team decided to impose a naval blockade around Cuba to prevent the arrival of any more Soviet nuclear weapons on the island.

On October 22, Kennedy announced to America and the world the discovery of the missile installations and the decision to quarantine the island. He also made the chilling statement that any nuclear missile launched from Cuba would be regarded as an attack on the United States by the Soviet Union, while demanding that the Soviets remove all of their offensive weapons from Cuba.

pan books   ILLUSTRATED

ROBERT F KENNEDY

**The Cuban Missile Crisis
October 1962**

13 DAYS

LEFT: Published after his death, Robert Kennedy's book about the missile crisis was direct, no-nonsense, revelatory, and a best seller.

RIGHT: John F. Kennedy receives an honorary doctorate from the University of California at Berkeley.

METRO-GOLDWYN-MAYER présente

en association avec SEVEN ARTS PRODUCTIONS **LOLITA** de JAMES B. HARRIS et STANLEY KUBRICK

JAMES MASON · SHELLEY WINTERS · PETER SELLERS

et **SUE LYON** dans le rôle de "Lolita"

Réalisation: **STANLEY KUBRICK** · Scénario: **VLADIMIR NABOKOV** · Production: **JAMES B. HARRIS**

LEFT: Sean Connery was the first James Bond to appear on the silver screen.

ABOVE: Stanley Kubrick's Lolita was an adaptation of Nabokov's controversial novel.

The year 1962 saw the screen debut of James Bond in *Dr. No.* Ian Fleming's suave agent appeared in the first of a long-running series of movies in the form of actor Sean Connery. But it was the form of Swiss beauty Ursula Andress—the first of the voluptuous "Bond girls"—striding, bikini-clad, out of the sea that has remained the film's enduring icon.

The French New Wave director François Truffaut captivated audiences and critics alike with *Jules et Jim*, the story of three people in love, but a love that does not affect their friendship over the years. Highlighting the fundamental impossibility of a *ménage-à-trois* relationship, even between three people who love each other dearly, the film broke new ground in terms of the subjects that could be addressed in the modern cinema.

Stanley Kubrick similarly tackled an area previously considered taboo when he adapted Vladimir Nabokov's *Lolita* for the silver screen, with James Mason as the unfortunate Humbert Humbert and Sue Lyon as the teenage "nymphette" who is the subject of his desire.

The screening of John Frankenheimer's *The Manchurian Candidate*, on the other hand, became an issue only in the light of subsequent events. The story of a Korean War hero who has been brainwashed by the Communists into assassinating a liberal presidential candidate, it was a sharply satirical look at America in the era of McCarthyism and paranoia. In the light of the Kennedy assassination in November 1963, however, the film was withdrawn from circulation. It had been acclaimed as one of the best Hollywood films of 1962—or any other year, for that matter.

237

THIS IS THE MODERN WORLD

Replacing the "Teddy Boy" fashions of the fifties, the United Kingdom saw a new, cooler style of male teenager emerge in the early sixties—the mod. The mods, or "modernists," despised the Teds as backward-looking and insular, while they had a cosmopolitan attitude and a taste for anything new. They wore Italian-style clothes, drank espresso coffee, and adopted the Italian motor scooter—Lambrettas or Vespas—as their preferred mode of transportation.

The style actually had its roots in Italy in the late fifties, where single-breasted jackets became popular among motor-scooter-driving young men about town in Rome and Milan. Sitting on a motor scooter, the jacket's hem did not crease, because it did not touch the seat. This was teamed with a crisp white shirt, a skinny dark tie, and narrow trousers. The shoes were narrow and thin-soled. Mod was born.

By 1962, middle-class teenagers in the United Kingom, and others with some money to burn, were more interested in modern jazz than pop music, preferred the new European movies, and began wearing the slick, pared-down styles of screen idols like Marcello Mastroianni and Jean-Paul Belmondo as well as jazz-style icons such as Dave Brubeck and Miles Davis.

The mods were self-consciously stylish, with Italian round-collar shirts, short, three-button jackets, no turnups on their narrow trousers, and pointed-toe (sometimes known as "winklepicker") shoes. Mod girls favored short hemlines, seam-less stockings, and high-heeled stiletto shoes.

When men's retailer John Stephen opened His Clothes on London's Carnaby Street, it was a magnet for the new style-conscious youth. Very soon he had three shops on the street, making it the fashion mecca for British teenagers into the midsixties, and he was called "The Mod Millionaire."

When R&B took over from modern jazz as the music of choice among the trendiest U.K. teenagers in 1962 and 1963, the mods were at the forefront. They were the style-setters who helped define the new rock 'n' roll revolution that was about to happen.

ABOVE: Although marketed as leisure machines, Vespas and Lambrettas became the transportation of choice for style-conscious mods.

RIGHT: Enrico Piaggio, whose company produced the iconic Vespa.

ALL ALONE AM I   BRENDA LEE

INCLUDING: I LEFT MY HEART IN SAN FRANCISCO • LOVER • MY COLORING BOOK

LOUIE LOUIE

The original "Louie Louie" was written in 1955 by Richard Berry and released as a single in 1957. The calypso-style record was a moderate success in Los Angeles, but Berry sold the publishing rights when he felt the song had run its course. Yet somehow, instead of fading into obscurity, "Louie Louie" was adopted by various American bar bands and became especially popular in the Pacific Northwest region.

Up in Tacoma, Washington, Rockin' Robin Roberts, a singer with a group called the Wailers, was the first to pick up on Berry's single and decided to cover the song in a completely new style. The band released the first rock 'n' roll version of it on their own Etiquette Records, and it became a regional hit in the Seattle-Tacoma area.

Next into the picture came two local bands based in Portland, Oregon: the Kingsmen and Paul Revere and the Raiders. Both bands caught the "Louie Louie" bug, deciding to record it themselves, and both recorded the song at Bob Lindahl's recording studio within a week of each other in April 1963.

Lyrical Investigations

The Kingsmen initially recorded the song as a demo for a gig on a cruise liner and hated the result, not even wanting it released. Apparently, singer Jack Ely had to sing his version of Berry's almost-incoherent lyrics into a microphone suspended near a 15-foot ceiling. Locally, the record came a poor second to the Paul Revere and the Raiders version, which made a greater impact across the Northwest area. Yet, six months later, the song was a huge hit across the nation, with the Kingsmen's version climbing to the number 2 position in the U.S. charts.

One reason for its success lay in the hardly decipherable lyrics, with lines like "Tell her I'll never leave her again" being interpreted by overprurient listeners as "Tell her I'll never lay her again," sparking a campaign to have the record banned (which it actually was in Indiana). The National Association of Broadcasters, the U.S. Department of Justice, and the Federal Communications Committee all launched investigations into the lyrics of the song, and at one stage, Federal Bureau of Investigation men were slowing down the 45 rpm disc to 33⅓ in order to unearth any hidden obscenities!

More important in the long run, the success it afforded the Kingsmen opened the door for the "garage bands" that flourished in America in the midsixties whose key common element was an abundance of raw energy and commitment rather than technical expertise. Inspired by the English Beat groups who invaded the U.S. charts in 1964, many of these bands, as teenage amateurs, rehearsed in their parents' garages. The basic rock 'n' roll sound of garage, typified by the Kingsmen's 1963 hit, was also heard in records by bands such as Sam the Sham and the Pharaohs (who scored with "Wooly Bully" in 1965), ? (Question Mark) and the Mysterians ("96 Tears" in 1966), and the Seeds, whose "Pushin' Too Hard" from 1967 is now considered a cult classic.

OPPOSITE: Paul Revere and the Raiders made their first impression on the charts with "Louie Louie." After releasing it on a small label in 1963, Columbia picked it up and re-released it.

ABOVE: The Kingsmen's "Louie Louie" lyrics were investigated by the Department of Justice.

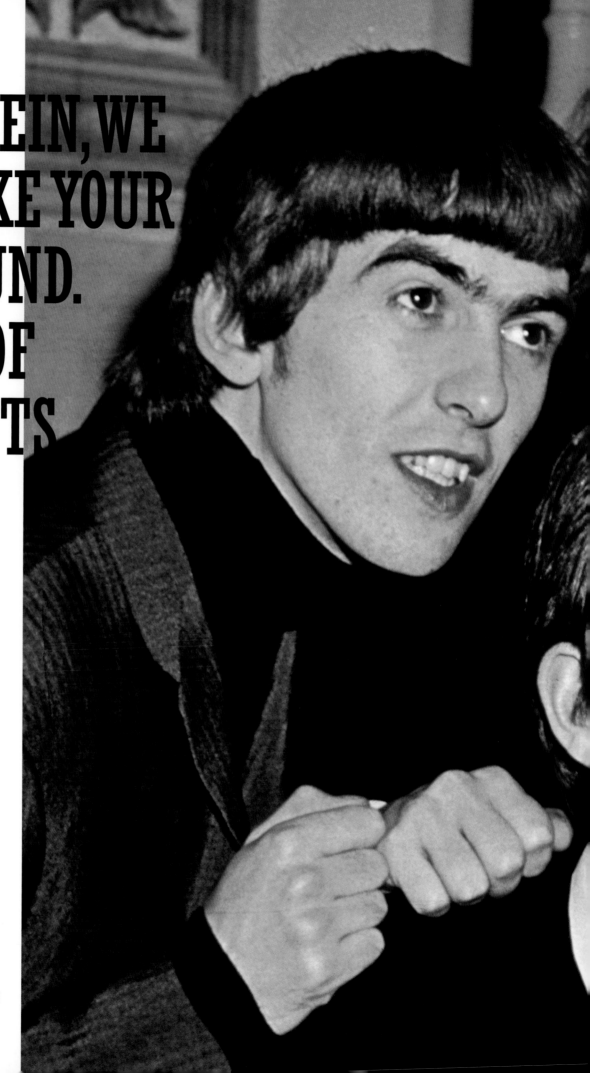

"MR. EPSTEIN, WE DON'T LIKE YOUR BOYS' SOUND. GROUPS OF GUITARISTS ARE ON THE WAY OUT."

DECCA RECORDS' 1962 LETTER TO THE BEATLES' MANAGER

At the start of 1963, the Beatles were hardly known outside their native Liverpool. By the end of the year, they had three consecutive U.K. chart-toppers, two number 1 albums, the fastest-selling U.K. single ever, and they had played for the Queen. The whole country fell in love with the Fab Four, and the press had a word for it—Beatlemania!

THE MERSEY BEAT

In the wake of the Beatles' success, scores of Beat groups emerged across the United Kingdom. This Beat boom was initially identified with the Beatles' home city of Liverpool, where it developed among the city's plethora of venues (the most famous of which was the Cavern Club). London record executives rushed up to the Northwest to sign more "Merseybeat" groups. Brian Epstein, who engineered the Beatles' meteoric rise, already had Gerry and the Pacemakers under contract and they became the first group to see their first three singles top the charts—"How Do You Do It?," "I Like It," and the Rodgers and Hammerstein standard "You'll Never Walk Alone," all in 1963. Epstein also managed singer Billy J. Kramer, whom he teamed with the Dakotas from nearby Manchester for a trio of 1963 hits, including the number 1 "Bad to Me."

The Searchers were the next Merseysiders to appear in the national best sellers, also debuting with a number 1, "Sweets for My

Sweet"—in August 1963, the same month that saw yet another Liverpool group, the Swingin' Blue Jeans, enter the Top 30. And another Epstein signing, the Foremost, made the Top 10 with a Lennon-McCartney number "Hello Little Girl" in September. Other Liverpool names that graced the charts less spectacularly in 1963 included the Big Three (also briefly managed by Epstein), the Dennisons, and the opportunistically named Merseybeats.

Meanwhile, in the capital, the Rolling Stones were being touted as "London's answer to the Beatles" although their actual music veered more toward Chicago-style rhythm and blues. They dented the charts (at number 21) with a Chuck Berry cover, "Come On," and made number 12 with Lennon and McCartney's "I Wanna Be Your Man," but it would be 1964 before they took the best-seller lists by storm.

The first serious competition from London came with Brian Poole and the Tremeloes, who crashed into the Top 5 with "Twist and Shout"

in July 1963 before topping the charts with "Do You Love Me" in September. Next there was the Dave Clark Five, whose second release, "Glad All Over," topped the chart in November 1963, their drum-thumping beat being dubbed "the Tottenham sound" after the London district where Clark was born.

Liverpool's neighboring city of Manchester produced three Top 5 hits by Freddie and the Dreamers in 1963, and the Hollies had the first of many Top 10 entries with "Stay" in November.

Cult Music

It seemed there were Beat and R&B groups all across the country waiting in the wings— groups that had come together through 1962 and 1963 and would find chart success in 1964. American R&B had become cult music for hundreds of aspiring blues-oriented bands in Britain, and the Rolling Stones were the first of many to make it into the charts. By the end of 1963, the embryonic R&B scene that had nurtured the Stones was now flourishing in basement clubs and rooms above pubs. In London alone, scores of groups like the Yard, Manfred Mann, the Kinks, and the Pretty Things were acquiring a fan following that would translate into record sales over the coming months.

In the Midlands, the Spencer Davis Group (with Ray Charles soundalike Stevie Winwood on keyboard and vocals), who would top the charts in 1965 with "Keep On Running," were part of a thriving Birmingham R&B circuit. At the same time, up in Newcastle, the Animals were crafting their homegrown version of African-American music—they'd crack the top spot in 1964 with their cover of "House of the Rising Sun." And over the Irish Sea in Belfast, 18-year-old Van Morrison was putting together Them, who would go on to chart with "Baby Please Don't Go" at the beginning of 1965.

Great Britain had gone "Beat group crazy" in 1963, but even the most optimistic soothsayer

of their fortunes could not have predicted that within a year or so, many of them—including the Animals, the Dave Clark Five, Herman's Hermits, Freddie and the Dreamers, the Moody Blues, the Kinks, Gerry and the Pacemakers, Wayne Fontana and the Mindbenders, and the Zombies, as well as brand-leaders the Beatles and Rolling Stones—would have become household names in the United States.

The British Beat boom of 1963 laid the foundations for the "British Invasion" of America, which would start when the Beatles landed early in 1964 and go on to revolutionize the rock 'n' roll music of the sixties.

OPPOSITE: Music magazines in 1963 went wild over the Beat Boom.

ABOVE: The Searchers came from the Beatles' hometown of Liverpool, on Merseyside.

THE BIRDS BOMBARD THE BEACH PARTY

In contrast to the delinquency featured in teen movies in the fifties, the early sixties saw the studios moving to a more wholesome image of youth when AIP (American International Pictures) recruited Frankie Avalon and Annette Funicello for a new style of teen flick. The result was Beach Party, a light comedy set in California's surf-and-sand community. When the film opened in August 1963, it was an immediate success, starting a new trend in teen movies. The brains behind the phenomenon was director William Asher, who went on to direct another four beach movies for the studio— Muscle Beach Party, Bikini Beach, Beach Blanket Bingo (all with Annette and Frankie), and How to Stuff a Wild Bikini. With bikini-clad girls and bronzed boys dancing the days away to the sounds of Jan and Dean or the Beach Boys, the films managed to be innocuous and sexy at the same time. Other studios jumped on the beach bandwagon with titles including Palm Springs Weekend, A Swingin' Summer, Surf Party, and (inevitably) The Beach Girls and the Monster.

The kids wouldn't stay long on the beach, though, if they had seen The Birds. Produced and directed by Alfred Hitchcock for Universal, The Birds was filmed in Bodega Bay, north of San Francisco, and showed what might happen when birds of all kinds decide to wage war on humans. A masterpiece of horror and suspense, the film became an instant classic.

"THE GREATEST LEADER OF OUR TIME HAS BEEN STRUCK DOWN BY THE FOULEST DEED OF OUR TIME."

LYNDON B. JOHNSON, NOVEMBER 27, 1963

Dealey Plaza, Dallas, Texas.
November 22, 1963, 12:30 p.m.
Central Standard Time

THE LONE GUNMAN

When the news was announced that President John F. Kennedy had been assassinated on November 22, 1963, America, and the rest of the world, was stunned into an almost unbelieving state of shock.

The scene was Dealey Plaza in Dallas, Texas, where the president and the first lady were riding in a presidential motorcade. It was 12:30 in the afternoon. As their open-top limousine passed the Texas School Book Depository on the plaza, shots rang out from the direction of the building. At first, many onlookers thought what they heard was the sound of firecrackers or a car backfiring, until the sight of the president slumped in the car with his terrified wife holding him told them differently. The scene that followed, captured on a silent 8 mm amateur film clip, has been shown again and again since that fateful day.

As the car slowed down, Clint Hill, a Secret Service agent riding in the car behind, leaped to the ground and began running to overtake the president's car and clamber aboard. He jumped onto the trunk of the car, when another shot struck the president in the head. Hill could see Mrs. Kennedy, apparently in a state of severe shock, crawling onto the trunk of the now-speeding limousine. Hill guided her back to the backseat where her husband lay and shielded them both with his body from additional firing.

Forlorn Hope

With the governor of Texas, John Connally, also seriously wounded in the shooting, the car sped out of Dealey Plaza to Parkland Memorial Hospital, where Kennedy was pronounced dead at 1 p.m. "We never had any hope of saving his life," one doctor recalled later. Kennedy's death was officially announced at 1:38 p.m., while Governor Connally was undergoing the first of two operations that saved his life.

Just after 2 p.m. the president's body was taken from the hospital and driven to the presidential aircraft *Air Force One*, which stood on the tarmac at Dallas's Love Field airport. Before the plane took off, Vice President Lyndon B. Johnson (who had been riding two cars behind the Kennedys in the Dallas motorcade) took the oath of office with Jacqueline Kennedy at his side.

As the news reverberated around the world, people in America huddled around radios and TVs; it was during the Cold War, and initially many feared it might be the start of a bigger attack on the country.

Not just in the United States but across the globe, people wept openly when they heard of the assassination. All three American TV networks canceled regular programs scheduled for the next three days, so they could provide nonstop news coverage of the assassination. Radio stations also canceled regular programming, some covering the assassination and others going off the air or just playing funeral music. Sporting events were canceled, and many cinemas and theaters closed on the day of the assassination, and many on the weekend after.

Murder Weapon Found

Soon after the assassination, a rifle was found on the sixth floor of the Texas Book Depository by two local law officers. Lee Harvey Oswald, a 24-year-old employee at the Depository, was apprehended, but only after he had shot and killed one of the arresting officers, J. D. Tippit. It was just 80 minutes since Kennedy had been shot.

Oswald denied being responsible for the assassination, insisting he had been set up for a crime he didn't commit, though he couldn't deny killing the policeman. But his case never came to court. Two days later he was shot while being transferred from police headquarters to a nearby jail. His assailant was Jack Ruby, a local nightclub owner—apparently obsessed with self-publicity—who got into the headquarters claiming to be a newspaper reporter. As Oswald was being walked through the building in front of the world's media, Ruby leapt out and shot him at close range with a handgun. Millions of TV viewers saw the shooting, which went down in history as the first live broadcast of a homicide on television.

After the shock of the assassination and its violent aftermath subsided, there was still a deep sense of trauma in the United States that couldn't be erased. The confidence that had characterized America through the fifties, and the optimism represented by the liberal reforms promised by Kennedy for the sixties—despite his involvement in Vietnam—were suddenly blown away in less than half a minute of gunfire.

It was one of those rare moments that causes everyone to remember exactly where they were and what they were doing when they heard the news.

Lee Harvey Oswald is escorted from Dallas Police Department headquarters on his way to jail. Moments later he was shot and killed.

PHOTO CREDITS